Journalism, Advertisement and Public Relations

Journalism, Advertisement and Public Relations

Shailendra Sengar

ANMOL PUBLICATIONS PVT. LTD.
NEW DELHI-110 002 (INDIA)

ANMOL PUBLICATIONS PVT. LTD.
H.O.: 4374/4B, Ansari Road, Darya Ganj,
New Delhi-110 002 (India)
Ph.: 23278000, 23261597

B.O.: No. 1015, Ist Main Road, BSK IIIrd Stage
IIIrd Phase, IIIrd Block
Bangalore - 560 085 (India)
Visit us at: www.anmolpublications.com

Journalism, Advertisement and Public Relations

First Published, 2008

ISBN 978-81-261-3432-8

PRINTED IN INDIA

Printed at Mehra Offset Press, Delhi.

Contents

Preface *vii*

1. Career in Journalism **1**

Journalism • A Career in Journalism • Journalism Jobs • Newspaper Journalist • Press Sub-editor • Magazine Journalist • News Analysts, Reporters and Correspondents • Writers and Editors • Interpreters and Translators • Photography • Press Photographer/Photo Journalist

2. Career in Broadcasting **63**

Broadcasting • Sound Engineering Technicians • Camera Operators and Editors • Prepress Technicians and Workers • Radio Jockey • Video Jockey • Broadcast Journalist • Broadcast Assistant, Radio • Floor Manager (Television) • Location Manager • Programme Researcher • Radio Producer • Television Production Assistant • Television/Film/Video Producer • Broadcast Engineer (Operational) • Film/Video Editor • Lighting Technician • Sound Technician • Television Camera Operator • Broadcast Presenter • Commissioning Editor

3. Career in Advertisement **187**

Advertising Jobs • Advertising and Marketing Communications • Advertising Sales Agents • Advertising and Public Relations Services • Advertising Executive

4. Career in Public Relations **219**

Public Relations • Career in Public Relations • Public Relations Officer • Public Relations Specialists • Demonstrators, Product Promoters and Models

Bibliography **247**

Index **253**

Preface

This Encyclopaedic Series of Career and Vocational Guidance Covers careers, describing jobs, places of employment, working conditions, qualifications, education and training. This has been developed to aid career and counsellors and job placement coordinators in planning activities for students and potential students about career vocational education programs. It contains a career and vocational guidance model which clarifies what career and vocational guidance services mean and what planners should include in their activities. The model shows an interrelatedness among major thrusts with career development being a central theme of vocational guidance. All of the thrusts depicted in the model represent essential services that should be available to students in career and vocational education programs. The encyclopaedia deals with various sections which correspond to the major thrusts identified in the model: (1) career development; (2) recruitment; (3) guidance and counselling; (4) placement; (5) follow-up and follow-through; and (6) consultation. Each section contains an outline of the perceived needs of the topic, an overview of the topic relative to career and vocational guidance, and some suggested activities and strategies that may be useful in meeting student needs.

It also contains current information about occupations, employment trends, and job searching. Materials on career decision-making, internships, and salaries are also located in each volume. This Series of Encyclopaedia helps students assess their potential for various careers.

Shailendra Sengar

1

Career in Journalism

Journalism

Journalism is concerned with collection and dissemination of news through the print media as well as the electronic media. This involves various areas of works like reporting, writing, editing, photographing, broadcasting or cable casting news items.

Journalism is classified into two on the basis of media: (i) Print Journalism and (ii) Electronic (Audio/Visual) Journalism. Print Journalism includes newspapers, magazines and journals. In print journalism one can work as editors, reporters, columnists, correspondents etc. Electronic journalism includes working for Radio, Television and the Web. In the web, skilled people are required to maintain sites by web newspapers (which cater only to the web and do not have print editions) and popular newspapers and magazines who have their own web editions. In electronic journalism one can be a reporter, writer, editor, researcher, correspondent and anchor.

Career in journalism is a prestigious profession as well as a highly paid one. Journalist play a major role in the development of nation. It is through them that we get information about daily happenings in the society. The purpose of journalism itself is to inform and interpret, educate and enlighten the people.

The opportunities for journalists are endless and at the same time the job has become more challenging, as the new world is proving the adage that "the pen (and the camera) is mightier than the sword." Simple reporting of events is no more sufficient, more specialisation and professionalism in reporting is required. Journalists specialize in diverse areas, such as politics, finance and economics, investigation, culture and sports for newspapers and periodicals.

Remuneration

The minimum salary as per government directive has to be Rs. 5500 to Rs. 9000 for reporters and senior reporters, Rs. 5000 to Rs. 10,500 for the chief reporters and sub-editors and Rs. 7500 to 12000 for editors. Actual salaries offered depend on the company one is working with and can be anything from very high to very low.

Travel and stay expenses as well as allowances are additional with all pay packets. Freelancers are paid for each piece of work they submit.

Eligibility & Course Areas

Educational Qualification: Bachelor's degree or postgraduate degree in journalism/mass communication is required to pursue a career in this field. Additional course work, specialized training or experience, fieldwork or internship increases one's opportunities in the field. There are a number of universities and institutes offering training in journalism.

Minimum eligibility for Bachelor degree in journalism is 10+2 and for Post graduate degree courses a Bachelor degree in journalism. Some institutes also provide one year certificate courses in journalism for which eligibility is 10+2. There are also courses in specialized areas of journalism like sports, television, photo, press law etc.

No course or training can claim to make one, a journalist. The courses train persons in the technical aspects only, to ensure one's success in the field one must have an inborn ability to write and produce new stories in correct, concise and interesting style. Latest trend in this regard is that big groups of newspapers advertise the posts of trainees for which all graduates are eligible. After conducting the entrance examination, suitable graduate trainees, with flair for writing are selected and employed. In other words, now the formal academic qualification for being a reporter, copy writer or correspondent is not essential.

Personal Attributes: To become a journalist one should have an inquisitive mind, will power, an aptitude for presenting information in an accurate, concise and effective manner, organize their thoughts and to express themselves clearly both orally and in writing. At the same time a journalist has to be tactful, confident and organised while interviewing people from all walks of life. They must have the ability to sift relevant facts from the irrelevant. The ability to accept criticism and willingness to do considerable rewriting are also necessary.

Job Prospects & Career Options

Job Prospects: They can find employment with newspapers, periodicals and magazines, central information service, press information bureau, websites, AIR and TV channels like Doordarshan, ZEE TV, Star TV etc. At the same time they can do freelancing. One can also take up this career as a part time employment along with any other field of work.

Career Options in Journalism: Journalists can work as editors, reporters, columnists, correspondents, staff or freelance writer, photojournalists, proofreaders, news analysts etc. in print (newspapers and magazines) and electronic (Radio, Television and Web) media.

Editing

Editor: In the editing field there are various positions :

Chief Editor/Resident Editor: Chief /resident editor is in charge of the overall functions of the publication. His primary responsibility is to supervise the functions of collection, selection and presentation of news. He reads and corrects copy for publication, decide on the editorial policy and the content of publications. Resident editor is in charge of a particular edition (*e.g.*. Chennai edition, Mumbai edition etc.).

Personal Attributes: He should have excellent journalistic vision- awareness of the major or minor political and current affairs, communication skills, leadership quality and long term experience as an editor.

Sub Editor: They assist chief editor in selecting & sorting the contents. Their job involves rewriting stories to fit the space assigned, improve the language, insert punctuation etc. They also give headlines and help in page layout. There are number of sub editors for each news paper. The chief sub editor is in charge of the team of sub editors- he assigns work and coordinates and supervises them. He act as a link between the chief editor and sub editors.

News /Feature Editor: He is the right-hand man of the chief editor. He decides on the news to be published in the newspaper each day. He collect news, controls the network of correspondents, reporting staff and other news sources, allocate assignments and attend editorial conferences.

Associate Editor: He directs the preparation of a section of a newspaper, magazine or a television or radio segment. He prepares news, feature articles and critical reviews and plans the layout of the publication, assigns reporting staff and photographers to obtain coverage of matters of news or interest related to his section.

Personal Attributes: Editors must have the ability to write & edit articles, take speedy decisions, a questioning mentality and an awareness of current affairs.

Job Prospectus: They can find job with newspaper groups, publishers of magazines and journals, Indian Information Service of the Government, websites etc.

Proofreader: A proofreader compare proofs and edited copy (Written, typed or printed material) to ensure that the final text is complete and accurate and that the spelling and punctuation are correct before final printing. They mark proofs for corrections, check revised proofs to ensure that the corrections have been made. They must have sound knowledge of spelling, punctuation and grammar, should be able to pay particular attention to detail and retain concentration for a long period.

Reporting

Reporter: He is the one who reports events as and when it occurs. The reporter is said to be the eyes & ears of the newspaper. Reporter attend press conferences, conduct interviews, visit sites of major occurrence and gather first hand report and present them in an unbiased manner. Their job involves a lot of travelling. A Chief reporter is in charge of the team of reporters and assigns work to the reporters. Main newspapers employ reporters in all major cities.

Personal Attributes: Reporter should have an analytic approach, perseverance, cool temperament, writing skill and self-confidence. He should have good contacts with various news resources and an ability to sense news.

Correspondent/Special Reporters: They are reporters for special purposes and their task involves reporting on a particular topic like politics, foreign affairs, sports, finance etc. They often report on news covering their area of expertise from a place where the particular event is happening. Their aim is to interpret or explain news and comment on the events, trends and causes behind it. Special correspondent must choose the concerned field in which he has special interest to make a success out of it. Usually one must have sufficient experience as a reporter to become a special correspondent.

Writing

Writer: A writer chooses themes or subjects for written work, conduct research into the subject, assemble background material and obtain other necessary data. Writers may specialise in- Journalism, fiction writing; children's books, educational textbook writing, historical writing and transferring oral histories into written form, humour or comedy writing and so on. In journalism, writers can be feature writers, leader writers, writers for multimedia and web and so on.

Feature Writer: Feature writers writes detailed stories or presents commentaries on specific news topics. They research and analyse facts and draw conclusions on a particular topic. They can cover any topic of public interest like interviews, organising data and evidence, feature story leads etc. Feature writing is more descriptive and detailed than news reporting.

Leader Writer: He gives ideas on news topics in the editorial columns of newspapers or magazines and discusses prospects of improvement with trainee writers.

Writing for Multimedia and the Web: Writers are required in multimedia and the worldwide Web for writing news and other articles. They must have a skill for writing precise text adaptive to the environment. If you can communicate your ideas through graphics, animation etc. it is an added advantage in this field.

Columnist: They are writers who contribute regularly to a publication. Usually one column on general or a specific topic is devoted to the writer. They writes a regular segment within their particular interest category, *e.g.* gardening, fashion, politics, films. The columnist usually projects a point of view and could either be a commentator or a critic. They review developments in special areas they write on & may contribute to a number of news papers at the same time.

Critic: A critic needs to be well read, have adequate knowledge and experience in his respective field. One can be a critic in various fields like film, art, drama etc. Only persons having good knowledge about the particular subject/art can authoritatively write about the subject.

Photography

Photo Journalist or News Photographer: They are the visual reporters. Photo journalists accompany reporters on assignments to take pictures that support a news story, feature or interview. They must know what makes a good news picture; be able to write accurate captions, work well with reporters, be quick and often work under difficult conditions. They must have good knowledge about technical aspects of photography like lighting, speed etc. to take photographs apt for the particular situation.

Others

Fashion Journalist: He is an overall in-charge of a fashion magazine. It is through him that the general public gets to know the latest fashion trends. He should have excellent taste for fashion and keeps himself abreast with latest fashion news, consumer reaction to new collections, fashion shows, current and future trends in colour, design and fabric. Today fashion journalist has a bright scope for employment as there is a need for exclusive articles and programmes with the development of fashion industry.

Cartoonists and illustrators make a social or political comment on public figures or events in the form of a cartoon that is funny as well as witty. A cartoon is one man's view of the world.

Other departments included in the publication of a newspaper or periodical are : production, advertising, legal affairs department, circulation and public relations.

A Career in Journalism

What's it About? : We are looking here at newspaper journalists, who research and write news stories and feature articles in order to inform readers about issues and events in the news.

What Skills do I Need?: To convince an editor that you are worth appointing, you will need to be able to demonstrate the following:

An interest in current affairs at all levels
A lively interest in people, places and events
An ability to write in a style which is easy to understand
Good spelling, grammar and punctuation
An appreciation of the part a local newspaper plays in the community
A willingness to accept irregular hours
An ability to work under pressure to meet deadlines
Determination and persistence

How do I Get into the Newspaper Industry?: Trainees come into the industry by a variety of routes. Some are recruited directly by regional or local newspapers and carry out their basic training under the terms of a training contract. This is known as direct entry. Within this category are those who may have secured employment with a newspaper company or a group of companies who run their own training programmes.

However, most trainees are recruited after attending full-time vocational education and training courses for post A-level students and graduates. Such courses are generally held at colleges accredited by the National Council for the Training of Journalists (NCTJ). Some of these courses are for graduates only. This route is known as pre-entry.

What Qualifications do I Need? : The usual entry requirement for newspaper journalism is a minimum of five GCSE passes (grades A-C) or equivalent. However, in recent years it has become rare for a trainee to come into the industry at this level. Over half the recruits are university graduates and many of the others have achieved at least two A-levels or equivalent. One of the passes at GCSE must be in English. Five GCSEs (grades A-C) is also the minimum NCTJ requirement for the pre-entry courses. However most colleges require two A-levels.

What Do I have to Study?: Current training courses lead to a variety of qualifications but all courses cover those aspects of law, public affairs and newspaper journalism necessary to enable a journalist to perform competently by the end of the training period. As well as demonstrating competence in these and other practical areas, trainees are expected to be able to achieve 100 wpm in an accredited shorthand system before obtaining an industry-recognised qualification.

Direct Entry: If you are recruited into the industry from school or university, you will be regarded as a direct entrant. Most companies expect you to enter into a two-year training contract, during which time basic training is carried out. The first six months of employment is likely to be a probationary period, during which you will be able to decide whether you have got what it takes to become a successful journalist. Most companies register you with the NCTJ and provide you with a distance learning foundation course to study.

After about six months, you should attend a block release course at college. Following a further period of work experience, you will have the opportunity to prove that you are competent to obtain the NCTJ's National Certificate or a National /Scottish Vocational Qualification at Level 4.

Trainees recruited by in-company training schemes undertake their off-the-job training at their company training centres. The NCTJ currently accredits one in-company training scheme: Midland News Association.

Pre-entry: If you attended a full-time journalism course before obtaining employment, you will probably enter into an 18-month training contract. The first three months is likely to be a probationary period. As with direct entrants, you will be expected to prove your competence after a period of work experience.

How Do I Get Started?

As a Direct Entrant: Apply direct to the editor of a regional or local newspaper for employment as a trainee. The names and addresses can be obtained from current editions of Benn's UK Media Directory and Willing's Press Guide Copies should be available at your local library under the reference section.

Journalism Jobs

Journalism is a discipline of gathering, affirming, reporting and analyzing information assembled regarding current events, consisting of issues, trends and people. In the present times, a large number of accredited Indian journalists (both in the field of electronic and print media) seek out, report on and publicize occurrences of consequence happening all across the globe. They are famous and their stories are carried out by numerous newspapers, magazines and periodicals, besides radio and television networks all around the world.,

The main activity of journalism is the reporting of events by stating who, what, when, where, why and how and explaining its significance and impact. People all around the world, in huge numbers, count on TV news, magazines, newspapers and radio to information, enlighten and even entertain them. Journalism exists in a number of media, like, newspapers, television, radio, magazines and the most famous and latest mediums, 'the Internet'.

Current Job Scenario: The purpose of journalism is to inform and interpret, educate and enlighten the general public. The opportunities for journalists are endless and at the same time the job is becoming more challenging. The job now requires more specialization and professionalism. The job market (both abroad and domestic) is good for those Indian Journalists who specialize in diverse areas, such as finance, politics, economics, investigation and sports & culture. They can find employment with numerous magazines, newspapers, periodicals, central information service, press information bureau, websites etc.

Career in Journalism: Career in journalism is a prestigious profession as well as a highly paid one. Various types of journalism are:

- Broadcast Journalism
- Business Journalism
- Alternative Journalism
- Investigative Journalism

Since, journalism is concerned with collection and dissemination of news through the print media as well as the electronic media, it can also be classified as:-

Print Journalism: Print journalism has been one of the oldest forms of journalism, it consists of newspapers, magazines and journals. In this profession there are many areas where one can work in, like, editors, reporters, columnists, correspondents etc.

Electronic Journalism: Electronic journalism includes communication mediums like television, radio, web, audio, video etc. With the growing network of TV, satellite communication, cable services, radio stations, etc., the future of this industry is very bright. In electronic journalism one can work in a number of fields, like, production, camera, graphics, editing, sound, programme research, script writing etc.

The Recruiters look for the following attributes:

The Must Have's:

- An inquisitive mind, determination and persistence
- An interest in current affairs at all levels
- An aptitude for presenting information in an accurate, concise and effective manner.
- A lively interest in people, places and events

- Ability to organize thoughts and to write in a style which is easy to understand.
- Ability to sift relevant facts from the irrelevant.
- A willingness to accept irregular hours
- Ability to accept criticism and willingness to do considerable rewriting are also necessary.
- An ability to work under pressure to meet deadlines

Eligibility: Employers in today's competitive world look for journalists who can write, edit and evaluate information and know how to communicate to a variety of audiences on a variety of communication platforms. However, recruiters give preference to those with strong liberal background at the graduation level and a Postgraduate degree from some renowned institute with specialization in the relevant field.

Newspaper Journalist

Job Description and Activities: Newspaper journalists or reporters source, research and write stories for publication in local, regional and national press.

Junior reporters are allocated work from the news desk and submit stories to the news editor, who passes it on to a team of copy tasters and subeditors. During the course of a career in journalism it is likely that you will move between functions. On smaller papers, some functions may merge into one.

Reporters cover all sorts of topics, including: news; items of cultural, sporting or scientific interest; local and national events; and entertainment, lifestyle and stories of 'human interest'.

Typical Work Activities: There is no such thing as a typical day in newspaper journalism, but as a junior reporter you may find yourself involved in the following:

- building contacts to maintain a steady flow of news, *e.g.* the police and emergency services, the local council, community organisations and health trusts;
- interviewing people in a range of very different circumstances—this may include those experiencing

distress or trauma (*e.g.*, bereaved relatives), good fortune (*e.g.*, lottery winners) or celebrity success, or those affected by or involved in making political decisions (*e.g.*, in relation to school closures or hospital reorganisation);

- reporting on business developments or events of cultural interest in the community;
- attending press conferences;
- attending local and council meetings and magistrates' court proceedings;
- attending other events, *e.g.* football matches;
- recording interviews and meetings using shorthand or technical equipment;
- producing final copy to deadlines - on a daily paper there may be several each day;
- writing 'fillers' or articles to entertain;
- researching and writing longer feature articles;
- working with photographers and editors to produce final copy according to the newspaper's house style.

Salary and Conditions

- The starting salary for a trainee reporter on a local/ regional paper may be as low as £10,000, but you can expect rises of £2,000 - £3,000 as you progress through the training period (and dissatisfaction with pay is often offset by enthusiasm for the job).
- The average salary for all journalists is £22,500, but there is wide variation between regional papers (£17,500) and national newspapers (£40,000) (salary data collected Jan. 06).
- Salaries for senior reporters, feature writers and sub-editors are dependent on the size and type of paper, rather than level of the post, but can range from £15,000 - £40,000 (salary data collected Jan. 06).
- The range of salaries for senior editors on regional daily papers is £50,000 - £80,000. On national papers, salaries can be even higher (salary data collected Jan. 06).

- Share options and bonuses, reflecting the paper's performance, can bolster salaries.
- Journalism has a long hours image. The 2002 survey Journalists at Work quotes the average working week as 41.6 hours, although 85% of journalists described their hours as reasonable. Early in your career you are likely to work an early or late shift pattern, but you will need to be flexible to accommodate breaking news and deadlines.
- Offices are usually open plan and may be noisy. You will spend much of your time working on a PC (or, more commonly, a Mac) and on the phone, but may need to travel to meet people or cover events.
- Many journalists spend part of their career working on a freelance basis. Demand for experienced freelancers is high, especially for feature writing and design. Young journalists often work freelance to build up experience and contacts; some retired journalists continue to work on a freelance basis. The National Union of Journalists (NUJ) issues a guide to freelance fees in their NUJ Freelance Fees Guide.
- Career breaks may be possible with returners sometimes moving back into the profession via a sub-editing role or through freelance work.
- The NUJ report a 60/40 male/female gender split in the industry. Women are increasingly represented at senior level.
- The profession is predominantly white, but efforts are being made to recruit from ethnic minority backgrounds.
- Opportunities with regional papers exist throughout the UK, but 70% of journalists working for national papers are based in London. Geographical mobility is important, especially at the beginning of a career in journalism.
- The role can be stressful. Your job is to ask 'why?', even if you risk making yourself look a fool, or, to quote John Humphreys, to 'challenge authority, find some answers and pass them on'.

- Because of the need to work long and unpredictable hours at times, you may find that your social and working life become intertwined.
- Travel within a working day can be common. Absence from home overnight is rarely required. There may be opportunities to work abroad.

Entry Requirements

The majority of new entrants to newspaper journalism are graduates and most will have gained a relevant pre-entry qualification.

Although an undergraduate degree in journalism may improve your chances of entry to the profession, there are pre-entry courses aimed at graduates of any discipline and personal qualities and experience are often considered as important as your actual degree subject. Pre-entry courses specifically for graduates of any discipline include:

- full-time one-year postgraduate courses;
- fast track 18/20 week postgraduate courses;
- courses approved by The National Council for the Training of Journalists (NCTJ).

Many pre-entry courses and undergraduate journalism degrees are accredited by the NCTJ and include their preliminary exams, which are necessary in order to sit the National Certificate Exam (NCE), required by many employers.

Entry with an HND or foundation degree only is possible if you also have relevant skills and experience. A few foundation degrees in journalism are recognised by the NCTJ. The Newspaper Society lists NCTJ-accredited courses on its website.

Although increasingly rare, direct entry is possible whereby individuals are recruited by newspapers that offer direct entry on to a two-year training contract. Anyone entering journalism this way would usually be required to sit the NCE early in their career. Potential candidates will need to show evidence of the following:

- the ability to be persuasive, with strong communication and social skills;

- a keen interest in news, current affairs and business;
- organisation skills and the ability to work under pressure to tight deadlines;
- an ability to grasp complex issues quickly and explain them in simple language;
- resilience, determination and motivation.

Competition for the limited number of places on graduate trainee schemes with large newspaper groups and national papers is extremely fierce. Programmes vary from year to year and details may not be widely circulated as editors rely on candidates to take the initiative to research opportunities. National newspapers who currently offer schemes include The Daily Telegraph, The Guardian, The Times and the Financial Times. Reuters recruits a handful of graduates each year into structured training schemes, including journalism in the financial sector. The Guardian Media Group sponsors graduates for postgraduate training and offers work experience through The Scott Trust Bursary Scheme.

You will need to present a good record of relevant work experience accompanied by a file of cuttings (*i.e.*, samples of your writing). Treat the task of building your personal portfolio professionally. Take every opportunity to write a selection of articles and reviews for local, free, national or specialist papers. Get involved in student newspapers and publications. Make use of publications such as the Writers and Artists Yearbook or the Guardian Media Directory, as well as informal sources to build up a network of contacts. Join the National Union of Journalists (NUJ) as a student and keep an eye on publications like the Media Guardian or the Press Gazette for work experience details. Pressure on work experience is greatest in June and July so be pro-active and try at other times in the year too. Do not despair at rejections - editors appreciate and respect persistence and the desire to succeed.

Initiatives like the George Viner Memorial Fund aim to support black and Asian students through training. The Journalism Diversity Fund supports the training of journalists from ethnically and socially diverse backgrounds. The Society of Editors also have a campaign backed by the Commission for

Racial Equality (CRE). From 1 October 2006 it will be illegal to discriminate against candidates on age grounds but, in practice, age may continue to be used in selection criteria by some employers.

You may be interested in further information about work experience and further study.

Training

After an initial probationary period, most trainee reporters follow basic journalism training under the terms of a training contract, usually lasting up to 18 months. All trainee journalists must pass preliminary exams to be eligible to sit The National Council for the Training of Journalists (NCTJ) National Certificate Exam (NCE), the professional qualification for senior newspaper journalists (and often seen as proof that a journalist has been properly trained). These include:

- newspaper journalism;
- public affairs (Parts I and II);
- dealing with handouts;
- law (Parts I and II);
- shorthand to 100 words per minute.

Trainees with large newspaper groups and national newspapers will also receive structured training in reporting, writing, proofreading, sub-editing, layout and design and production. Smaller newspapers may not be able to provide opportunities to train in these areas to the same extent. Courses run by the NCTJ are well recognised in the industry and can lead to a variety of further qualifications, including N/SVQs.

Career Development

Most journalists start work on local or regional newspapers. After a few years as a general reporter, many people move on, specialising in a certain area such as politics, crime or education.

Some become district reporters, covering a distinct geographical area. Other career options include moving into news management by joining the news desk, or a move into production, working on page layout and headlines as a sub-editor. It may also be possible to move overseas as a foreign correspondent, where knowledge of the language and culture is essential.

Career development depends on individual performance and initiative. The skills learned on a local or regional newspaper (or through a training scheme) are relevant to reporting in all media and there is more movement out to other types of journalism from newspapers than vice versa.

Many senior journalists work freelance across print, broadcast and online journalism. As news is increasingly a significant feature of both radio and television broadcasting, it offers newspaper journalists off-screen opportunities as researchers, writers and production assistants on the reporting or editing side of news programmes. The internet provides an increasing number of opportunities in news reporting.

Employees in news agencies such as Reuters can sometimes enter directly as trainees but it is more common to start in newspapers and then move to agency work. Working for an agency can provide experience in a range of different media, as agency reporters may provide tapes for local radio, features for magazines and news items for national daily newspapers, teletext and other digital media providers. Because of the range of work available, this can be a good stepping stone to freelance work.

Press Sub-editor

Job Description and Activities: Press sub-editors are journalists who work for:

- national daily or weekly newspapers;
- local and regional newspapers;
- magazines.

They are responsible for ensuring that the tone, style and layout of final copy matches the publication's house style and target market.

The role involves processing all the copy before it is published to ensure that it is accurate, makes sense and reads well. They also lay out the story on the page and may also be involved with overall page design. As with many roles in journalism, sub-editing is a demanding role that requires constant attention to detail within a fast-paced working environment.

Typical Work Activities: Work activities vary and can depend on the extent to which production and layout work falls within a sub-editor's remit. Only senior sub-editors would be expected to have much legal knowledge, but there are common activities that form much of the work of most sub-editors. These include:

- editing copy to remove spelling mistakes and grammatical errors;
- rewriting material so that it flows or reads better and adheres to the house style of a particular publication;
- ensuring that a story fits a particular word count by cutting or expanding material as necessary;
- writing headlines that capture the essence of the story or are clever or amusing;
- writing stand-firsts (brief introductions which sum up the story);
- liaising with reporters or journalists to clarify facts and details about a story;
- editing press releases or reports;
- compiling routine information, such as tables of sports results or financial data;
- checking stories to ensure they are accurate, do not break the law or go against the publication's policy;
- cropping photos and deciding where to use them for best effect;
- writing the captions for pictures;
- discussing concerns with editors;
- proofreading complete pages produced by other sub-editors;
- working to a page plan to ensure that the right stories appear in the correct place on each page;
- laying out pages and, depending on the nature of the role, playing a part in page design;

- adding last minute news stories;
- keeping up to date with sector issues, *e.g.* by reading related publications.

Salary and Conditions

- Starting salaries range from £13,000 to £16,000 on a local paper or small magazine and £18,000 for a larger regional or national paper (salary data collected Oct. 05). Salaries can be lower than this, simply because it is such a popular sector and this can drive entry salaries down.
- Salaries for senior sub-editors range from £22,000 to £37,000, again depending on the publication concerned. A chief sub-editor for a national newspaper could earn £50,000+ (salary data collected Oct. 05).
- The work is definitely not nine to five, with hours varying according to workload. Depending on whether you are working for a daily, weekly or monthly title, work cycles build up to a frenetic peak just before the paper is due to go to print. Working late to meet deadlines is all part of the job. Sub-editors working for national dailies may have to work unsocial hours and some early or late shifts.
- The work is desk-based, but can include visits to meetings, launches and other events.
- On smaller publications there is a fair degree of flexibility and variety of work. More specialised, but narrower, roles are likely with a larger paper or magazine. However, many sub-editors find that work activities are generally fluid, which means that it can be easy to become involved in more writing, design and production, so that once you progress beyond being a basic sub-editing role, the work is often varied.
- The work environment can be competitive and stressful, with high levels of stress as deadlines approach. Despite this, job satisfaction is often high because your work is readily visible.
- Freelance work is an option for sub-editors with experience. This can offer increased flexibility and the chance to earn a higher salary.

- The role can offer a route into other areas of journalism and publishing, though it is often something people move into after gaining experience as a reporter.
- Travel within a working day is occasional. Overseas work or travel is uncommon.

Entry Requirements

A degree is not essential, but it is often difficult to get into the profession without a relevant degree or postgraduate course and/or a vocational qualification. Graduates from a range of backgrounds can gain entry on to training courses, but relevant degree subjects include:

- English;
- media studies.

To some extent, any degree that helps to develop excellent written communication skills will be of an advantage. For later career development, for example on a specialist magazine, your degree subject may be relevant: a science or engineering subject for a technical journal; history or economics for a current affairs magazine, etc.

The National Council for the Training of Journalists (NCTJ) accredits many degree and postgraduate pre-entry courses, so it is worth checking what the accreditation status of any particular course is when making your application.

Entry with HND only is possible, since the only stated requirement for anyone to undergo training is to hold three GCSEs at grade C or above. The reality is that the competitive nature of this industry means graduates and postgraduates are in a far stronger position than those with an HND or other equivalent qualification.

Pre-entry experience is crucial, for example via a work-based placement or through voluntary experience with a local paper.

Potential candidates will need to show evidence of the following:

- a pro-active, determined attitude;
- a resilient outlook;

- a good eye for detail;
- the ability to work under pressure;
- the ability to apply an understanding of law to your work;
- excellent communication skills.

For many jobs and certainly to be considered by any of the relevant recruitment agencies, competency with Quark Xpress is essential. Having basic Photoshop skills is also a real plus. If you do not have these, then at least being highly IT literate shows that you are likely to succeed on any relevant training courses.

As with all roles in journalism, competition is fierce. Selection procedures for courses or for jobs as sub-editors often involve copy-subbing exercises, so it is useful to practise this skill by summarising reports, précising lengthy articles, or simply trying to rewrite something in a more communicative way.

This is an area of work where maturity is often appreciated. Commonly, people move into sub-editing roles having first gained experience as a reporter.

You may be interested in further information about work experience and further study.

Training

Sub-editors will have either completed a course accredited by The National Council for the Training of Journalists (NCTJ) before they enter journalism, or they will study for an approved course while they are working. It is possible to gain entry to this role without prior training, though previous experience in a relevant setting is a must. New entrants are likely to have the support of a more experienced collegue.

Many of the large newspaper groups run in-house training programmes.

There is a wide range of approved courses, but all cover the basics of journalism, including the law, as well as the practical skills of journalism, including sub-editing. Approved courses are listed on the NCTJ website. Courses are available at foundation, undergraduate and postgraduate degree levels.

Whilst degree-level and postgraduate courses in journalism include sub-editing as one of the core skills, it is really learned on the job. Experience and expertise in this area are gained, for example, by starting with the basics, such as editing out typing errors and spelling mistakes and adjusting word counts and then moving on to writing headlines and learning to lay out a story on the page.

Newspaper groups send their sub-editors on a range of in-company or external training courses. These are offered by the NCTJ and other relevant professional bodies. They cover all aspects of the role, including:

- restructuring features;
- tackling technical copy;
- stand-firsts and captions;
- making the most of the page in terms of design and overall effect.

Opportunities for advanced IT training also help sub-editors to update their skills and keep up with industry developments.

Career Development

The most junior post for a sub-editor is that of copy sub, which is all based on dealing with the written text. Being given greater responsibility for page design and layout is the next step up.

A typical career for a really successful sub-editor is:

- editorial assistant;
- sub-editor;
- production editor;
- chief sub-editor;
- editor.

However, since every publication has only one editor, not every sub is going to achieve, or wish to achieve, this position.

The sub-editing role provides an excellent opportunity to gain an insight into all aspects of journalism, with exposure to writing, design and production skills. Sub-editors with a little experience often get the opportunity to write features, especially if they have been subbing copy for a specific section, such as sport, the arts, business or finance. This is very valuable experience for anyone aiming to write for a career. Sub-editors can also move into a more full-time design and production role.

Journalism for the web is another possible career move where the sub-editor's ease with technical issues and good writing ability can be a valuable combination. This is a growing area of the industry.

Magazines and small newspapers have less clear-cut definitions between journalists, sub-editors and production editors, so a move to a smaller publication can be very useful to develop a real breadth of experience.

Many of the largest newspaper groups own titles all over the country and one way to gain promotion is to apply for more senior posts within your own newspaper group.

Like other journalists, sub-editors can also find employment as press officers for companies or working with public relations (PR) agencies, writing the kind of copy that is likely to be accepted by other media.

Geographic mobility and a willingness to move companies can aid successful career development. The ability to maintain industry contacts and respond quickly to new opportunities is also very useful.

Magazine Journalist

Job Description and Activities

Magazine journalists research and write news and feature articles suited to a magazine's reader profile. The readership of a magazine is often defined by a common need or interest.

There are over 9,000 magazine titles in the UK covering a diverse range of topics and varying from glossy magazines to trade newsletters. Most fall into one of four categories:

- business;
- professional;
- consumer;
- specialist consumer.

The three main branches of magazine journalism are news writing, feature writing and sub-editing. Although generally in paper format, many magazine publishers increasingly produce material in new media (for example, CD, web, or audio) in addition to hard copy.

Typical Work Activities: The work can vary considerably depending on the size of the organisation and the subject matter covered by the publication. It can also vary depending on the medium through which the magazine is produced. Typical work activities include:

- researching a subject and story;
- talking to people;
- atttending seminars, conferences and fairs (some magazine publishers hold exhibitions and events to allow advertisers to meet their readership);
- generating ideas for stories;
- meeting with colleagues to plan the content of the edition and the character of the publication.

Journalists, particularly freelancers, will also spend time networking and building relationships with publications and their staff. A commissioning editor will also be involved in monitoring the work of others.

Producing text that reads well and that is in keeping with the mood of the readership is important, but generating interesting ideas for subjects to cover is probably more significant overall.

On smaller magazines, the role might include all of these activities plus administrative work; in a larger team the role will probably be more strictly defined.

Salary and Conditions

- For those entering the profession at graduate level, job titles will include staff writer, graduate writer and journalism trainee. Starting salaries range from £18,000-£24,000, although many graduates have to work for free, sometimes for long periods of time, before securing a paid job (salary data collected May 06).

- For those with some experience, salaries are often negotiable, depending on the level of experience. Senior staff (senior staff writer, sub editor or features editor) usually earn between £19,000 and £35,000 (salary data collected May 06).
- For those working for the biggest publications, or who become editor in chief of a magazine, salaries can be anything from £22,000 to £63,000+ (salary data collected May 06).
- Freelance fees vary according to experience and ability, but the average freelance fee per 1,000 words is £224 (data collected May 06).
- Salary levels depend mainly on the location, size and popularity of the magazine. Salaries in London and the South-East are generally higher and opportunities more plentiful. Experience and ability will also influence pay.
- This is not a nine to five job; copy deadlines may mean irregular hours. Unsocial hours are common.
- Part-time work and career breaks are possible.
- With much of magazine journalism now being outsourced, freelancing is more common (up to 80% of magazine copy is written by freelancers). Many people make successful careers as freelance magazine journalists, contributing pieces to a wide variety of publications.
- The magazine industry is largely (although not exclusively) based in London and the South-East.
- Women are well represented on consumer magazines.
- There is the opportunity to meet a wide variety of people outside the organisation but long hours, tight deadlines and writing for the public domain can be stressful and it is sometimes necessary to subordinate your private life to the calls of the job. News happens irregularly, but media coverage appears regularly and deadlines have to be met.
- There is frequent travel within the working day and occasional absence from home at night. Overseas work and travel is not uncommon.

Entry Requirements

More than 70% of entrants to journalism are now graduates. Some specialist magazines may require subject knowledge relating to a particular degree, *e.g.* engineering, science, or computing. Entry without a degree or HND is sometimes possible. Experience, determination and good contacts may substitute for a degree/HND and will enhance any application.

A pre-entry certificate or postgraduate qualification in journalism, though not usually essential, will give you a good grounding in writing and an awareness of journalistic law.

While a degree and a relevant qualification may get you started, it is your personal aptitude that will determine your success. Pre-entry experience, either paid or unpaid, is essential as you will gain first-hand knowledge of the industry and will demonstrate to employers your ability to thrive in a pressured environment.

Potential candidates will need to show evidence of the following:

- literacy;
- a familiarity with current affairs;
- a pro-active approach to finding things out;
- resilience;
- strong interpersonal skills;
- a demonstrable interest in/passion for the subject of the magazine.

IT skills, such as HTML, Java, Perl, Quark Xpress, e-mail and familiarity with the internet are all valued in this field.

Get involved in student newspapers, magazines, radio stations and internal television circuits. Write to magazines, showing an enthusiasm for their subject matter and ask for some work experience. Very few structured work experience or training schemes exist. Contact magazines directly to enquire whether they have a scheme.

Entry into journalism in general is very competitive, with several people applying for every training vacancy. The industry is growing, but the number of training vacancies is not increasing proportionately. This is because much of the growth is in small publishers, which do not run training schemes. Entry into popular consumer magazines is also very competitive, but slightly easier to specialist technical and scientific journals, or trade and business magazines.

Many opportunities are not advertised at all and applications submitted on speculation are a common way of securing a job. Where there is no central recruiting point, you should apply directly to the editor of the magazine or journal. Freelancers and speculative job-hunters rely on directories such as the Writers and Artists Yearbook to find editors' details. Try to build up your own personalised list of contacts.

If you are considering freelancing, make sure you target the right magazines for your article. Telephone editors with an idea for an article relevant to their publication. Keep an eye out for events or stories with a local interest and you may be able to persuade your local newspaper to publish your work. Even reviewing products, theatre or films can add to your portfolio.

In an attempt to offset the scarcity of black journalists, the National Union of Journalists (NUJ) has set up the George Viner Memorial Fund to help those who want to take industry-recognised pre-entry courses, but lack the money to do so.

From 1 October 2006 it will be illegal to discriminate against candidates on age grounds but, in practice, age may continue to be used in selection criteria by some employers. You may be interested in further information about work experience and further study.

Training

Trainees with big publishing houses receive structured training in reporting, writing, proof-reading, sub-editing, layout and design, production and law for journalists leading to N/SVQs. Smaller organisations that recruit directly may not be able to provide such opportunities.

The Periodicals Training Council (PTC) is the training arm of The Periodical Publishers Association (PPA) and is funded and recognised by the government as the industry training organisation responsible for the magazine publishing sector. Its objective is to enhance the performance of the sector by identifying training needs, setting occupational standards and developing N/SVQs.

It also accredits courses run by colleges and universities and acts as a focal point for information and guidance on good practice.

Courses run by The National Council for the Training of Journalists (NCTJ), throughout the country and online, are also well recognised in the industry. Although mainly focused on newspaper journalism, it does run a distance learning course in periodical journalism and sub-editing and all its courses are accredited by the National Union of Journalists (NUJ).

Another option is the London College of Communication, the media branch of the University of the Arts, London, which runs respected short, as well as undergraduate and postgraduate, courses in journalism and other media industries.

Career Development

There is no fixed path of/career progression in magazine journalism. You may progress from staff writer to sub-editor/ chief sub/section head, or you may move across into newspapers, TV journalism or public relations. Freelancing is a realistic option, allowing more flexible working patterns and (perhaps) greater control over your own work.

Journalism is a fast-moving and fast-changing career where it pays to keep abreast of new developments in media and communications. Other major factors affecting career development are the contacts you make in the industry - editors are more likely to give work to someone they know they can trust - and your willingness to be flexible about the work you take on.

The industry is characterised by a move away from specialisms towards multi-skilling and there are more opportunities for people to move between media. Increasingly, journalists are also writing for online publications, so knowledge and expertise of writing for the web can be very helpful.

Commercial awareness is essential for progression in order to sell your work as a freelancer or, if you work for a magazine, to increase your readership.

News Analysts, Reporters and Correspondents

Significant Points: Competition will be keen for jobs at large metropolitan and national newspapers, broadcast stations and magazines; most entry-level openings arise at small broadcast stations and publications.

Most employers prefer individuals with a bachelor's degree in journalism or mass communications and experience gained at school newspapers or broadcasting stations or through internships with news organizations.

Jobs often involve irregular hours, night and weekend work and pressure to meet deadlines.

Slower than average employment growth is expected.

Nature of the Work: News analysts, reporters and correspondents gather information, prepare stories and make broadcasts that inform us about local, State, national and international events; present points of view on current issues; and report on the actions of public officials, corporate executives, interest groups and others who exercise power.

News analysts—also called *news-casters* or *news-anchors*—examine, interpret and broadcast news received from various sources. News anchors present news stories and introduce video-taped news or live transmissions from on-the-scene reporters. Newscasters at large stations and networks usually specialize in a particular type of news, such as sports or weather. *Weather-casters*, also called weather reporters, report current and forecasted weather conditions.

They gather information from national satellite weather services, wire services and local and regional weather bureaus. Some weather casters are trained meteorologists and can develop their own weather forecasts. *Sports-casters* select, write and deliver sports news. This may include interviews with sports personalities and coverage of games and other sporting events. *News correspondents* report on news occurring in the large U.S. and foreign cities where they are stationed.

In covering a story, *reporters* investigate leads and news tips, look at documents, observe events at the scene and interview people. Reporters take notes and also may take photographs or shoot videos. At their office, they organize the material, determine the focus or emphasis, write their stories and edit accompanying video material. Many reporters enter information or write stories using laptop computers and electronically submit the material to their offices from remote locations. In some cases, *newswriters* write a story from information collected and submitted by reporters. Radio and television reporters often compose stories and report "live" from the scene. At times, they later tape an introduction to or commentary on their story in the studio. Some journalists also interpret the news or offer opinions to readers, viewers, or listeners. In this role, they are called *commentators* or *columnists.*

General-assignment reporters write about newsworthy occurrences—such as accidents, political rallies, visits of celebrities, or business closings—as assigned. Large newspapers and radio and television stations assign reporters to gather news about specific topics, such as crime or education. Some reporters specialize in fields such as health, politics, foreign affairs, sports, theatre, consumer affairs, social events, science, business, or religion. Investigative reporters cover stories that may take many days or weeks of information gathering. Some publications use teams of reporters instead of assigning each reporter one specific topic, allowing reporters to cover a greater variety of stories. News teams may include reporters, editors, graphic artists and photographers working together to complete a story. Reporters on small publications cover all aspects of the news. They take photographs, write headlines, lay out pages, edit wire-service stories and write editorials. Some also solicit advertisements, sell subscriptions and perform general office work.

Working Conditions: The work of news analysts, reporters and correspondents is usually hectic. They are under great pressure to meet deadlines. Broadcasts sometimes are aired with little or no time for preparation. Some news analysts, reporters and correspondents work in comfortable, private offices; others work in large rooms filled with the sound of keyboards and computer printers, as well as the voices of other reporters. Curious onlookers, police, or other emergency workers can distract those reporting from the scene for radio and television. Covering wars, political uprisings, fires, floods and similar events is often dangerous.

Working hours vary. Reporters on morning papers often work from late afternoon until midnight. Radio and television reporters usually are assigned to a day or evening shift. Magazine reporters usually work during the day.

Reporters sometimes have to change their work hours to meet a deadline or to follow late-breaking developments. Their work demands long hours, irregular schedules and some travel. Because many stations and networks are on the air 24 hours a day, newscasters can expect to work unusual hours.

Training, Other Qualifications and Advancement: Most employers prefer individuals with a bachelor's degree in journalism or mass communications, but some hire graduates with other majors. They look for experience at school newspapers or broadcasting stations and internships with news organizations. Large-city newspapers and stations also may prefer candidates with a degree in a subject-matter specialty such as economics, political science, or business. Some large newspapers and broadcasters may hire only experienced reporters.

More than 1,200 institutions offer programmes in communications, journalism and related programmes. In 2004, 104 of these were accredited by the Accrediting Council on Education in Journalism and Mass Communications. About three-fourths of the courses in a typical curriculum are in liberal arts; the remaining courses are in journalism. Examples of journalism courses are introductory mass media, basic reporting and copy editing, history of journalism and press law and ethics. Students planning a career in broadcasting take courses in radio and television news and production. Those planning newspaper or magazine careers usually specialize in news-editorial journalism. To create stories for online media, they need to learn to use computer software to combine online story text with audio and video elements and graphics.

Some schools also offer a master's or Ph.D. degree in journalism. Some graduate programmes are intended primarily as preparation for news careers, while others prepare journalism teachers, researchers and theorists and advertising and public relations workers. A graduate degree may help those looking to advance.

High school courses in English, journalism and social studies provide a good foundation for college programmes. Useful college liberal arts courses include English with an emphasis on writing, sociology, political science, economics, history and psychology. Courses in computer science, business and speech are useful as well. Fluency in a foreign language is necessary in some jobs.

Reporters typically need more than good word-processing skills. Computer graphics and desktop-publishing skills also are useful. Computer-assisted reporting involves the use of computers to analyze data in search of a story. This technique and the interpretation of the results require computer skills and familiarity with databases. Knowledge of news photography also is valuable for entry-level positions, which sometimes combine the responsibilities of a reporter with those of a camera operator or photographer.

Employers report that practical experience is the most important part of education and training. Upon graduation many students already have gained much practical experience through part-time or summer jobs or through internships with news organizations. Most newspapers, magazines and broadcast news organizations offer reporting and editing internships. Work on high school and college newspapers, at broadcasting stations, or on community papers or U.S. Armed Forces publications also provides practical training. In addition, journalism scholarships, fellowships and assistantships awarded to college journalism students by universities, newspapers, foundations and professional organizations are helpful. Experience as a stringer or freelancer—a part-time reporter who is paid only for stories printed—is advantageous.

Reporters should be dedicated to providing accurate and impartial news. Accuracy is important, both to serve the public and because untrue or libelous statements can lead to lawsuits. A nose for news, persistence, initiative, poise, resourcefulness, a good memory and physical stamina are important, as is the emotional stability to deal with pressing deadlines, irregular hours and dangerous assignments. Broadcast reporters and news analysts must be comfortable on camera. All reporters must be at ease in unfamiliar places and with a variety of people. Positions involving on-air work require a pleasant voice and appearance.

Most reporters start at small publications or broadcast stations as general assignment reporters or copy editors. They are usually assigned to cover court proceedings and civic and club meetings, summarize speeches and write obituaries. With experience, they report more difficult assignments or specialize in a particular field. Large publications and stations hire few recent graduates; as a rule, they require new reporters to have several years of experience.

Some news analysts and reporters can advance by moving to larger newspapers or stations. A few experienced reporters become columnists, correspondents, writers, announcers, or public relations specialists. Others become editors in print journalism or programme managers in broadcast journalism, who supervise reporters. Some eventually become broadcasting or publishing industry managers.

Employment: News analysts, reporters and correspondents held about 64,000 jobs in 2004. About 61 percent worked for newspaper, periodical, book and directory publishers. Another 25 percent worked in radio and television broadcasting. About 7 percent of news analysts, reporters and correspondents were self-employed.

Job Outlook: Competition will continue to be keen for jobs on large metropolitan and national newspapers, broadcast stations and networks and magazines. Most job opportunities will be with small-town and suburban newspapers and radio and television stations. Talented writers who can handle highly specialized scientific or technical subjects have an advantage.

Also, newspapers increasingly are hiring stringers and freelancers.

Journalism graduates have the background for work in closely related fields such as advertising and public relations and many take jobs in these fields. Other graduates accept sales, managerial, or other nonmedia positions.

Employment of news analysts, reporters and correspondents is expected to grow more slowly than average for all occupations through the year 2014. Many factors will contribute to the limited job growth in this occupation. Consolidation and convergence should continue in the publishing and broadcasting industries. As a result, companies will be better able to allocate their news analysts, reporters and correspondents to cover news stories. Constantly improving technology also is allowing workers to do their jobs more efficiently, another factor that will limit the number of workers needed to cover a story or certain type of news. However, the continued demand for news will create some job opportunities. For example, some job growth likely will occur in newer media areas, such as online newspapers and magazines. Job openings also will result from the need to replace workers who leave their occupations permanently; some news analysts, reporters and correspondents find the work too stressful and hectic or do not like the lifestyle and transfer to other occupations.

The number of job openings in the newspaper and broadcasting industries—in which news analysts, reporters and correspondents are employed—is sensitive to economic ups and downs because these industries depend on advertising revenue.

Earnings: Salaries for news analysts, reporters and correspondents vary widely. Median annual earnings of reporters and correspondents were $31,320 in May 2004. The middle 50 percent earned between $22,900 and $47,860. The lowest 10 percent earned less than $18,470 and the highest 10 percent earned more than $68,250. Median annual earnings of reporters and correspondents were $30,070 in newspaper, periodical, book and directory publishers and $34,050 in radio and television broadcasting.

Median annual earnings of broadcast news analysts were $36,980 in May 2004. The middle 50 percent earned between $25,560 and $68,440.

The lowest 10 percent earned less than $19,040 and the highest 10 percent earned more than $122,800. Median annual earnings of broadcast news analysts were $37,840 in radio and television broadcasting.

Writers and Editors

Significant Points: Most jobs in this occupation require a college degree in communications, journalism, or English, although a degree in a technical subject may be useful for technical-writing positions.

The outlook for most writing and editing jobs is expected to be competitive because many people are attracted to the occupation.

Online publications and services are growing in number and sophistication, spurring the demand for writers and editors, especially those with Web experience.

Nature of the Work: Communicating through the written word, writers and editors generally fall into one of three categories. *Writers and authors* develop original fiction and nonfiction for books, magazines, trade journals, online publications, company newsletters, radio and television broadcasts, motion pictures and advertisements. *Editors* examine proposals and select material for publication or broadcast.

They review and revise a writer's work for publication or dissemination. *Technical writers* develop technical materials, such as equipment manuals, appendixes, or operating and maintenance instructions. They also may assist in layout work.

Most writers and editors have at least a basic familiarity with technology, regularly using personal computers, desktop or electronic publishing systems, scanners and other electronic communications equipment. Many writers prepare material directly for the Internet. For example, they may write for electronic newspapers or magazines, create short fiction or poetry, or produce technical documentation that is available only online. Also, they may write text for Web sites. These writers should be knowledgeable about graphic design, page layout and multimedia software. In addition, they should be familiar with interactive technologies of the Web so that they can blend text, graphics and sound together.

Writers—especially of nonfiction—are expected to establish their credibility with editors and readers through strong research and the use of appropriate sources and citations. Sustaining high ethical standards and meeting publication deadlines are essential.

Creative writers, poets and lyricists, including novelists, playwrights and screen writers, create original works—such as prose, poems, plays and song lyrics—for publication or performance. Some works may be commissioned by a sponsor; others may be written for hire (on the basis of the completion of a draft or an outline).

Nonfiction writers either propose a topic or are assigned one, often by an editor or publisher. They gather information about the topic through personal observation, library and Internet research and interviews. Writers then select the material they want to use, organize it and use the written word to express ideas and convey information. Writers also revise or rewrite sections, searching for the best organization or the right phrasing. *Copy writers* prepare advertising copy for use by publication or broadcast media or to promote the sale of goods and services. *Newsletter writers* produce information for distribution to association memberships, corporate employees, organizational clients, or the public.

Freelance writers sell their work to publishers, publication enterprises, manufacturing firms, public relations departments, or advertising agencies. Sometimes, they contract with publishers to write a book or an article. Others may be hired to complete specific assignments, such as writing about a new product or technique.

Bloggers write for the Internet. Most bloggers write personal reflections on a subject of close personal or professional interest. Some blogs take the form of a personal diary; others read like reports from the field—first-hand, subjective accounts of an event or an activity. Most blogs are written for recreational reasons with little expectation of earning a fee; however, some blogs promote a business or support a cause and may generate interest or income through other activities.

Editors review, rewrite and edit the work of writers. They may also do original writing. An editor's responsibilities vary with the employer and type and level of editorial position held. Editorial duties may include planning the content of books, technical journals, trade magazines and other general-interest publications. Editors also decide what material will appeal to readers, review and edit drafts of books and articles, offer comments to improve the work and suggest possible titles. In addition, they may oversee the production of the publications. In the book-publishing industry, an editor's primary responsibility is to review proposals for books and decide whether to buy the publication rights from the author.

Major newspapers and newsmagazines usually employ several types of editors. The *executive editor* oversees *assistant editors,* who have responsibility for particular subjects, such as local news, international news, feature stories, or sports. Executive editors generally have the final say about what stories are published and how they are covered. The *managing editor* usually is responsible for the daily operation of the news department. *Assignment editors* determine which reporters will cover a given story. *Copy editors* mostly review and edit a reporter's copy for accuracy, content, grammar and style.

In smaller organizations, such as small daily or weekly newspapers or the membership or publications departments of non-profit or similar organizations, a single editor may do everything or share responsibility with only a few other people. Executive and managing editors typically hire writers, reporters and other employees. They also plan budgets and negotiate contracts with freelance writers, sometimes called "stringers" in the news industry. In broadcasting companies, *programme directors* have similar responsibilities.

Editors and programme directors often have assistants, many of whom hold entry-level jobs. These assistants, such as copy editors and *production assistants*, review copy for errors in grammar, punctuation and spelling and check the copy for readability, style and agreement with editorial policy. They suggest revisions, such as changing words and rearranging sentences, to improve clarity or accuracy. They also carry out research for writers and verify facts, dates and statistics. Production assistants arrange page layouts of articles, photographs and advertising; compose headlines; and prepare copy for printing. *Publication assistants* who work for publishing houses may read and evaluate manuscripts submitted by freelance writers, proofread printers' galleys and answer letters about published material. Production assistants on small newspapers or in radio stations compile articles available from wire services or the Internet, answer phones and make photocopies.

Technical writers put technical information into easily understandable language. They prepare operating and maintenance manuals, catalogues, parts lists, assembly instructions, sales promotion materials and project proposals. Many technical writers work with engineers on technical subject matters to prepare written interpretations of engineering and design specifications and other information for a general readership. Technical writers also may serve as part of a team conducting usability studies to help improve the design of a product that still is in the prototype stage. They plan and edit technical materials and oversee the preparation of illustrations, photographs, diagrams and charts.

Science and medical writers prepare a range of formal documents presenting detailed information on the physical or medical sciences. They convey research findings for scientific or medical professions and organize information for advertising or public relations needs. Many writers work with researchers on technical subjects to prepare written interpretations of data and other information for a general readership.

Working Conditions: Some writers and editors work in comfortable, private offices; others work in noisy rooms filled with the sound of keyboards and computer printers, as well as the voices of other writers tracking down information over the telephone. The search for information sometimes requires that writers travel to diverse workplaces, such as factories, offices, or laboratories, but many find their material through telephone interviews, the library and the Internet.

Advances in electronic communications have changed the work environment for many writers. Laptop computers and wireless communications technologies allow growing numbers of writers to work from home and even on the road. The ability to e-mail, transmit and download stories, research, or editorial review materials using the Internet allows writers and editors greater flexibility in where and how they complete assignments.

Some writers keep regular office hours, either to maintain contact with sources and editors or to establish a writing routine, but most writers set their own hours. Many writers, especially freelance writers, are paid per assignment; therefore, they work any number of hours necessary to meet a deadline. As a result, writers must be willing to work evenings, nights, or weekends to produce a piece acceptable to an editor or client by the publication deadline. Those who prepare morning or weekend publications and broadcasts also may regularly work nights and weekends.

While many freelance writers enjoy running their own businesses and the advantages of working flexible hours, most routinely face the pressures of juggling multiple projects with competing demands and the continual need to find new work in order to earn a living. Deadline pressures and long, erratic work hours—often part of the daily routine in these jobs—may cause stress, fatigue, or burnout; use of computers for extended periods may cause some individuals to experience back pain, eyestrain, or fatigue.

Training, Other Qualifications and Advancement: A college degree generally is required for a position as a writer or editor. Although some employers look for a broad liberal arts background, most prefer to hire people with degrees in communications, journalism, or English. For those who specialize in a particular area, such as fashion, business, or law, additional background in the chosen field is expected. Knowledge of a second language is helpful for some positions.

Increasingly, technical writing requires a degree in, or some knowledge about, a specialized field—for example, engineering, business, or one of the sciences. In many cases, people with good writing skills can acquire specialized knowledge on the job. Some transfer from jobs as technicians, scientists, or engineers. Others begin as research assistants or as trainees in a technical information department, develop technical communication skills and then assume writing duties.

Writers and editors must be able to express ideas clearly and logically and should love to write. Creativity, curiosity, a broad range of knowledge, self-motivation and perseverance also are valuable. Writers and editors must demonstrate good judgment and a strong sense of ethics in deciding what material to publish. Editors also need tact and the ability to guide and encourage others in their work.

For some jobs, the ability to concentrate amid confusion and to work under pressure is essential. Familiarity with electronic publishing, graphics and video production equipment increasingly is needed. Use of electronic and wireless communications equipment to send e-mail, transmit work and review copy often is necessary. Online newspapers and magazines require knowledge of computer software used to combine online text with graphics, audio, video and animation.

High school and college newspapers, literary magazines, community newspapers and radio and television stations all provide valuable, but sometimes unpaid, practical writing experience. Many magazines, newspapers and broadcast stations have internships for students. Interns write short pieces, conduct research and interviews and learn about the publishing or broadcasting business.

In small firms, beginning writers and editors hired as assistants may actually begin writing or editing material right away. Opportunities for advancement can be limited, however. Many writers look for work on a short-term, project-by-project basis. Many small or not-for-profit organizations either do not have enough regular work or cannot afford to employ writers on a full-time basis. However, they routinely contract out work to freelance writers.

In larger businesses, jobs usually are more formally structured. Beginners generally do research, fact checking, or copy editing. Advancement to full-scale writing or editing assignments may occur more slowly for newer writers and editors in larger organizations than for employees of smaller companies. Advancement often is more predictable, though, coming with the assignment of more important articles.

Advancement for freelancers often means working on larger, more complex projects for more money. Building a reputation and establishing a track record for meeting deadlines also makes it easier to get future assignments, as does instituting long-term freelance relationships with the same publications.

The growing popularity of blogs could allow some writers to get their work read; a few well-written blogs may garner some recognition for the author and may lead to a few paid pieces in other print or electronic publications. However, most bloggers do not earn much money writing their blogs.

Employment: Writers and editors held about 320,000 jobs in 2004. More than one-third were self-employed. Writers and authors held about 142,000 jobs; editors, about 127,000 jobs; and technical writers, about 50,000 jobs. About one-half of the salaried jobs for writers and editors were in the information sector, which includes newspaper, periodical, book and directory publishers; radio and television broadcasting; software publishers; motion picture and sound-recording industries; Internet service providers, Web search portals and data-processing services; and Internet publishing and broadcasting. Substantial numbers also worked in advertising and related services, computer systems design and related services and public and private educational services. Other salaried writers and editors worked in computer and electronic product manufacturing; government agencies; religious organizations; and business, professional, labour, political and similar organizations.

Jobs with major book publishers, magazines, broadcasting companies, advertising agencies and public relations firms are concentrated in New York, Chicago, Los Angeles, Boston, Philadelphia and San Francisco; however, many writers work elsewhere and travel regularly to meet with personnel at the headquarters. Jobs with newspapers, business and professional journals and technical and trade magazines are more widely dispersed throughout the country.

Thousands of other individuals work as freelance writers, earning some income from their articles, books and, less commonly, television and movie scripts. Most support themselves with income derived from other sources.

Job Outlook: Employment of writers and editors is expected to grow about as fast as the average for all occupations through the year 2014. The outlook for most writing and editing jobs is expected to be competitive because many people with writing or journalism training are attracted to the occupation.

Employment of salaried writers and editors for newspapers, periodicals, book publishers and non-profit organizations is expected to increase as demand grows for these publications. Magazines and other periodicals increasingly are developing market niches, appealing to readers with special interests. Businesses and organizations are developing newsletters and websites and more companies are experimenting with publishing materials directly on the Internet. Online publications and services are growing in number and sophistication, spurring the demand for writers and editors, especially those with Web experience. Advertising and public relations agencies, which also are growing, should be another source of new jobs.

Opportunities should be best for technical writers and those with training in a specialized field. Demand for technical writers and writers with expertise in areas such as law, medicine, or economics is expected to increase because of the continuing expansion of scientific and technical information and the need to communicate it to others. Legal, scientific and technological developments and discoveries generate demand for people to interpret technical information for a more general audience. Rapid growth and change in the high-technology and electronics industries result in a greater need for people to write users' guides, instruction manuals and training materials. This work requires people who not only are technically skilled as writers, but also are familiar with the subject area.

In addition to job openings created by employment growth, some openings will arise as experienced workers retire, transfer to other occupations, or leave the labour force. Replacement needs are relatively high in this occupation; many freelancers leave because they cannot earn enough money.

Earnings: Median annual earnings for salaried writers and authors were $44,350 in May 2004. The middle 50 percent earned between $31,720 and $62,930. The lowest 10 percent earned less than $23,330 and the highest 10 percent earned more than $91,260. Median annual earnings were $54,410 in advertising and related services and $37,010 in newspaper, periodical, book and directory publishers.

Median annual earnings for salaried editors were $43,890 in May 2004. The middle 50 percent earned between $33,130 and $58,850. The lowest 10 percent earned less than $25,780 and the highest 10 percent earned more than $80,020. Median annual earnings of those working for newspaper, periodical, book and directory publishers were $43,620.

Median annual earnings for salaried technical writers were $53,490 in May 2004. The middle 50 percent earned between $41,440 and $68,980. The lowest 10 percent earned less than $32,490 and the highest 10 percent earned more than $86,780. Median annual earnings in computer systems design and related services were $54,710.

According to the Society for Technical Communication, the median annual salary for entry level technical writers was $42,500 in 2004. The median annual salary for midlevel non-supervisory technical writers was $51,500 and for senior non-supervisory technical writers, $66,000.

Interpreters and Translators

Significant Points: 15 percent of these workers are self-employed. Work is often sporadic and many interpreters and translators work part time.

Although training requirements can vary, most interpreters and translators have a bachelor's degree.

Job outlook varies by specialty and language combination.

Nature of the Work: Interpreters and translators enable the cross-cultural communication necessary in today's society by converting one language into another. However, these language specialists do more than simply translate words—they relay concepts and ideas between languages. They must thoroughly understand the subject matter in which they work so that they are able to convert information from one language, known as the source language, into another, the target language. In addition, they must remain sensitive to the cultures associated with their languages of expertise.

Interpreters and translators are often discussed together because they share some common traits. For example, both need a special ability, known as language combination. This enables them to be fluent in at least two languages—a native, or active, language and a secondary, or passive, language; a small number of interpreters and translators are fluent in two or more passive languages. Their active language is the one that they know best and into which they interpret or translate and their passive language is one of which they have nearly perfect knowledge.

Although some people do both, interpretation and translation are different professions. Each requires a distinct set of skills and aptitudes and most people are better suited for one or the other. While interpreters often work into and from both languages, translators generally work only into their active language.

Interpreters convert one spoken language into another—or, in the case of sign-language interpreters, between spoken communication and sign language. This requires interpreters to pay attention carefully, understand what is communicated in both languages and express thoughts and ideas clearly. Strong research and analytical skills, mental dexterity and an exceptional memory also are important.

The first part of an interpreter's work begins before arriving at the jobsite. The interpreter must become familiar with the subject matter that the speakers will discuss, a task that may involve research to create a list of common words and phrases associated with the topic. Next, the interpreter usually travels to the location where his or her services are needed. Physical presence may not be required for some work, such as telephone interpretation. But it is usually important that the interpreter see the communicators in order to hear and observe the person speaking and to relay the message to the other party.

There are two types of interpretation: simultaneous and consecutive. Simultaneous interpretation requires interpreters to listen and speak (or sign) at the same time. In simultaneous interpretation, the interpreter begins to convey a sentence being spoken while the speaker is still talking. Ideally, simultaneous interpreters should be so familiar with a subject that they are able to anticipate the end of the speaker's sentence. Because they need a high degree of concentration, simultaneous interpreters work in pairs, with each interpreting for 20- to 30-minute segments. This type of interpretation is required at international conferences and is sometimes used in the courts.

In contrast to simultaneous interpretation's immediacy, consecutive interpretation begins only after the speaker has verbalized a group of words or sentences. Consecutive interpreters often take notes while listening to the speakers, so they must develop some type of note-taking or shorthand system. This form of interpretation is used most often for person-to-person communication, during which the interpreter sits near both parties.

Translators convert written materials from one language into another. They must have excellent writing and analytical ability. And because the documents that they translate must be as flawless as possible, they also need good editing skills.

Translators' assignments may vary in length, writing style and subject matter. When they first receive text to convert into another language, translators usually read it in its entirety to get an idea of the subject. Next, they identify and look up any unfamiliar words. Multiple additional readings are usually needed before translators begin to actually write and finalize the translation. Translators also might do additional research on the subject matter if they are unclear about anything in the text. They consult with the text's originator or issuing agency to clarify unclear or unfamiliar ideas, words, or acronyms.

Translating involves more than replacing a word with its equivalent in another language; sentences and ideas must be manipulated to flow with the same coherence as those in the source document so that the translation reads as though it originated in the target language. Translators also must bear in mind any cultural references that may need to be explained to the intended audience, such as colloquialisms, slang and other expressions that do not translate literally.

Some subjects may be more difficult than others to translate because words or passages may have multiple meanings that make several translations possible. Not surprisingly, translated work often goes through multiple revisions before final text is submitted.

The way in which translators do their jobs has changed with advancements in technology. Today, nearly all translation work is done on a computer and most assignments are received and submitted electronically. This enables translators to work from almost anywhere and a large percentage of them work from home. The Internet provides advanced research capabilities and valuable language resources, such as specialized dictionaries and glossaries. In some cases, use of machine-assisted translation—including memory tools that provide comparisons of previous translations with current work—helps save time and reduce repetition.

The services of interpreters and translators are needed in a number of subject areas. While these workers may not completely specialize in a particular field or industry, many do focus on one area of expertise. Some of the most common areas are described below; however, interpreters and translators also may work in a variety of other areas, including business, social services, or entertainment.

Conference interpreters work at conferences that involve non-English-speaking attendees. This work includes international business and diplomacy, although conference interpreters also may interpret for any organization that works with foreign language speakers. Employers prefer high-level interpreters who have the ability to translate from at least two passive languages into one active (native) language—for example, the ability to interpret from Spanish and French into English. For some positions, such as those with the United Nations, this qualification is mandatory.

Much of the interpreting performed at conferences is simultaneous; however, at some meetings with a small number of attendees, consecutive interpreting also may be used. Usually, interpreters sit in soundproof booths, listening to the speakers through headphones and interpreting into a microphone what is said. The interpreted speech is then relayed to the listener through headsets. When interpreting is needed for only one or two people, the interpreter generally sits behind or next to the attendee and whispers a translation of the proceedings.

Guide or escort interpreters accompany either U.S. visitors abroad or foreign visitors in the United States to ensure that they are able to communicate during their stay. These specialists interpret on a variety of subjects, both on an informal basis and on a professional level. Most of their interpretation is consecutive and work is generally shared by two interpreters when the assignment requires more than an 8-hour day. Frequent travel, often for days or weeks at a time, is common, an aspect of the job that some find particularly appealing.

Judiciary interpreters and translators help people appearing in court who are unable or unwilling to communicate in English. These workers must remain detached from the content of their work and not alter or modify the meaning or tone of what is said. Legal translators must be thoroughly familiar with the language and functions of the U.S. judicial system, as well as other countries' legal systems. Court interpreters work in a variety of legal settings, such as attorney-client meetings, preliminary hearings, depositions, trials and arraignments. Success as a court interpreter requires an understanding of both legal terminology and colloquial language. In addition to interpreting what is said, court interpreters also may be required to translate written documents and read them aloud, also known as sight translation.

Literary translators adapt written literature from one language into another. They may translate any number of documents, including journal articles, books, poetry and short stories. Literary translation is related to creative writing; literary translators must create a new text in the target language that reproduces the content and style of the original. Whenever possible, literary translators work closely with authors in order to best capture their intended meanings and literary characteristics.

This type of work often is done as a sideline by university professors; however, opportunities exist for well-established literary translators. As is the case with writers, finding a publisher and maintaining a network of contacts in the publishing industry is a critical part of the job. Most aspiring literary translators begin by submitting a short sample of their work, in the hope that it will be printed and give them recognition. For example, after receiving permission from the author, they might submit to a publishing house a previously unpublished short work, such as a poem or essay.

Localization translators constitute a relatively recent and rapidly expanding specialty. Localization involves the complete adaptation of a product for use in a different language and culture. At its earlier stages, this work dealt primarily with software localization, but the specialty has expanded to include the adaptation of Internet sites and products in manufacturing and other business sectors.

Translators working in localization need a solid grasp of the languages to be translated, a thorough understanding of technical concepts and vocabulary and a high degree of knowledge about the intended target audience or users of the product. The goal of these specialists is for the product to appear as if it were originally manufactured in the country where it will be sold and supported. Because software often is involved, it is not uncommon for people who work in this area of translation to have a strong background in computer science or computer-related work experience.

Providing language services to health care patients with limited English proficiency is the realm of *medical interpreters and translators*. Medical interpreters help patients to communicate with doctors, nurses and other medical staff. Translators working in this specialty primarily convert patient materials and informational brochures, issued by hospitals and medical facilities, into the desired language. Medical interpreters need a strong grasp of medical and colloquial terminology in both languages, along with cultural sensitivity regarding how the patient receives the information. They must remain detached but aware of the patient's feelings and pain.

Sign language interpreters facilitate communication between people who are deaf or hard of hearing and people who can hear. Sign language interpreters must be fluent in English and in American Sign Language (ASL), which combines signing, finger spelling and specific body language. ASL has its own grammatical rules, sentence structure, idioms, historical contexts and cultural nuances. Sign language interpreting, like foreign language interpreting, involves more than simply replacing a word of spoken English with a sign representing that word.

Most sign language interpreters either interpret, aiding communication between English and ASL, or transliterate, facilitating communication between English and contact signing—a form of signing that uses a more English language-based word order. Some interpreters specialize in oral interpreting for deaf or hard of hearing persons who lip-read instead of sign. Other specialties include tactile signing, which is interpreting for persons who are blind as well as deaf by making manual signs into a person's hands; cued speech; and signing exact English.

Self-employed and freelance interpreters and translators need general business skills to successfully manage their finances and careers. They must set prices for their work, bill customers, keep financial records and market their services to attract new business and build their client base.

Working Conditions: Working environments of interpreters and translators vary. Interpreters work in a variety of settings, such as hospitals, courtrooms and conference centres. They are required to travel to the site—whether it is in a neighbouring town or on the other side of the world—where their services are needed. Interpreters who work over the telephone generally work on call, often in call centres in urban areas and keep to a standard 5-day, 40-hour workweek. Interpreters for deaf students in schools usually work in a school setting for 9 months out of the year.

Translators usually work alone and they must frequently perform under pressure of deadlines and tight schedules. Many translators choose to work at home; however, technology allows translators to work from virtually anywhere.

Because many interpreters and translators freelance, their schedules are often erratic, with extensive periods of no work interspersed with others requiring long, irregular hours. For those who freelance, a significant amount of time must be dedicated to looking for jobs. In addition, freelancers must manage their own finances and payment for their services may not always be prompt. Freelancing, however, offers variety and flexibility and allows many workers to choose which jobs to accept or decline.

The number of work-related accidents in these occupations is relatively low. The work can be stressful and exhausting and translation can be lonesome or dull. However, interpreters and translators may use their irregular schedules to pursue other interests, such as travelling, dabbling in a hobby, or working a second job. Many interpreters and translators enjoy what they do and value the ability to control their schedules and workloads.

Training, Other Qualifications and Advancement: The educational backgrounds of interpreters and translators vary. Knowing a language in addition to a native language is essential. Although it is not necessary to have been raised bilingual to succeed, many interpreters and translators grew up speaking two languages.

In high school, students can prepare for these careers by taking a broad range of courses that include English writing and comprehension, foreign languages and basic computer proficiency. Other helpful pursuits include spending time abroad, engaging in comparable forms of direct contact with foreign cultures and reading extensively on a variety of subjects in English and at least one other language.

Beyond high school, there are many educational options. Although a bachelor's degree is often required, interpreters and translators note that it is acceptable to major in something other than a language. However, specialized training in how to do the work is generally required. A number of formal programmes in interpreting and translation are available at colleges nationwide and through non-university training programmes, conferences and courses. Many people who work as conference interpreters or in more technical areas—such as localization, engineering, or finance—have master's degrees, while those working in the community as court or medical interpreters or translators are more likely to complete job-specific training programmes.

There is currently no universal form of certification required of all interpreters and translators in the United States, but there are a variety of different tests that workers can voluntarily take to demonstrate proficiency. The American Translators Association provides accreditation in more than 24 language combinations for its members; other options include a certification programme offered by The Translators and Interpreters Guild. Many interpreters are not certified. Federal courts have certification for Spanish, Navajo and Haitian Creole interpreters and many State and municipal courts offer their own forms of certification. The National Association of Judiciary Interpreters and Translators also offers certification for court interpreting.

The U.S. Department of State has a three-test series for interpreters, including simple consecutive interpreting (for escort work), simultaneous interpreting (for court or seminar work) and conference-level interpreting (for international conferences). These tests are not referred to directly as certification, but successful completion often indicates that a person has an adequate level of skill to work in the field.

The National Association of the Deaf and the Registry of Interpreters for the Deaf (RID) jointly offer certification for general sign interpreters. In addition, RID offers specialty tests in legal interpreting, speech reading and deaf-to-deaf interpreting—which includes interpreting between deaf speakers with different native languages and from ASL to tactile signing.

Experience is an essential part of a successful career in either interpreting or translation. In fact, many agencies or companies use only the services of people who have worked in the field for 3 to 5 years or who have a degree in translation studies or both.

A good way for translators to learn first-hand about the profession is to start out working in-house for a company; however, such jobs are not very numerous. Persons seeking to enter interpreter or translator jobs should begin by getting experience whatever way they can—even if it means doing informal or unpaid work. All translation can be used as examples for potential clients, even translation done as practice. Mentoring relationships and internships are other ways to build skills and confidence.

Escort interpreting may offer an opportunity for inexperienced candidates to work alongside a more seasoned interpreter. Interpreters might also find it easier to break into areas with particularly high demand for language services, such as court or medical interpretation. Once interpreters and translators have gained sufficient experience, they may then move up to more difficult or prestigious assignments, may seek certification, may be given editorial responsibility, or may eventually manage or start their own translation agency.

Employment: Interpreters and translators held about 31,000 jobs in 2004. However, the actual number of interpreters and translators is probably significantly higher because many work in the occupation only sporadically. Interpreters and translators are employed in a variety of industries, reflecting the diversity of employment options in the field. About 9,900 worked in public and private educational institutions, such as schools, colleges and universities. About 4,100 worked in health care, many of which worked for hospitals. Another 3,400 worked in other areas of government, such as Federal, State and local courts. Other employers of interpreters and translators include publishing companies, telephone companies, airlines and interpreting and translating agencies.

About 4,600 interpreters and translators are self-employed. To find work, these interpreters and translators may submit resumes to many different employment agencies and then wait to be contacted when an agency matches their skills with a job. After establishing a few regular clients, interpreters and translators may receive enough work from a few clients to stay busy and they often hear of subsequent jobs by word of mouth or through referrals from existing clients. Many who freelance in the occupation work only part time, relying on other sources of income to supplement earnings from interpreting or translation.

Job Outlook: Employment of interpreters and translators is projected to increase faster than the average for all occupations over the 2004-14 period, reflecting strong growth in the industries employing interpreters and translators. Higher demand for interpreters and translators in recent years has resulted directly from the broadening of international ties and the increase in the number of foreign language speakers in the United States. Both of these trends are expected to continue, contributing to relatively rapid growth in the number of jobs for interpreters and translators. Demand will remain strong for translators of the languages referred to as "PFIGS"—Portuguese, French, Italian, German and Spanish—and the principal Asian languages—Chinese, Japanese and Korean. In addition, current events and changing political environments, often difficult to foresee, will increase the need for persons who can work with other languages. For example, homeland security needs are expected to drive increasing demand for interpreters and translators of Middle Eastern and North African languages, primarily in Federal Government agencies.

Technology has made the work of interpreters and translators easier. However, technology is not likely to have a negative impact on employment of interpreters and translators because such innovations are incapable of producing work comparable with work produced by these professionals.

Urban areas, especially those in California and New York and Washington, DC, provide the largest numbers of employment possibilities, especially for interpreters; however, as the immigrant population spreads into more rural areas, jobs in smaller communities will become more widely available.

Job prospects for interpreters and translators vary by specialty. In particular, there should be strong demand for specialists in localization, driven by imports and exports, the expansion of the Internet and demand in other technical areas, such as medicine or law. Rapid employment growth among interpreters and translators in health services industries will be fuelled by the implementation of relatively recent guidelines regarding compliance with Title VI of the Civil Rights Act, which require all health care providers receiving Federal aid to provide language services to non-English speakers.

Similarly, the Americans with Disabilities Act and other laws, such as the Rehabilitation Act, mandate that, in certain situations, an interpreter must be available for people who are deaf or hard of hearing. Given the shortage of interpreters and translators meeting the desired skill level of employers, interpreters for the deaf will continue to have favourable employment prospects. On the other hand, job growth is expected to be limited for both conference interpreters and literary translators.

Earnings: Salaried interpreters and translators had median hourly earnings of $16.28 in May 2004. The middle 50 percent earned between $12.40 and $21.09. The lowest 10 percent earned less than $9.67 and the highest 10 percent earned more than $27.45.

Earnings depend on language, subject matter, skill, experience, education, certification and type of employer and salaries of interpreters and translators can vary widely. Interpreters and translators with language skills for which there is a greater demand, or for which there are relatively few people with the skills, often have higher earnings. Interpreters and translators with specialized expertise, such as those working in software localization, also generally command higher rates. Individuals classified as language specialists for the Federal Government earned an average of $71,625 annually in 2005. Limited information suggests that some highly skilled interpreters and translators—for example, high-level conference interpreters—working full time can earn more than $100,000 annually.

For those who are not salaried, earnings may fluctuate, depending on the availability of work. Furthermore, freelancers do not have any employer-paid benefits. Freelance interpreters usually earn an hourly rate, whereas translators who freelance typically earn a rate per word or per hour.

Photography

Photography is a unique and creative medium of self-expression. It is an art form requiring aesthetic sense as well as technical expertise. A hobby that can be made profitable by going professional by the talented.

With the explosion of the communication network, the growth of advertising and media and the fashion boom and digital photography, it has now become a profession with great commercial value. Photos are an essential part in both print and electronic media. So this is an area offering great scope for those who have an interest and attributes needed to be a professional.

Being a creative medium, photography requires more of inherent talent for success than formal training. However training hones the inherent skills and help to shine in this competitive field with various specializations like portraiture, fashion and advertising photography, journalistic photography, wildlife and outdoors photography etc. Creating a commercial quality photograph requires the skill for choosing and presenting a subject in a way to achieve the maximum effect with the appropriate equipment. One should have a definite know how of the angle, lighting and the latest equipments and technology to make a name in the field.

Remuneration

Photographers can start working as assistants to senior photographers, in which capacity they are paid around Rs. 3,500 - 6,000. Your earnings can go up to 25,000, depending upon the designation and the organisation likewise and maybe more once you have established yourself as a freelancer.

Eligibility: Educational: There are no specific academic requirements for full time courses in photography, however, candidates who have cleared the 10+2 exam are eligible for the diploma/certificate courses in photography. There are many students who learn photography along with their college degree, doing a part-time course. Besides the Certificate and Diploma courses in the field, Photography is also offered as an optional subject for a bachelor's degree in Fine arts. Some institutes offer full fledged B.A. courses in photography of three year duration.

Besides the academic requirements, having a background in computers or electronics, related work experience and training is beneficial for making a break in the field.

Personal attributes: Successful photographers are creative individuals who can think and communicate in visual terms. They are able to interpret a client's needs, translating their ideas into images that work. Thus photography basically requires a keen, observant eye and an intelligent, curious and perceptive mind. A photographer must have full knowledge and command over the variety of cameras, lights and props and all kinds of photographic techniques. They should have a sense of light and shade and the magic of colours. Photographer must have creativity, determination and good powers of observation. They must also have the ability to work quickly under pressure, in difficult conditions and irregular hours.

Job Prospects & Career Options

Job Prospects: One of the most exciting aspects of photography is the variety of jobs available in the field, ranging from highly specialized, technical work to jobs that require creativity and Visual literacy.

One can begin your career as an assistant of a senior or professional photographer, so that he/she can grasp the finer points of photography. Photographers can specialize in areas such as portrait, commercial and industrial, advertising, scientific, fashion, news, wildlife photography etc. They have the option to either take up jobs with news papers, magazines, advertising agencies, government agencies, industrial houses or work as free lancers. The government employs photographers on a regular pay scale to do general photography documentation, for covering day-to-day events and functions and for making photo features and captioning. Fashion photographers can find employment with fashion houses, designers, fashion journals and news papers.

Career Options: Press photographers are also known as photojournalists. Press photographers supply pictures to the national and local press and must be versatile with an ability to photograph all kinds of subjects. They must have journalistic instincts, know what makes a good news picture, be able to write accurate captions, work well with reporters, be quick and often work under difficult conditions.

Feature photography essentially involves telling a story in pictures and therefore requires knowledge of the subject. Feature Photographers cover an entire theme or subject with a set of photographs. The work is varied and leads to assignments at any time and in any place-photographing people at home, or life in foreign parts, or schools at work, anything that makes a story. Photographers specialise in the photography of wildlife, sports travel, environment etc. They may work with news reporters or work as freelancers and take independent assignments on environment, wild life etc.

Editorial Photographers work normally for magazines and periodicals, nearly always as freelancers. The main task of an editorial photographer is to pictorially illustrate what is written in the article or report. Work can be varied, depending on the article or report, which needs illustration.

Commercial/ Industrial photographer takes pictures of merchandise, exteriors and interiors of factories and machinery both indoors and outdoors to be used for company brochures, annual reports and in advertising and selling. An industrial photographer's main emphasis is on taking pictures for a single company or firm. The main intention is to make the company's factory, machines or products look good.

Portrait/Wedding Photographers: They take pictures of individuals or small groups. Portrait subjects like pets, children, families, weddings, functions and activities of sports and social clubs. However, there is an increasing demand for portraits in the home, garden or workplace, especially in the case of children's portraits. Portrait photographers may work for a studio or be self-employed.

Advertising photographs are either taken by the photographic departments of advertising agencies, by photographic studios, or by freelance photographers. A large number of photographers do catalogue work, while some studios specialize in 'mail order' photography. This is the best paid and most competitive branch; success in this sphere depends entirely on ability, efficiency and the right personality. Advertising photographers are usually provided with instructions as to what exactly has to be photographed. However they are also expected to suggest their own ideas for new angles.

Fashion photography as a career developed recently in India. It is an extremely creative and well paid profession. Most fashion photography is done by specialist studios or freelancers who are commissioned by fashion houses or advertising agencies. They usually work under the direction of a fashion expert. The bulk of fashion photography is carried out in either Mumbai or Delhi and involves by highly sophisticated and well-equipped studios by freelancers who are commissioned by fashion houses of advertising agencies. They can also find employment with fashion houses, designers, fashion journals and news papers.

Fine arts photographers sell their photographs as fine artwork. In addition to technical proficiency, fine arts photographers need artistic talent and creativity.

Digital photography involves the use of a digital camera. The images are captured on a disk, floppy or directly on to the computer. In conventional methods of photography the images were captured on film which had to be processed and then scanned with the help of a scanner onto the computer for any further changes or effects that the image may need. Digital photography saves time and money that goes into scanning images. Digital photography is used largely in the media, as digital images can be stored easily and conveyed quickly over long distances. Nature and Wildlife Photography involves taking photographs of animals, birds, plants and landscapes. While photos of rare species are in great demand, nature photographs are also widely used as pictures for calendars or covers. Romantic sunsets, flowers, trees, lakes and waterfalls, etc., all make interesting subjects for a nature photographer.

Forensic Photography : A crime scene must be photographed from every angle clearly to show detail, with the emphasis on accurately recording the size and distance of objects. They can find employment with law enforcement agencies, police, legal system and in the investigative services of the government and also private detective agencies.

Freelancing has been the most popular career choice among photographers. Photographers who want to be self-employed need to have business management skills. They must have good communication, problem solving skills and be able to work independently. They can do freelancing in any of the above fields.

Press Photographer/Photo Journalist

Press photographers/photojournalists take pictures for local, regional and national newspapers, magazines and news agencies. Some press photographers specialise in a particular area of press photography, such as sports, human interest, business and commercial.

Work Activities: Press photographers/photojournalists work for local, regional and national newspapers, magazines, periodicals, technical journals or news agencies. They often start their careers by working for local newspapers, covering items of local interest, before moving on to either national publications, specialist publications, or freelance work.

Press photographers must be able to put people at ease so that they can set up a picture to complement a story effectively. A lot of the photographs they take are of events such as cheque presentations and church fetes so they need to think of an angle to make the picture interesting. Often, photographers are required to 'set up' a picture, posed by models, of something that could not be photographed as it was happening, for example,

a mugging. Press photographers may also have to write their own stories.

Press photographers/photojournalists constantly work to meet deadlines and may find that their schedules change to keep up with events happening throughout the day. They may be required to travel locally, nationally and even internationally.

Some press photographers/photojournalists specialise in a particular type of photography as they gain more experience. Examples are sports coverage or supplying material for celebrity gossip columns.

Photojournalists often have their work published in Sunday newspaper colour supplements. They aim to tell a story in as much visual detail as possible. Assignments may include producing an in-depth travel feature or covering a major political event. As well as taking pictures, press photographers usually develop and print their own work.

Personal Qualities and Skills: You will need to combine technical ability with creative flair and the ability to decide what makes a newsworthy picture. The ability to respond quickly and accurately to situations is important. Patience is an essential quality as you may have to wait for a long time for a photo opportunity that lasts for a few seconds. You also need to be determined and resourceful enough to get a better picture than your rivals. Business skills are important if you work freelance.

Pay and Opportunities: Pay rates for press photographers/photojournalists vary depending on whether they are employed or self-employed. The pay rates given below are approximate. Press photographers/photojournalists earn in the range of £14,500 - £17,000 a year, rising to around £21,500 - £27,000. Higher earners can make around £39,000 a year.

Working hours can vary. You may work shifts or be on call to follow up news that breaks at any time during the day or night. Many press photographers work irregular hours, which may include early starts, late finishes and work at weekends and on public holidays.

Although publishers of newspapers and magazines employ a large proportion of press photographers, many are self-

employed. Publishers often use picture agencies, which generate a lot of work for freelance photographers. Getting a job on a national newspaper is difficult.

Entry is very competitive and usually only open to experienced people.

The following information is sourced from government statistics. The government's definition of types of job is slightly different to that used in this programme. For this type of job, the most relevant Government-defined occupation is 'Photographers and audiovisual equipment operators'.

In 2001 there were 3,000 people working as 'Photographers and audiovisual equipment operators' in Scotland. 14 in every 10,000 employees working in Scotland were employed as 'Photographers and audiovisual equipment operators'.

Entry Routes and Training: Press photography/ photojournalism has a structured training scheme run by the National Council for the Training of Journalists (NCTJ). The NCTJ courses are journalism based rather than photographically based; they aim to develop a news-sense as well as an ability to use photographic equipment.

One method of entry is to find employment on a newspaper and qualify by following the NCTJ training scheme of planned practical experience and a twelve-week block-release course at The Sheffield College (Norton College), the only approved centre in Great Britain. Alternatively, it is possible to train by doing the full-time pre-entry course in Press Photography at The Sheffield College (Norton College) followed by a period of on- and off-the-job training. However, competition for the limited number of places is fierce. Evidence of enthusiasm and commitment is essential.

SVQs in Newspaper Journalism (Press Photography) are also available at levels 3 and 4.

Qualifications: For direct entry to employment as a press photographer/photojournalist with block-release training at The Sheffield College (Norton College), the usual minimum requirement is Standard Grade English and 4 other subjects at Standard Grade (1-3). The minimum requirements for entry

to the full-time pre-entry courses are 1/2 Highers (A-C) plus 4 Standard Grades (1-3).

Applicants must be able to present a good portfolio of work. Due to fierce competition, candidates usually have more than the specified minimum requirements.

Adult Opportunities: This is an extremely competitive field. Relevant experience and/or qualifications are usually preferred. Having a portfolio of photographic work is important.

Photography can be studied on a full- or part-time basis, or it can develop from a hobby. It is useful to update your skills by taking short courses in photographic techniques and methods.

Relevant courses in photography and photo journalism, at various levels, are offered by a number of centres, by distance learning.

Many colleges relax the normal academic entry requirements for adult applicants, especially those with relevant experience.

- 57% of people who work in occupations such as press photographer/photojournalist are self-employed.
- 22% work part-time.
- 9% have flexible hours.
- 2% of employees work on a temporary basis.

2

Career in Broadcasting

Broadcasting

Significant Points: Keen competition is expected for many jobs, particularly in large metropolitan areas, because of the large number of jobseekers attracted by the glamour of this industry.

Job prospects will be best for applicants with a college degree in broadcasting or a related field and relevant experience, such as work at college radio and television stations or internships at professional stations.

In this highly competitive industry, broadcasters are less willing to provide on-the-job training and instead seek candidates who can perform the job immediately.

Many entry-level positions are at smaller broadcast stations; consequently, workers often must change employers and sometimes relocate, in order to advance.

Nature of the Industry: The broadcasting industry consists of radio and television stations and networks that create content or acquire the right to broadcast taped television and radio programmes. Networks transmit their signals from broadcasting studios via satellite signals to local stations or cable distributors. Broadcast signals then travel over cable television lines, satellite distribution systems, or the airwaves from a station's transmission tower to the antennas of televisions and radios. Anyone in the signal area with a radio or television can receive the programming. Most Americans receive their television broadcasts through cable and other pay television providers.

• Although cable television stations and networks are included in this statement, cable and other pay television distributors are classified in the telecommunications industry.

Radio and television stations and networks broadcast a variety of programmes, such as national and local news, talk shows, music programmes, movies, other entertainment and advertisements. Stations produce some of these programmes, most notably news programmes, in their own studios; however, much of the programming is produced outside the broadcasting industry. Establishments that produce filmed or taped programming for radio and television stations and networks-but do not broadcast the programming-are in the motion picture industry. Many television networks own production companies that produce their many shows.

Cable and other programme distributors compensate local television stations and cable networks for rebroadcast rights. For popular cable networks and local television stations, distributors pay a fee per subscriber and/or agree to broadcast a less popular channel owned by the same network. Revenue for radio and television stations and networks also comes from the sale of advertising time. The rates paid by advertisers depend on the size and characteristics (age, gender and median income, among others) of a program's audience. Educational and non-commercial stations generate revenue primarily from donations by individuals, foundations, government and corporations. These stations generally are owned and managed by public broadcasting organizations, religious institutions, or school systems.

Changes in Federal Government regulation and communication technology have affected the broadcast industry. The Telecommunications Act of 1996 relaxed ownership restrictions, an action that has had a tremendous impact on the industry. Instead of owning only one radio station per market, companies can now purchase up to eight radio stations in a single large market. These changes have led to a large-scale consolidation of radio stations. In some areas, five FM and three AM radio stations are owned by the same company and share the same offices. The ownership of commercial radio stations is increasingly concentrated. In television, owners are permitted two stations in larger markets and are restricted in the total number of stations nationwide (in terms of percent of all viewers).

The U.S. Federal Communications Commission (FCC) is a proponent of digital television (DTV), a technology that uses digital signals to transmit television programmes. Digital signals consist of pieces of simple electronic code that can carry more information than conventional analog signals. This code allows for the transmission of better quality sound and higher resolution pictures, often referred to as high-definition television (HDTV). FCC regulations require all stations to broadcast digital signals as well as conventional analog signals. The current goal of the FCC is to have all stations stop broadcasting analog signals by 2007. However, because of the number of viewers who do not yet own television sets that are compatible with DTV, full implementation of the change from analog to digital broadcasting may take longer. After the switch is complete, any viewers using an analog TV and over-the-air signals will need a converter box to change the signal from digital to analog. Most television stations are currently broadcasting digital signals in response to FCC regulations. Many digital cable systems and satellite television providers already broadcast all their channels digitally, with some channels in high definition.

The transition to HDTV broadcasting has also accelerated the conversion of other aspects of television and radio production from analog to digital. Many stations have replaced specialized hardware with less specialized computers equipped with software that performs the same functions. Stations may use digital cameras, edit with computers and store video on computer servers. Many major network shows now use HDTV cameras and editing equipment.

The transition to digital broadcasting also is occurring in radio. Most stations already store music, edit clips and broadcast their analog signals with digital equipment. Satellite radio services, which offer 100 channels of digital sound, operate on a subscription basis, like pay television services. To compete, some radio stations are embedding a digital signal into their analog signals. With a specially equipped radio, these digital services offer better quality sound and display some limited text, such as the title of the song and the artist.

Working Conditions: Most employees in this industry work in clean, comfortable surroundings in broadcast stations and studios. Some employees work in the production of shows and broadcasting while other employees work in advertising, sales, promotions and marketing.

Television news teams made up of reporters, camera operators and technicians travel in electronic news-gathering vehicles to various locations to cover news stories. Although such location work is exciting, some assignments, such as reporting on military conflicts or natural disasters, may be dangerous. These assignments may also require outdoor work under adverse weather conditions.

Camera operators working on such news teams must have the physical stamina to carry and set up their equipment. Broadcast technicians on electronic news-gathering trucks must ensure that the mobile unit's antenna is correctly positioned for optimal transmission quality and to prevent electrocution from power lines. Field service engineers work on outdoor transmitting equipment and may have to climb poles or antenna towers; their work can take place under a variety of weather conditions.

Broadcast technicians who maintain and set up equipment may have to do heavy lifting. Technological changes have enabled camera operators also to fulfil the tasks of broadcast technicians, operating the transmission and editing equipment on a remote broadcasting truck. News operations, programming and engineering employees work under a great deal of pressure in order to meet deadlines. As a result, these workers are likely to experience varied or erratic work schedules, often working on early morning or late evening news programmes.

Sales workers may face stress meeting sales goals. Aside from sometimes erratic work schedules, management and administrative workers typically find themselves in an environment similar to any other office.

For many people, the excitement of working in broadcasting compensates for the demanding nature of the work. Although this industry is noted for its high pressure and long hours, the work is generally not hazardous.

Employment: Broadcasting provided about 327,000 wage and salary jobs in 2004. Although more than half of all establishments employed fewer than 10 people, most jobs were in large establishments; about 73 percent of all jobs were in establishments with at least 50 employees. Broadcasting establishments are found throughout the country, but jobs in larger stations are concentrated in large cities.

Occupations in the Industry: Occupations at large broadcast stations and networks fall into five general categories: Programme production, news-related, technical, sales and general administration. At small stations, jobs are less specialized and employees often perform several functions. Although on-camera or on-air positions are the most familiar occupations in broadcasting, the majority of employment opportunities are behind the scenes table.

Programme production occupations. Most television programmes are produced by the motion picture and video industry; actors, directors and producers working on these prerecorded programmes are not employed by the broadcasting industry. Employees in programme production occupations at television and radio stations create programmes such as news, talk and music shows.

Assistant producers provide clerical support and background research; assist with the preparation of musical, written and visual materials; and time productions to make sure that they do not run over schedule. Assistant producers also may operate cameras and other audio and video equipment.

Video editors select and assemble pre-taped video to create a finished programme, applying sound and special effects as necessary. Conventional editing requires assembling pieces of video-tape in a linear fashion to create a finished product. The editor first assembles the beginning of the programme and then, works sequentially towards the end. Newer computerized editing allows an editor to electronically cut and paste video segments. This electronic technique is known as nonlinear editing because the editor is no longer restricted to working sequentially; a segment may be moved at any time to any location in the programme.

Producers plan and develop live or taped productions, determining how the show will look and sound. They select the script, talent, sets, props, lighting and other production elements. Producers also coordinate the activities of on-air personalities, production staff and other personnel. Web site or Internet producers, a relatively new occupation in the broadcasting industry, plan and develop Internet sites that provide news updates, programme schedules and information about popular shows. These producers decide what will appear on the Internet sites and design and maintain them.

Announcers read news items and provide other information, such as programme schedules and station breaks for commercials or public service information. Many radio announcers are referred to as disc jockeys; they play recorded music on radio stations. Disc jockeys may take requests from listeners; interview guests; and comment on the music, weather, or traffic. Most stations now have placed all of their advertisements, sound bites and music on a computer, which is used to select and play or edit the items. Technological advances have simplified the monitoring and adjusting of the transmitter, leaving disc jockeys responsible for most of the tasks associated with keeping a station on the air. Traditional tapes and CDs are used only as backups in case of a computer failure. Announcers and disc jockeys need a good speaking voice; the latter also need a significant knowledge of music.

Programme directors are in charge of on-air programming in radio stations. Programme directors decide what type of music will be played, supervise on-air personnel and often select the specific songs and the order in which they will be played. Considerable experience, usually as a disc jockey, is required, as well as a thorough knowledge of music.

News-related occupations. News, weather and sports reports are important to many television stations because these reports attract a large audience and account for a large proportion of revenue. Many radio stations depend on up-to-the-minute news for a major share of their programming. Programme production staff, such as producers and announcers, also work on the production of news programmes.

Reporters gather information from various sources, analyze and prepare news stories and present information on the air. Correspondents report on news occurring in U.S. and foreign cities in which they are stationed. Newswriters write and edit news stories from information collected by reporters. Newswriters may advance to positions as reporters or correspondents.

Broadcast news analysts, also known as news anchors, analyze, interpret and broadcast news received from various sources. News anchors present news stories and introduce video-taped news or live transmissions from on-the-scene reporters. Newscasters at large stations may specialize in a particular field. Weather-casters, also called weather reporters, report current and forecasted weather conditions. They gather information from national satellite weather services, wire services and local and regional weather bureaus. Some weather-casters are trained atmospheric scientists and can develop their own weather forecasts. Sports-casters, who are responsible for reporting sporting events, usually select, write and deliver the sports news for each newscast.

Assistant news directors supervise the newsroom; they coordinate wire service reports, tape or film inserts and stories from individual newswriters and reporters. Assignment editors assign stories to news teams, sending the teams on location if necessary.

News directors have overall responsibility for the news team made up of reporters, writers, editors and newscasters as well as studio and mobile unit production crews. This senior administrative position entails responsibilities that include determining what events to cover and how and when they will be presented in a news broadcast.

Technical occupations. Employees in these occupations operate and maintain the electronic equipment that records and transmits radio or television programmes. The titles of some of these occupations use the terms "engineer," "technician," and "operator" interchangeably.

Radio operators manage equipment that regulates the signal strength, clarity and range of sounds and colours of broadcasts. They also monitor and log outgoing signals and operate transmitters. Audio and video equipment technicians operate equipment to regulate the volume, sound quality, brightness, contrast and visual quality of a broadcast. Broadcast technicians set up and maintain electronic broadcasting equipment. Their work can extend outside the studio, as when they set up portable transmitting equipment or maintain stationary towers.

Television and video camera operators set up and operate studio cameras, which are used in the television studio and electronic news gathering cameras, which are mobile and used outside the studio when a news team is pursuing a story at another location. Camera operators need training in video production as well as some experience in television production.

Master control engineers ensure that all of the radio or television station's scheduled programme elements, such as on-location feeds, prerecorded segments and commercials, are smoothly transmitted. They also are responsible for ensuring that transmissions meet FCC requirements.

Technical directors direct the studio and control room technical staff during the production of a programme. They need a thorough understanding of both the production and technical aspects of broadcasting; this knowledge often is acquired by working as a lighting director or camera operator, or as another type of broadcast worker.

Network and computer systems administrators and network systems and data communications analysts design, set up and maintain systems of computer servers. These servers store recorded programmes, advertisements and news clips.

Assistant chief engineers oversee the day-to-day technical operations of the station. Chief engineers or directors of engineering are responsible for all of the station's technical facilities and services. These workers need a bachelors' degree in electrical engineering, technical training in broadcast engineering and years of broadcast engineering experience.

Employment of Wage and Salary Workers in Broadcasting by Occupation, 2004 and Projected Change, 2004-14. (Employment in Thousands)

Occupation	*Employment, 2004 Number*	*Percent change, 2004-14*	*Percent*
All occupations	327	100.0	10.7
Management, business and financial occupations	34	10.5	13.8
General and operations managers	9	2.8	10.2
Sales managers	4	1.3	8.8
Accountants and auditors	3	0.8	13.5
Professional and related occupations	159	48.6	5.4
Computer support specialists	2	0,7	39.4
Network and computer systems administrators	2	0.6	48.7
Electronics engineers, except computer	2	0.5	12.0
Electrical and electronic engineering technicians	2	0.7	20.2
Producers and directors	21	6.5	10.0
Radio and television announcers	39	11.9	-7.3
Broadcast news analysts	6	1.8	2.4
Reporters and correspondents	11	3.3	2.2
Public relations specialists	3	1.0	6.7
Editors	4	1.3	7.0
Writers and authors	3	0.9	7.2
Broadcast and sound engineering technicians and radio operators	29	8.8	5.2
Audio and video equipment technicians	4	1.2	5.9
Broadcast technicians	22	6.9	5.2
Sound engineering technicians	2	0.7	5.8
Photographers	4	1.1	0.1
Camera operators, television, video, and motion picture	9	2.9	5.3
Film and video editors	4	1.1	10.7
Sales and related occupations	46	14.0	7.0
First-line supervisors/managers of non-retail sales workers	3	0.9	-0.3
Advertising sales agents	32	9.7	2.7
Sales representatives, services, all other	4	1.1	36.2
Office and administrative support occupations	61	18.6	13.2

Contd...

Occupation	*Employment, 2004 Number*		*Percent change, 2004-14 Percent*
First-line supervisors/managers of office and administrative support workers	5	1.4	9.7
Bookkeeping, accounting and auditing clerks	4	1.3	0.6
Customer service representatives	14	4.2	48.4
Receptionists and information clerks	3	1.0	3.3
Dispatchers, except police, fire and ambulance	2	0.6	31.8
Production, planning and expediting clerks	2	0.7	16.1
Executive secretaries and administrative assistants	6	1.8	10.0
Secretaries, except legal, medical and executive	4	1.1	-8.5
Office clerks, general	9	2.9	3.7
Installation, maintenance and repair occupations	23	7.1	42.7
Telecommunications equipment installers and repairers, except line installers	4	1.4	47.2
Telecommunications line installers and repairers	11	3.4	46.9

Note: May not add to totals due to omission of occupations with small employment.

Sales, promotions and marketing occupations. Most workers in this category are advertising sales agents, sometimes known as account executives. They sell advertising time to sponsors, advertising agencies and other buyers. Sales representatives must have a thorough knowledge of the size and characteristics of their network's or station's audience, including income levels, gender, age and consumption patterns.

Sales work has expanded beyond the traditional role of simply selling advertising to a wide range of marketing efforts. For instance, stations earn additional revenue by broadcasting from a business, such as a dance club. Businesses also sponsor concerts or other promotions that are organized by a station. In return for sponsorship, the businesses are usually allowed to set up a booth or post large signs at the event.

Continuity directors schedule and produce commercials. Continuity directors carefully schedule commercials, taking into account both the timeslot in which a commercial is to be played, as well as competing advertisements. For example, two car dealership advertisements should not be played during the same commercial break. Continuity directors also create and produce advertisements for clients who do not produce their own.

Large stations and networks generally have several workers who spend all of their time handling sales. Sales worker supervisors, who may handle a few large accounts personally, supervise these workers. In small stations, part-time sales personnel or announcers often handle sales responsibilities during hours when they are not on the air.

General Administration: General managers or station managers coordinate all radio and television station activities. In very small stations, the manager and a bookkeeper may handle all of the accounting, purchasing, hiring and other routine office work. In larger stations, the general administrative staff includes business managers, accountants, lawyers, personnel workers, public relations workers and others. These professionals are assisted by office and administrative support workers, such as secretaries, word processors, typists and financial clerks.

Training and Advancement: Professional, management and sales occupations generally require a college degree; technical occupations often do not. It is easier to obtain employment and gain promotions with a degree, especially in larger, more competitive markets. Advanced schooling generally is required for supervisory positions-including technical occupations-having greater responsibility and higher salaries.

Entry-level jobs in news or programme production increasingly require a college degree and some broadcast experience. More than 1,200 institutions offer programmes in communications, journalism and related programmes. As of 2004, there were 104 schools accredited by the Accrediting Council on Education in Journalism and Mass Communications (ACEJMC). Some community colleges offer 2-year programmes in broadcasting. Broadcast trade schools offer courses that last 6 months to a year and teach radio and television announcing, writing and production.

Individuals pursuing a career in broadcasting often gain initial experience through work at college radio and television stations or through internships at professional stations.

Although these positions usually are unpaid, they sometimes provide college credit or tuition. More importantly, they provide hands-on experience and a competitive edge when applying for jobs. In this highly competitive industry, broadcasters are less willing to provide on-the-job training and instead seek candidates who can perform the job immediately.

Some technical positions require only a high school diploma. However, many broadcast stations seek individuals with training in broadcast technology, electronics, or engineering from a technical school, community college, or 4-year college. An understanding of computer networks and software will become increasingly important as industry use of digital technology expands. Supervisory technical positions and jobs in large stations generally require a college degree.

The Society of Broadcast Engineers (SBE) issues certification to technicians who pass a written examination. Several classes of certification are available, requiring increasing levels of experience and knowledge for eligibility. The Telecommunications Act of 1996 mandated that the FCC drop its licensing requirements for transmitter maintenance; SBE certification has filled the void left by the elimination of this license.

Employees in the radio and television broadcasting industry often find their first job in broadcast stations that serve smaller markets. Competition for positions in large metropolitan areas is stronger and stations in these areas usually seek highly experienced personnel. Because many radio and television stations are small, workers in this industry often must change employers to advance. Relocation to other parts of the country frequently is necessary for advancement.

Outlook: Employment in broadcasting is expected to increase 11 percent over the 2004-14 period, more slowly than the 14 percent projected for all industries combined. Factors contributing to the relatively slow rate of growth include industry consolidation, introduction of new technologies and competition from other media outlets. Keen competition is expected for many jobs, particularly in large metropolitan areas, because of the large number of jobseekers attracted by the glamour of this industry. Job prospects will be best for applicants with a college degree in broadcasting, journalism, or a related field as well as relevant work experience.

Consolidation of individual broadcast stations into large networks, especially in radio, has increased as the result of relaxed ownership regulations. This trend will continue to limit employment growth as networks use workers more efficiently. For example, a network can run eight radio stations from one office, producing news programming at one station and then using the programming for broadcast from other stations, thus eliminating the need for multiple news staffs. Similarly, technical workers, upper level management and marketing and advertising sales workers are pooled to work for several stations simultaneously. In the consolidation of the radio industry, several major companies have purchased numerous stations nationwide. These companies plan to achieve cost savings through consolidation and economies of scale, limiting employment growth.

The introduction of new technology also is slowing employment growth. Conventional broadcast equipment used to be relatively specialized; each piece of equipment served a separate function and required an operator with specialized knowledge. Newer computerized equipment often combines the functions of several older pieces of equipment and does not require specialized knowledge for operation. This reduces the need for certain types of workers, including those responsible for editing, recording and creating graphics. In addition, increased use of remote monitoring equipment allows technical workers in one location to operate and monitor transmissions at a remote station.

Job growth also is being constrained by the use of radio and television programming created by services outside the broadcasting industry. These establishments provide prepared programming, including music, news, weather, sports and professional announcer services. The services can easily be accessed through satellite connections and reduce the need for programme production and news staff at radio and television stations.

Radio broadcasters expect continued growth in revenues as national media companies that own multiple cable stations, network television stations and/or radio stations use their combined marketing power to include radio advertising packages with other marketing deals. The new national scope of radio networks allows radio to more effectively sell advertising to large national advertisers to better compete with television networks. The major threats to the radio industry, especially smaller, marginal stations, are from car CD (compact disk) players and from satellite radio, which functions like cable television with subscribers paying a monthly fee.

Earnings: Weekly earnings of non-supervisory workers in broadcasting averaged $703 in 2004, higher than the average of $529 for all private industry. As a common rule, earnings of broadcast personnel are highest in large metropolitan areas. Earnings in selected occupations in broadcasting for May 2004 appear in table.

Median Hourly Earnings of the Largest Occupations in Broadcasting

Occupation	*Broadcasting, except Internet*	*All industries*
General and operations managers	$42.73	$37.22
Producers and directors	21.58	25.40
Advertising sales agents	19.08	19.37
Telecommunications line installers and repairers	17.35	19.39
Reporters and correspondents	16.37	15.06
Camera operators, television, video and motion picture	14.60	18.08
Customer service representatives	14.00	12.99
Broadcast technicians	12.35	13.47
Office clerks, general	12.15	10.95
Radio and television announcers	10.51	10.64

The principal unions representing employees in broadcasting are the National Association of Broadcast Employees and Technicians (NABET), the International Brotherhood of Electrical Workers (IBEW), the International Alliance of Theatrical Stage Employees (IATSE) and the American Federation of Television and Radio Artists (AFTRA).

Sound Engineering Technicians

Significant Points: Job applicants will face keen competition for jobs in major metropolitan areas, where pay generally is higher; prospects are expected to be better in small cities and towns.

Technical school, community college, or college training in broadcast technology, electronics, or computer networking provides the best preparation.

About 30 percent work in broadcasting, mainly for radio and television stations and 17 percent work in the motion picture, video and sound recording industries.

Evening, weekend and holiday work is common.

Nature of the Work: Broadcast and sound engineering technicians and radio operators set up, operate and maintain a wide variety of electrical and electronic equipment involved in almost any radio or television broadcast, concert, play, musical recording, television show, or movie. With such a range of work, there are many specialized occupations within the field.

Audio and video equipment technicians set up and operate audio and video equipment, including microphones, sound speakers, video screens, projectors, video monitors, recording equipment, connecting wires and cables, sound and mixing boards and related electronic equipment for concerts, sports events, meetings and conventions, presentations and news conferences. They also may set up and operate associated spotlights and other custom lighting systems.

Broadcast technicians set up, operate and maintain equipment that regulates the signal strength, clarity and range of sounds and colours of radio or television broadcasts. These technicians also operate control panels to select the source of the material. Technicians may switch from one camera or studio to another, from film to live programming, or from network to local programming.

Sound engineering technicians operate machines and equipment to record, synchronize, mix, or reproduce music, voices, or sound effects in recording studios, sporting arenas, theatre productions, or movie and video productions.

Radio operators mainly receive and transmit communications using a variety of tools. These workers also repair equipment, using such devices as electronic testing equipment, handtools and power tools. One of their major duties is to help to maintain communication systems in good condition.

The transition to digital recording, editing and broadcasting has greatly changed the work of broadcast and sound engineering technicians and radio operators. Software on desktop computers has replaced specialized electronic equipment in many recording and editing functions. Most radio and television stations have replaced videotapes and audio-tapes with computer hard drives and other computer data storage systems. Computer networks linked to specialized equipment dominate modern broadcasting. This transition has forced technicians to learn computer networking and software skills.

Broadcast and sound engineering technicians and radio operators perform a variety of duties in small stations. In large stations and at the networks, technicians are more specialized, although job assignments may change from day to day. The terms "operator," "engineer," and "technician" often are used interchangeably to describe these jobs. Workers in these positions may monitor and log outgoing signals and operate transmitters; set up, adjust, service and repair electronic broadcasting equipment; and regulate fidelity, brightness, contrast, volume and sound quality of television broadcasts.

Technicians also work in programme production. *Recording engineers* operate and maintain video and sound recording equipment. They may operate equipment designed to produce special effects, such as the illusions of a bolt of lightning or a police siren. *Sound mixers* or *re-recording mixers* produce soundtracks for movies or television programmes. After filming or recording is complete, these workers may use a process called "dubbing" to insert sounds. *Field technicians* set up and operate portable transmission equipment outside the studio. Because television news coverage requires so much electronic equipment and the technology is changing so rapidly, many stations assign technicians exclusively to news.

Chief engineers, transmission engineers and *broadcast field supervisors* oversee other technicians and maintain broadcasting equipment.

Working Conditions: Broadcast and sound engineering technicians and radio operators generally work indoors in pleasant surroundings. However, those who broadcast news and other programmes from locations outside the studio may work outdoors in all types of weather. Technicians doing maintenance may climb poles or antenna towers, while those setting up equipment do heavy lifting.

Technicians at large stations and the networks usually work a 40-hour week under great pressure to meet broadcast deadlines and may occasionally work overtime. Technicians at small stations routinely work more than 40 hours a week. Evening, weekend and holiday work is usual because most stations are on the air 18 to 24 hours a day, 7 days a week. Even though a technician may not be on duty when the station is broadcasting, some technicians may be on call during non-work hours; these workers must handle any problems that occur when they are on call.

Technicians who work on motion pictures may be on a tight schedule and may work long hours to meet contractual deadlines.

Training, Other Qualifications and Advancement: The best way to prepare for a broadcast and sound engineering technician job is to obtain technical school, community college, or college training in broadcast technology, electronics, or computer networking. In the motion picture industry, people are hired as apprentice editorial assistants and work their way up to more skilled jobs. Employers in the motion picture industry usually hire experienced freelance technicians on a picture-by-picture basis. Reputation and determination are important in getting jobs.

When starting out, broadcast and sound engineering technicians learn skills on the job from experienced technicians and supervisors. These beginners often start their careers in small stations and, once experienced, move on to larger ones. Large stations usually hire only technicians with experience. Experienced technicians can become supervisory technicians or chief engineers. A college degree in engineering is needed in order to become chief engineer at a large television station. Many employers pay tuition and expenses for courses or seminars to help technicians keep abreast of developments in the field.

Audio and video equipment technicians generally need a high school diploma. Many recent entrants have a community college degree or other forms of post-secondary degrees, although they are not always required. These technicians may substitute on-the-job training for formal education requirements. Working in a studio as an assistant is a great way of gaining experience and knowledge.

Radio operators usually are not required to complete any formal training. This is an entry-level position that generally requires on-the-job training.

Licensing is not required for broadcast technicians. However, certification by the Society of Broadcast Engineers is a mark of competence and experience. The certificate is issued to experienced technicians who pass an examination.

Prospective technicians should take high school courses in math, physics and electronics. Building electronic equipment from hobby kits and operating a "ham," or amateur, radio are good experience, as is working in college radio and television stations.

Broadcast and sound engineering technicians and radio operators must have manual dexterity and an aptitude for working with electrical, electronic and mechanical systems and equipment.

Employment: Broadcast and sound engineering technicians and radio operators held about 95,000 jobs in 2004. Their employment was distributed among the following detailed occupations:

Audio and video equipment technicians	46,000
Broadcast technicians	34,000
Sound engineering technicians	13,000
Radio operators	2,000

About 30 percent worked in broadcasting (except Internet) and 17 percent worked in the motion picture, video and sound recording industries. About 7 percent were self-employed. Television stations employ, on average, many more technicians than radio stations. Some technicians are employed in other industries, producing employee communications, sales and training programmes. Technician jobs in television and radio are located in virtually all cities; jobs in radio also are found in many small towns. The highest paying and most specialized jobs are concentrated in New York City, Los Angeles, Chicago and Washington, DC—the originating centres for most network or news programmes. Motion picture production jobs are concentrated in Los Angeles and New York City.

Job Outlook: People seeking entry-level jobs as technicians in broadcasting are expected to face keen competition in major metropolitan areas, where pay generally is higher and the number of qualified jobseekers typically exceeds the number of openings. Prospects for entry-level positions are expected to be better in small cities and towns for beginners with appropriate training.

Overall employment of broadcast and sound engineering technicians and radio operators is expected to grow about as fast as average for all occupations through the year 2014. Job growth in radio and television broadcasting will be limited by consolidation of ownership of radio and television stations and by labour-saving technical advances, such as computer-controlled programming and remotely controlled transmitters. The Federal Communications Commission (FCC) is required to examine its media ownership rules quadrennially.

Thus, the rules can change periodically. In 2005, FCC regulations stated that a single owner could own up to eight radio stations in a single large market and that a single owner could not own television stations that would reach more than 39 percent of households. Revisions to these rules have been passed by the FCC, but have not been implemented because of legal challenges. When broader common ownership is allowed, stations often are consolidated and operated from a single location, reducing employment because one or a few technicians can provide support to multiple stations. Technicians who know how to install transmitters will be in demand as television stations install digital transmitters. Although most television stations are broadcasting in both analog and digital formats and plan to switch entirely to digital, radio stations are only beginning to broadcast digital signals.

Employment of broadcast and sound engineering technicians in the cable and pay television portion of the broadcasting industry is expected to grow as the range of products and services expands, including cable Internet access and video-on-demand. Employment of these workers in the motion picture industry is expected to grow rapidly. However, job prospects are expected to remain competitive because of the large number of people who are attracted by the glamour of working in motion pictures.

Projected job growth varies among detailed occupations in this field. Employment of audio and video equipment technicians and sound engineering technicians is expected to grow faster than the average for all occupations. Not only will these workers have to set up audio and video equipment, but they will have to maintain and repair it as well.

Employment of broadcast technicians is expected to grow about as fast as the average for all occupations through 2014, as advancements in technology enhance the capabilities of technicians to produce higher quality radio and television programming. Employment of radio operators, on the other hand, is projected to decline as more stations control programming and operate transmitters remotely.

In addition to employment growth, job openings also will result from the need to replace experienced technicians who leave this field. Some of these workers leave for other jobs that require knowledge of electronics, such as computer repairer or industrial machinery repairer.

Earnings: Television stations usually pay higher salaries than radio stations; commercial broadcasting usually pays more than public broadcasting; and stations in large markets pay more than those in small markets.

Median annual earnings of audio and video equipment technicians in May 2004 were $32,570. The middle 50 percent earned between $24,180 and $44,290. The lowest 10 percent earned less than $19,110 and the highest 10 percent earned more than $58,620. Median annual earnings in motion picture and video industries, which employed the largest number of audio and video equipment technicians, were $33,670.

Median annual earnings of broadcast technicians in May 2004 were $28,010. The middle 50 percent earned between $19,240 and $42,760. The lowest 10 percent earned less than $14,960 and the highest 10 percent earned more than $62,850. Median annual earnings in radio and television broadcasting, which employed the largest number of broadcast technicians, were $25,220.

Median annual earnings of sound engineering technicians in May 2004 were $38,110. The middle 50 percent earned between $25,470 and $56,320. The lowest 10 percent earned less than $19,180 and the highest 10 percent earned more than $80,450.

Median annual earnings of radio operators in May 2004 were $32,720. The middle 50 percent earned between $23,960 and $43,850. The lowest 10 percent earned less than $17,960 and the highest 10 percent earned more than $57,420.

Camera Operators and Editors

Significant Points: Workers acquire their skills through on-the-job or formal post-secondary training.

Technical expertise, a good eye, imagination and creativity are essential.

Keen competition for job openings is expected because many talented peopled are attracted to the field.

Nature of the Work: *Television, video and motion picture camera operators* produce images that tell a story, inform or entertain an audience, or record an event. *Film and video editors* edit soundtracks, film and video for the motion picture, cable and broadcast television industries. Some camera operators do their own editing.

Making commercial-quality movies and video programmes requires technical expertise and creativity. Producing successful images requires choosing and presenting interesting material, selecting appropriate equipment and applying a good eye and a steady hand to ensure smooth, natural movement of the camera.

Camera operators use television, video, or motion picture cameras to shoot a wide range of material, including television series, studio programmes, news and sporting events, music videos, motion pictures, documentaries and training sessions. Some camera operators film or video-tape private ceremonies and special events, such as weddings and conference programme sessions. Those who record images on video-tape are often called *videographers*.

Many are employed by independent television stations; local affiliate stations of television networks; large cable and television networks; or smaller, independent production companies. *Studio camera operators* work in a broadcast studio and usually video-tape their subjects from a fixed position. *News camera operators*, also called *electronic news gathering (ENG) operators*, work as part of a reporting team, following newsworthy events as they unfold. To capture live events, they must anticipate the action and act quickly. ENG operators sometimes edit raw footage on the spot for relay to a television affiliate for broadcast.

Camera operators employed in the entertainment field use motion picture cameras to film movies, television programmes and commercials. Those who film motion pictures also are known as *cinematographers*. Some specialize in filming cartoons or special effects. Cinematographers may be an integral part of the action, using cameras in any of several different mounts. For example, the camera operator can be stationary and shoot whatever passes in front of the lens, or the camera can be mounted on a track, with the camera operator responsible for shooting the scene from different angles or directions. Wider use of digital cameras has enhanced the number of angles and the clarity that a camera operator can provide. Other camera operators sit on cranes and follow the action while crane operators move them into position. *Steadicam operators* mount a harness and carry the camera on their shoulders to provide a clear picture while they move about the action. Camera operators who work in the entertainment field often meet with directors, actors, editors and camera assistants to discuss ways of filming, editing and improving scenes.

Working Conditions: Working conditions for camera operators and editors vary considerably. Those employed by television and cable networks and advertising agencies usually work a 5-day, 40-hour week; however, they may work longer hours to meet production schedules. ENG operators often work long, irregular hours and must be available to work on short notice. Camera operators and editors working in motion picture production also may work long, irregular hours.

ENG operators and those who cover major events, such as conventions or sporting events, frequently travel locally and stay overnight or travel to distant places for longer periods. Camera operators filming television programmes or motion pictures may travel to film on location.

Some camera operators—especially ENG operators covering accidents, natural disasters, civil unrest, or military conflicts—work in uncomfortable or even dangerous surroundings. Many camera operators must wait long hours in all kinds of weather for an event to take place and must stand or walk for long periods while carrying heavy equipment. ENG operators often work under strict deadlines.

Training, Other Qualifications and Advancement: Employers usually seek applicants with a good eye, imagination and creativity, as well as a good technical understanding of how the camera operates. Television, video and motion picture camera operators and editors usually acquire their skills through on-the-job training or formal post-secondary training at vocational schools, colleges, universities, or photographic institutes. Formal education may be required for some positions.

Many universities, community and junior colleges, vocational-technical institutes and private trade and technical schools offer courses in camera operation and videography. Basic courses cover equipment, processes and techniques.

Bachelor's degree programmes, especially those including business courses, provide a well-rounded education. Film schools also may provide training on the artistic or aesthetic aspects of film-making.

Individuals interested in camera operations should subscribe to videographic newsletters and magazines, join audio-video clubs and seek summer or part-time employment in cable and television networks, motion picture studios, or camera and video stores.

Camera operators in entry-level jobs learn to set up lights, cameras and other equipment. They may receive routine assignments requiring adjustments to their cameras or decisions on what subject matter to capture. Camera operators in the film and television industries usually are hired for a project on the basis of recommendations from individuals such as producers, directors of photography and camera assistants from previous projects or through interviews with the producer. ENG and studio camera operators who work for television affiliates usually start in small markets to gain experience.

Camera operators need good eyesight, artistic ability and hand-eye coordination. They should be patient, accurate and detail oriented. Camera operators also should have good communication skills and, if needed, the ability to hold a camera by hand for extended periods.

Camera operators who run their own businesses, or freelance, need business skills as well as talent. These individuals must know how to submit bids, write contracts, get permission to shoot on locations that normally are not open to the public, obtain releases to use film or tape of people, price their services, secure copyright protection for their work and keep financial records.

With experience, operators may advance to more demanding assignments or to positions with larger or network television stations. Advancement for ENG operators may mean moving to larger media markets. Other camera operators and editors may become directors of photography for movie studios, advertising agencies, or television programmes. Some teach at technical schools, film schools, or universities.

Employment: Television, video and motion picture camera operators held about 28,000 jobs in 2004 and film and video editors held about 20,000. Many are employed by independent television stations, local affiliate stations of television networks or broadcast groups, large cable and television networks, or smaller independent production companies. About 1 in 5 camera operators were self-employed. Some self-employed camera operators contracted with television networks, documentary or independent filmmakers, advertising agencies, or trade show or convention sponsors to work on individual projects for a set fee, often at a daily rate.

Most of the salaried camera operators were employed by television broadcasting stations or motion picture studios. More than half of the salaried film and video editors worked for motion picture studios. Most camera operators and editors worked in large metropolitan areas.

Job Outlook: Television, video and motion picture camera operators and editors can expect keen competition for job openings because the work is attractive to many people. The number of individuals interested in positions as videographers and movie camera operators usually is much greater than the number of openings. Those who succeed in landing a salaried job or attracting enough work to earn a living by freelancing are likely to be the most creative and highly motivated people, able to adapt to rapidly changing technologies and adept at operating a business. Related work experience or job-related training also can benefit prospective camera operators.

Employment of camera operators and editors is expected to grow about as fast as the average for all occupations through 2014. Rapid expansion of the entertainment market, especially motion picture production and distribution, will spur growth of camera operators. In addition, computer and Internet services will provide new outlets for interactive productions. Growth will be tempered, however, by the increased offshore production of motion pictures. Camera operators will be needed to film made-for-the-Internet broadcasts, such as live music videos, digital movies, sports features and general information or entertainment programming. These images can be delivered directly into the home either on compact discs or as streaming video over the Internet. Job growth in radio and television broadcasting will be tempered by the use of robocams and Parkervision systems for studio broadcasts; cameras in these systems are automated and under the control of a single person working either on the studio floor or in a director's booth.

Earnings: Median annual earnings for television, video and motion picture camera operators were $37,610 in May 2004. The middle 50 percent earned between $22,640 and $56,400. The lowest 10 percent earned less than $15,730 and the highest 10 percent earned more than $76,100. Median annual earnings were $48,900 in the motion picture and video industries and $29,560 in radio and television broadcasting.

Median annual earnings for film and video editors were $43,590 in May 2004. The middle 50 percent earned between $29,310 and $63,890. The lowest 10 percent earned less than $21,710 and the highest 10 percent earned more than $93,950. Median annual earnings were $44,710 in the motion picture and video industries, which employed the largest numbers of film and video editors.

Many camera operators who work in film or video are freelancers, whose earnings tend to fluctuate each year. Because most freelance camera operators purchase their own equipment, they incur considerable expense acquiring and maintaining cameras and accessories. Some camera operators belong to unions, including the International Alliance of Theatrical Stage Employees and the National Association of Broadcast Employees and Technicians.

Prepress Technicians and Workers

Significant Points: Most prepress technician jobs now require formal post-secondary graphic communications training in the various types of computer software used in digital imaging.

Employment is projected to decline as the increased use of computers in typesetting and page layout requires fewer prepress technicians.

Nature of the Work: The printing process has three stages—prepress, press and binding or postpress. In small print shops, *job printers* are usually responsible for all three stages. They check proofs for errors and print clarity and correct mistakes, print the job and attach each copy's pages together. In most printing firms, however, each of the stages is the responsibility of a specialized group of workers. *Prepress technicians and workers* are responsible for the first stage, preparing the material for printing presses. They perform a variety of tasks involved with transforming text and pictures into finished pages and making printing plates of the pages.

Advances in computer software and printing technology continue to change prepress work. Most customers today are able to provide printers with pages of material that look like the desired finished product they want printed and bound in volume. Using a process called "desktop publishing," customers are increasingly using their own computers to do much of the typesetting and page layout work formerly done by designers on art-boards.

Much of this work is now done by desktop publishers or graphic designers with knowledge of publishing software. It is increasingly common for prepress technicians or other printing workers to receive files from the customer on a computer disk or submitted electronically via e-mail or "file transfer protocol", known as "ftp", that contains typeset material already laid out in pages.

Prepress work is now done with the use of digital imaging technology by prepress technicians known as "preflight technicians" or production coordinators. Using this technology, these technicians take the electronic files received from customers, check it for completeness and format it into pages using electronic page layout systems. Even though the pages may already be laid out, they still may have to be formatted to fit the dimensions of the paper stock to be used.

When colour printing is required, the technicians use digital colour page-makeup systems to electronically produce an image of the printed pages, then use off-press colour proofing systems to print a copy, or "proof," of the pages as they will appear when printed. The technician then has the proofs delivered or mailed to the customer for a final check. Once the customer gives the

"OK to print," technicians use laser "image-setters" to expose digital images of the pages directly onto thin aluminum printing plates.

Platemakers for a long time used a photographic process to make printing plates. The flat, a layout sheet onto which a negative has been attached, was placed on top of a thin metal plate coated with a light-sensitive resin. Exposure to ultraviolet light activated the chemical in parts of the plate not protected by the film's dark areas. The plate was then developed in a solution that removes the unexposed nonimage area, exposing bare metal. The chemical on areas of the plate exposed to the light hardened and became water repellent. The hardened parts of the plate form the text and images to be printed. Now, the printing industry has largely moved to technology known as "direct-to-plate", by which the prepress technicians send the data directly to a plating system, bypassing the need for stripping film onto a flat.

During the printing process, the plate is first covered with a thin coat of water. The water adheres only to the bare metal nonimage areas and is repelled by the hardened areas that were exposed to light. Next, the plate comes in contact with a rubber roller covered with oil-based ink. Because oil and water do not mix, the ink is repelled by the water-coated area and sticks to the hardened areas. The ink covering the hardened text is transferred to paper.

Working Conditions: Prepress technicians and workers usually work in clean, air-conditioned areas with little noise. Some workers may develop eyestrain from working in front of a video display terminal, or musculoskeletal problems such as backaches. Those platemakers who still work with toxic chemicals face the hazard of skin irritations. Workers are often subject to stress and the pressures of short deadlines and tight work schedules.

Prepress employees usually work an 8-hour day. Some workers—particularly those employed by newspapers—work night shifts, weekends and holidays.

Training, Other Qualifications and Advancement: Digital imaging technology has largely replaced cold type print technology. Instead of painstakingly taping pieces of photographic negatives to flats, today's prepress technicians use computer software skills to electronically modify and lay out the material; in some cases, the first time the material appears on paper is when the final product rolls off the printing press.

Traditionally, prepress technicians and workers started as helpers and were trained on the job, with some jobs requiring years of experience performing the detailed handwork to become skilful enough to perform even difficult tasks quickly. Today, persons seeking to enter prepress technician jobs require formal post-secondary graphic communications training in the various types of computer software used in digital imaging.

Post-secondary graphic communications programmes are available from a variety of sources. For beginners, 2-year associate degree programmes offered by community and junior colleges and technical schools and some 4-year bachelor's degree programmes in graphic design colleges teach the latest prepress skills and allow students to practice applying them. However, bachelor's programmes usually are intended for students who may eventually move into management positions in printing or design jobs.

Community and junior colleges, 4-year colleges and universities, vocational-technical institutes, industry-sponsored update and retraining programmes and private trade and technical schools all also offer prepress-related courses for workers who do not wish to enrol in a degree programme. Many workers with experience in other printing jobs take a few college graphic communications courses to upgrade their skills and qualify for prepress jobs. Prepress training designed to train skilled workers already employed in the printing industry also is offered through unions in the printing industry.

Many employers view individuals with a combination of experience in the printing industry and formal training in the new digital technology as the best candidates for prepress jobs. The experience of these applicants in printing press operator or other jobs provides them with an understanding of how printing plants operate, familiarizes them with basic prepress functions and demonstrates their reliability and interest in advancing in the industry.

Employers prefer workers with good communication skills, both oral and written, for prepress jobs. Prepress technicians and workers should be able to deal courteously with people because, when prepress problems arise, they sometimes have to contact the customer to resolve them. Also, in small shops, they may take customer orders. Persons interested in working for firms using advanced printing technology need to know the basics of electronics and computers. Mathematical skills also are essential for operating many of the software packages used to run modern, computerized prepress equipment. At times, prepress personnel may have to perform computations in order to estimate job costs.

Prepress technicians and workers need good manual dexterity and they must be able to pay attention to detail and work independently. Good eyesight, including visual acuity, depth perception, field of view, colour vision and the ability to focus quickly, also are needed assets. Artistic ability is often a plus. Employers also seek persons who possess an even temperament and an ability to adapt, important qualities for workers who often must meet deadlines and learn how to use new software or operate new equipment.

Employment: Prepress technicians and workers overall held about 141,000 jobs in 2004. Of these, approximately 63,000 were employed as job printers; the remainder was employed as prepress technicians and other prepress workers. Most prepress jobs are found in the printing industry, while newspaper publishing employs the second largest number of prepress technicians and workers.

The printing and publishing industries are two of the most geographically dispersed in the United States and prepress jobs are found throughout the country. However, jobs are concentrated in large metropolitan areas such as Chicago, Los Angeles–Long Beach, New York City, Minneapolis–St. Paul, Philadelphia, Boston and Washington, DC.

Job Outlook: Overall employment of prepress technicians and workers is expected to decline through 2014. Demand for printed material should continue to grow, spurred by rising levels of personal income, increasing school enrollments, higher levels of educational attainment and expanding markets. But the use of computers and publishing software—often by the clients of the printing company—will result in rising productivity of prepress technicians.

Computer software now allows office workers to specify text typeface and style and to format pages at a desktop computer terminal, shifting many prepress functions away from the traditional printing plants into advertising and public relations agencies, graphic design firms and large corporations. Many companies are turning to in-house desktop publishing as page layout and graphic design capabilities of computer software have improved and become less expensive and more user-friendly. Some firms are finding it less costly to prepare their own newsletters and other reports than to send them out to trade shops. At newspapers, writers and editors also are doing more composition using publishing software. Rapid growth in the use of desktop publishing software already has eliminated most prepress typesetting and composition technician jobs associated with the older technologies, such as cold-type. However, opportunities will be favourable for prepress technicians with strong computer skills, such as preflight technicians, who are employed to check materials prepared by clients and adapt it for printing.

In order to compete in the desktop publishing environment, commercial printing companies are adding desktop publishing and electronic prepress work to the list of services they provide. Electronic prepress technicians, digital proofers, platemakers and graphic designers are using new equipment and ever-changing software to design and layout publications and complete their printing more quickly. The increasing range of services offered by printing companies using new digital technologies mean that opportunities in prepress work will be best for those with computer backgrounds who have completed Post-secondary programmes in printing technology or graphic communications. Workers with this background will be better able to adapt to the continuing evolution of publishing and printing technology.

Earnings: Median hourly earnings of prepress technicians and workers were $15.30 in May 2004. The middle 50 percent earned between $11.69 and $20.01 an hour. The lowest 10 percent earned less than $9.06 and the highest 10 percent earned more than $24.82 an hour.

For job printers, median hourly earnings were $15.41 in May 2004. The middle 50 percent earned between $12.00 and $20.04 an hour. The lowest 10 percent earned less than $9.57, while the highest 10 percent earned more than $24.05 an hour.

Median hourly earnings in commercial printing, the industry employing the largest number of prepress technicians and workers, were $15.91 in May 2004, while the figure for these workers in the newspaper, periodical and book publishing industry was $14.22 an hour. For job printers, median hourly earnings in commercial printing in May 2004 were $15.67, while in the newspaper, periodical and book publishing industry median hourly earnings were $15.63.

Wage rates for prepress technicians and workers vary according to occupation, level of experience, training, location, size of firm and union membership status.

Radio Jockey

Though the popularity of radio had suffered badly with the arrival of Television and Internet, the opening of the FM radio to private channels has infused a new life to radio. Radio Jockeying is an exciting, promising and challenging career for those who have a passion for music. It is the only profession in which one may be recognized by their voice.

Radio Jockeys are those who anchor music programmes on radio. The task of a RJ is to entertain the listeners by playing music or conveying messages in a most attractive and sophisticated way. They play requests from listeners, interview guests, manage contests and also provide information on the music, weather and traffic. This is a profession which requires a lot of hard work and presence of mind. It is the performance of these Radio Jockeys that makes or mars the radio station. Mostly youngsters are preferred in this field as they have new ideas, concepts and are bubbling with enthusiasm.

Every successful Radio Jockey has their own style of communicating. To make an imprint in the listeners heart, apart from a good voice, the Radio Jockey should be warm, friendly, spontaneous, dynamic and must possess good communication skills. One who is interested in this field must keep on observing how the RJ's handle the calls, interact with the listeners, how they answer tricky and awkward questions and comments from the listeners etc. Prospective candidates must listen to a lot of radio, try and come up with innovative ideas and pack their voice with energy.

Eligibility: Radio Jockeying is a talent based field. Even though no formal educational qualification is required, a degree or at least plus two is generally a pre requisite.

The most essential factor for a Radio Jockey is a good voice with the ability to modulate as per the occasion. Apart from that, an RJ should have a clear diction, accurate pronunciation, flare and fluency in the language. They should be able to control the pitches of their voice and learn to use them to the best effect. Another distinguishing characteristic to become a successful radio jockey is the speed of response, good sense of humour, individuality, creativity of mind, spontaneity and an intensive knowledge of music. Successful RJs have the ability to twist and turn their speech according to the situation.

Staying updated is very important for a radio jockey. An RJ needs to keep track of the happenings in and around the city. People will enjoy listening to an RJ, if they can sound different on the show. So qualities like mimicry, local dialects and comedy or humour items will help the RJ to carry on their shows.

Personal Skills - Radio Jockeys should be diplomatic in character as they have to interact with people of different nature. They must maintain a down-to-earth and approachable attitude so that listeners can comfortably make calls and speak their hearts out.

Job Prospects & Career Options: The job of a Radio Jockey is of diversifying nature depending on the subject matter of the programme. They do not have a regular 9 to 5 job. They can be called to host or anchor a show anytime of the day or night. Their job profile includes selecting music, scripting and presenting radio shows. The success of the RJ depends the way they present a programme as it can increase or decrease the listeners of the show. The way of anchoring should be original and the presentation should be interesting to the listeners, one has to give variations and punch to ones voice wherever necessary.

A Radio Jockey should also be able to write scripts for a show and should be aware about the latest movies and songs. As Radio jockeys have to deal with sound equipment and computers, they should be familiar with them.

Radio Jockeys can find work in organisations like AIR (All India Radio), Times FM, Radio Mid-Day and other independent radio stations. The two options for entering into this field are by audition or by approaching a software producing company.

AIR (All India Radio) holds auditions for RJs every 3 months in their radio stations in various cities especially in metros. The selection is highly competitive and the selected RJs are given in-house training for 2 months in everything from CD players to mixers to digital audio technology etc. The software companies generally prefer people with 2-3 years experience. A few radio software producers in Mumbai are Radiostar, Radio Midday and Radio Wani.

Because of their voice standard, RJ can do voice-overs for television and radio advertisements. They can also lend their voices to audio magazines and documentaries. RJs also can anchor or compeer TV shows or live shows or events.

Remuneration: Radio Jockeys are in much demand with the opening of the air waves to the private sector. The beginners in the initial stage can earn between Rs. 7,000 to Rs. 15,000 per month. For sponsored programmes, software producing companies may pay between Rs 1400 to Rs 2500 per show. After a few years of experience, the earnings can be raised double and depending on the popularity of their shows, RJ's can earn between Rs 15,000 up to Rs 85,000 per month. If you are recognised, then you will have all the right to demand your own price.

As a radio jockey, besides getting contractual good money you earn by doing Ad commercials. You can earn more by doing voice-overs for television and radio advertisements. RJ's can earn Rs 2,000-3,000 per hour by doing shows for the Indian diaspora on foreign radio. Another well-paid and upcoming option is radio broadcasting on the Net, which could earn you between Rs 40,000 to 50,000 per month.

Video Jockey

With the advent of various music channels on TV, Video jockeying is becoming an exciting career option for the music crazy generation. The main job of the VJ is to introduce music videos and host music related shows on Television. But as competition increases, music channels are on the trend of incorporating many diverse shows to attract the public, especially the youth. So the VJ's area of work involves apart from introducing videos; hosting game to travel shows to youth forums, chatting with the public, doing interviews with artists and music celebrities etc. In short, they act as intermediary figures between the audience and the musicians or music videos. It may also involve off- camera work like deciding on the theme and choosing the songs to suit the theme of the show, participating in promotionals like road shows, attending theme parties and with experience, even writing script for the show at times.

VJs must constantly keep up-to-date on the latest trends in music, all the latest videos and information about music stars and other celebrities. In that sense, they take upon a more journalistic role. They also should have a well-rounded knowledge of all types of music and also should be informed about a bit of everything from films to politics to travel whatever the theme the show demands. Some of them specialize in a particular area or genre of music. They must be able to answer any queries about music and must fulfil their roles as experts. Vj's interact with the viewers through telephone, e-mail or fax.

Jockeying generally involves three areas and as such Jockeys are called a Video Jockey (VJ), Radio Jockey (RJ) and Disc Jockey (DJ). They all deal with music but while VJ's present shows on TV, RJ's do it on Radio and DJ's in live shows in clubs, restaurants, Music stores etc.

Eligibility: No specific educational background or formal training is required to be a VJ, except some personal attributes. However a background in mass communication, visual communication or the performing arts comes in handy.

An interest and love for music is an essential aspect. Along with that, excellent body language and dress sense, a pleasant voice, good command over the required language depending on the medium, presence of mind and a good knowledge of music anyone can aspire to be a VJ. One has to get to know about the various styles of music, musicians and albums. With the changing trends one also needs to be well informed generally on topics like politics, travel and what is new.

Command over language is important as video jockey needs to talk a lot. Some amount of voice training would definitely help as VJs need a voice that's clear, pleasant and strong. He should be able to take split second decisions, answer promptly, be energetic and have a wonderful sense of humour to make the show interesting. He may also need to work erratic hours and travel extensively.

Job Prospects & Career Options: VJs are mainly employed by Music channels, Producers of music shows and film based programmes.

Besides popular prospective employers like MTV, Channel V, B4U music, MCM Asia etc., there are many number of channels including regional ones who are in demand of VJ's. But it is not easy to get a break in the field. You may be employed on a contract basis per show or on a full time basis. There will be paper adds calling VJ's or VJ hunts advertised on TV. The selection will be tough, which may include a test on paper, on voice modulation or facing the camera. Your screen presence, physique and voice and ability to stand out in the crowd will go a long way in being selected.

Once you are selected, there is no such thing as hierarchy in this profession. Beginners with talent may get to handle their own shows within the first 6 months. It mainly depends on your ability. Besides the excellent pay, you get to host shows in the country or abroad, meet celebrities and be on the glam walk of life. Keeping up the popularity for long is not easy and as such this profession is a short lived one. The rule is make hay while it lasts. But the profession gives you ample scope to diversify to various fields such as Modelling, Theatre (direction/ acting), Film (acting), Music videos (directing/acting/ choreography), Anchoring, News casting, PR etc. that generally VJ's do. The more popular you get through veejaying the more the choices you may have.

Remuneration: There is a great scope for the profession with the explosion of satellite channels and more and more music channels being launched. The success of the music show depends entirely on the VJ's ability to connect with the audience and make them come back for more. Although this is a short lived career, within that short time span, a successful VJ can earn between 10,000 to 25000, running up to lakhs depending upon the popularity of the show. Apart from the earnings, the glamour and popularity associated with the profession attracts youngsters to the field.

Broadcast Journalist

Broadcast journalism involves generating story ideas or picking up on leads, then pitching the story to the programme editor. Broadcast journalists may then research the article and interview those connected to the story, who could be:

- victims of crime, or their relatives;
- politicians;
- celebrities;
- members of the public.

Articles must then be written in the appropriate style for the organisation and the audience. Broadcast journalists are often responsible for arranging the content and order of news bulletins and making sure timings are exact. They may brief a presenter before the bulletin in television or present the news themselves in radio.

Typical Work Activities: The extent and range of duties will vary considerably between jobs. There may be different job titles and descriptions depending on whether you are employed in television or radio and which company you work for.

Tasks typically involve:

- monitoring news-wires for breaking stories and updates;
- keeping track of the latest developments, such as court decisions and press conferences;
- identifying stories for follow-up and marketing your ideas to the editor;
- researching news items and establishing useful contacts;
- assessing the situation on location and deciding on the best way to present a story;
- setting up and conducting interviews, on or off camera/ tape;
- preparing scripts;
- supervising the editing of the final tape or film report;
- working autocue, running scripts or fetching tapes;
- selecting stories for bulletins and making appropriate changes when new stories break;
- deciding on the best order for stories within the programme, based on their nature/content;
- using specialised computer software and studio equipment;
- preparing exact timings for the reading of each news item;
- monitoring timings during broadcast and keeping presenters advised of timings;
- making necessary changes during the programme;
- giving technical directions;
- presenting directly in radio, studio or direct to camera;
- contributing programme ideas.

Salary and Conditions

- Range of typical starting salaries: £12,000 - £20,000 (salary data collected May 05).
- Range of typical salaries at senior level/with experience

(*e.g.*, after 10-15 years in the role): £24,000 - £45,000 (salary data collected May 05).

- Pay tends to be higher in TV than radio (the lower end of the starting salary range would be relevant to some independent local radio posts). Additional allowances may be paid for shift work and unsocial hours. In London, a weighting may be available. Salaries for the experienced vary considerably, although correspondents tend to earn more in general. Reporters are often on individually negotiated National Union of Journalists (NUJ) contracts.
- Working hours typically include regular unsocial hours. Shift work is common and prospective broadcast journalists need to be flexible about the hours they work: you may start early in the morning to cover regional news on breakfast radio/TV shows; alternatively, you may start mid morning and work until evening. Weekend work is often required and most broadcasters do not take public holidays. On-air presenters are less likely to go out on location to cover stories and their working hours may be more predictable/social.
- Jobs are quite widely available. Work for national stations may be regionally or London based. There are far more posts as local journalists on regional stations, especially in radio. Digital audio broadcasting (DAB) has opened up even more opportunities in radio.
- It is often necessary to take work on short-term contracts (permanent contracts are rare and competition is high). It may be necessary to move around to secure a new contract when one finishes.
- Women are well represented in regional and national reporting jobs but under-represented at senior management level.
- The work can be stressful due to regular deadlines, working with minimal preparation time and the need to originate stories. You may be in contact with members of the public or celebrities at times of crisis in their lives, which can be stressful for the interviewer.

- There is frequent travel within a working day and absence from home at night. Overseas work or travel is occasional.

Entry Requirements

Although this area of work is open to all graduates, the following degree subjects may improve your chances:

- politics/government/public administration;
- economics.

There is some debate in the industry about how undergraduate media courses are viewed, so it is worth researching the destinations of previous students on specific media courses.

Entry is not generally possible with HND only. A degree is required for entry to the BBC and ITN training schemes. The official minimum entry qualification of five GCSEs belies the fact that more than 70% of entrants are now graduates, though occasionally there are opportunities for non-graduates with specialist knowledge or substantial relevant experience.

A postgraduate course in print or broadcast journalism, or one recognised by The National Council for the Training of Journalists (NCTJ) or the Broadcast Journalism Training Council, is becoming increasingly important. See the AGCAS Vocational Course Survey Journalism for details of courses.

Broadly speaking, the two main entry routes are direct entry or via a pre-entry or postgraduate course. Selectors for courses and for direct entry to jobs use similar methods: an application form; a test for English, writing ability and general knowledge; and an interview. Pre-entry experience, such as in the BBC or independent local radio stations, is essential, although it can be difficult to gain.

Potential candidates will need to show evidence of the following:

- motivation and perseverance;
- a clear, authoritative broadcast voice and manner;
- the ability to stay calm when things go wrong on air;
- the ability to analyse, clarify and present information under pressure;

- knowledge and expertise of writing for the web;
- an exceptional interest in and grasp of current affairs.

Student newspapers, magazines, radio stations and internal television circuits are now present in most universities and colleges, so take advantage of opportunities for work experience. Applications that are backed up by cuttings look stronger than those without (cuttings will also make it easier for a selector to judge your potential). Freelancing for local papers can be useful experience in developing your own news sense, ideas, style and contacts. You could cover weekend sporting fixtures or arts events for a local paper or radio station.

Contacts are important in the media and your ability to network will impress potential employers. During your vacations write to local papers, radio and television stations, explaining your interest in journalism. Visit an organisation to research background information.

Television journalism is a relatively small industry and competition for jobs can be fierce. Initially, you may need to approach employers for short-term contract work or unpaid work experience. Determination, tenacity and a willingness to start with a small organisation doing a variety of tasks (sometimes menial) may be necessary.

Many jobs are not advertised so it is necessary to make speculative applications. Identify an appropriate person to target with your focused CV, *e.g.* a producer, editor, or head of news. You should avoid writing to personnel, as this often proves fruitless. Enclose a short audio-tape, with a recording of you reading a brief news article, to demonstrate that you have an appropriate voice for broadcast journalism.

In an attempt to offset the scarcity of British Black and Asian journalists, the National Union of Journalists (NUJ) has set up the George Viner Memorial Fund to support those who want to take industry-recognised pre-entry courses.

From 1 October 2006 it will be illegal to discriminate against candidates on age grounds but, in practice, age may continue to be used in selection criteria by some employers. Although the majority of new entrants into broadcast journalism tend to be in their mid to late 20s, mature entry is less difficult if established in print journalism. You may be interested in further information about work experience and further study.

Training

Initial training in broadcast journalism is possible through completing one of the many postgraduate courses available. Most cover journalism for radio and television. Alternatively, those with some experience from student media or voluntary placements can start in print journalism and radio before progressing to television. It is also possible to enter straight into a trainee role within the television sector, but this is extremely competitive.

On-the-job training includes both informal and formal training. Through informal training, the trainee can learn about the dynamics of the news team, what the producers are looking for and how the news should be set out. They may start by doing basic tasks, such as working autocue or fetching tapes, before progressing to interviewing, initially off camera and finally on camera. Formal training may also be received for use of specialist software or technical equipment.

At the BBC, there is a wide range of training available. This includes voice training, creative package training or access to facilities for online training.

Career Development

Many broadcast journalists will gain initial experience in regional radio, where they will be given early responsibility and exposure to a wide range of tasks. This environment tends to be an ideal grounding for those who wish to move across into television journalism.

Many television journalists work as reporters for news or current affairs programmes. Some journalists start in the newsroom and progress quickly to reporting; a minority become correspondents or presenters once they are suitably experienced. Multi-skilling is becoming more important and there is a move towards flexibility, with staff able to work as journalist and presenter.

Movement into work in documentaries or investigative journalism is one option for progression. Another is to move from a regional television station to a more high profile role with a national company, such as ITN or the BBC. If management is a strength, progression to the head of news may be an option. Some might combine their journalistic skills and experience in related job roles, *e.g.* as a television producer.

Broadcast journalists are often presented with opportunities to expand their portfolio of skills through exposure to the range of journalistic activity, such as writing, researching, reporting and presenting. This might also be through helping on the technical and administrative side. Teletext and most recently, online news, require written journalist skills. The development of these services may be advantageous for print journalists trying to break through into television.

Broadcast Assistant, Radio

Job Description and Activities: Broadcast assistants provide vital support in the development and day-to-day production of local and national radio. In giving practical support to programme producers and presenters, they ensure that shows run as smoothly as possible by managing a range of activities in a busy environment.

Broadcast assistants undertake key administrative activities as well as assisting in planning, researching and producing live and prerecorded radio programmes. They often have creative input in the development of new shows or features.

The broad scope of the role means that it is a common starting point for a career in radio.

Typical Work Activities: The job can vary widely between radio stations and even between different programmes within a single station. In particular, day-to-day activities will vary between speech and music radio stations. The breadth of duties undertaken may also differ depending upon the size of the station and production team. Most broadcast assistants will be expected to provide some degree of administrative, technical and production support, but some posts may be more closely related to assistant producer or producer roles.

Typical work activities are likely to include:

- undertaking general research for programmes;
- arranging and overseeing guest visits and freelance staff;
- maintaining up-to-date contact lists;
- producing transcripts, programme logs and running orders;
- recording programme costs;
- preparing contracts and payments for guests and contributors;
- answering and archiving details of calls for 'phone ins' and competitions;
- booking resources, facilities, studio time and equipment;
- editing audio 'packages' with digital editing software;
- assisting the studio producer with time-keeping;
- assisting with the recording of transmissions;
- 'driving the desk' for some prerecorded or live programmes;
- contributing to the creative input of a show, for example writing cues and updating scripts;
- liaising with publicity departments about programme trailers and competition prizes.
- updating the programme/station website and ensuring that the on-air and online content are the same.

You will normally have the opportunity to undertake other ad hoc duties and contribute your ideas. If you work for a smaller station, you may have more creative input and your role could include more high-profile activities, such as:

- researching and interviewing guests;
- choosing music;
- presenting shows or small sections of a programme, such as news items and reviews of music, films or books.

Salary and Conditions

- Range of typical starting salaries: £15,000 - £23,000 in London; £13,000 - £19,000 in the rest of the UK (salary data collected Dec. 05).

- Range of typical salaries at senior level/with experience (*e.g.*, after 10-15 years in the role): £17,000 - £25,000 (salary data collected Dec. 05).
- Salary levels are fairly low in many parts of the industry.
- Working hours are usually long. The shifts you work will vary depending on the programmes you are working on, but typically include some evening and weekend work and overnight shifts. Tight deadlines may require you to work overtime.
- The working day is often unpredictable and is generally led by how well a recording is progressing. Work on live programmes can be more predictable.
- Working shifts and unpredictable hours means that your personal life will often have to fit around your job. You will also need to be prepared to cover for colleagues who are on holiday or absent through sickness.
- The atmosphere is informal and sociable, but the work can be pressured with tight deadlines.
- Posts are available all over the UK in towns and cities where there are local BBC and commercial radio stations. National BBC and commercial radio stations broadcast from London, although the BBC's 'Out of London' project will see some radio stations, including Five Live, relocated to Manchester by 2010.
- Geographic mobility can be beneficial when developing a career in this area.
- Self-employment and freelance work are commonly possible. Broadcast assistants in both the BBC and independent radio are often employed on a freelance or short-term contract basis.
- Travel within a working day in the UK is occasionally necessary, but overseas work or travel is rarely a feature of the job.

Entry Requirements

Although this area of work is open to all graduates and Diplomates, a degree, HND or foundation degree in radio or media production may improve your chances.

Graduates from a wide variety of degree, HND and foundation degree disciplines aim for careers in radio broadcasting. Knowledge of a specialist subject, such as science or politics, may give you the edge for certain types of programmes. Generally, however, the subject you study is less important than relevant practical experience and energy and enthusiasm for the industry, combined with the right personality, are often more important to employers than education.

Entry without a degree, HND or foundation degree is sometimes possible, but candidates will need considerable relevant experience in programme-making, often gained through voluntary work.

Postgraduate study is not essential, although some entrants complete a postgraduate Diploma or MA in Radio or Media Production. Others opt for short practical courses to improve their chances. Skillset (Sector Skills Council for the Audio Visual Industries) provide advice on what to look for when choosing a course.

Pre-entry experience is vital for developing additional technical skills and demonstrating commitment to the industry. This can be obtained through placements and voluntary, holiday or part-time work.

Potential candidates will need to show evidence of the following:

- creative flair;
- a flexible attitude;
- strong written and oral communication skills;
- a strong interest in radio;
- technical skills;
- the ability to work as part of a team;
- the ability to plan, prioritise and work under pressure.

A good radio voice can be an asset. Computer literacy is desirable - requirements vary between radio stations.

A good overall knowledge of the radio industry and the specific output of the station you wish to join is crucial. Keep up to date with developments in the sector by reading Media Guardian, Broadcast and Radio Magazine. Listen to a variety of radio genres via analogue (FM and AM), digital audio broadcasting (DAB), cable, satellite and digital TV and the internet. The Radio Academy organises one-day radio masterclass sessions at universities/higher education institutions for students and others, thinking about a job in radio, which offer a valuable insight into the industry.

The Commercial Radio Companies Association maintains a Work Placement Digest. BBC Work Experience regularly advertises work experience opportunities online. Other opportunities for building up experience can be found through student, hospital, community or in-store radio stations. Undertaking a period of work experience will help you to make contacts and get known in an industry in which, according to Skillset, 40% of people work in jobs that were never advertised. Membership of professional organisations, such as the Student Radio Association (SRA) and the Women's Radio Group, may provide further opportunities to make contacts.

BBC Training and Development also offers a range of online and face-to-face courses. Trainee posts may also be advertised on BBC Jobs. However, there is a high level of competition for posts and recruitment is not on a regular basis.

From I October 2006 it will be illegal to discriminate against candidates on age grounds but, in practice, age may continue to be used in selection criteria by some employers. You may be interested in further information about work experience and further study.

Training

There are few formal trainee schemes. Training is likely to be unstructured and delivered on the job or through short courses. Many entering a career at this level will seek to gain skills and support from colleagues, such as other broadcast assistants, researchers, producers and presenters. Most stations will expect you to start with a good working knowledge of the broadcasting environment and programme production. Any training available usually focuses on the technical aspects of the job: 'driving the desks' and using specific types of recording and editing systems.

Together, the British Film Institute (BFI) and Skillset (Sector Skills Council for the Audio Visual Industries) maintain a Media Courses and Multimedia Courses Directory of over 5,000 media courses across the UK. Skillset also subsidises a range of short courses for freelancers.

BBC Training and Development offers online and face-to-face courses in a range of technical and operational radio skills. The BBC also offers mid-career training to broadcast assistants.

Career Development

Career progression is achieved by gaining work on a variety of programmes and stations and providing additional support when required. Taking advantage of any opportunities to broaden your skills or to try out other areas of work is very important. This may include offering to cover for colleagues who are on holiday or absent through sickness, or undertaking an attachment.

The BBC 'attachments' system provides the opportunity for staff to work in a related role for up to six months. Attachments are frequently used to extend skills, make contacts and as a way to move on to a different type of role or programme. Following an attachment, broadcast assistants may be able to progress to roles as producers or presenters.

Relevant professional bodies, such as The Radio Academy, may offer additional information and support about possible career development. The Academy provides annual 'Fast Track' conferences aimed at professionals under 25, or those in the first five years of their radio career, to help them clarify and plan their career progression.

Broadcast assistants looking to progress may also undertake additional training courses. See the Skillset (Sector Skills Council for the Audio Visual Industries) website to investigate emerging skills shortages in the sector and the British Film Institute (BFI)/Skillset Media Courses and Multimedia Courses Directory to investigate relevant courses.

In local radio in particular, the turnover of staff is fairly rapid (the average stay in local radio is around two to three years), with many using it as a stepping stone to either network radio or television work.

Floor Manager (Television)

Job Description and Activities: Floor managers ensure that sets, props and technical equipment are safe, ready to use and in the right position prior to filming. They are also responsible for the audience (if there is one) being seated in good time.

In studio settings, the floor manager is the link between the director (up in the gallery) and the floor below. The floor manager is responsible for passing on cues to presenters and guests to ensure timings are met and the broadcast goes smoothly.

The work is mainly studio-based, but may also include outside broadcasts, depending on the production.

Typical Work Activities: Typical activities include:

- checking that equipment, *e.g.* microphones and earpieces, are working before the show;
- seating the audience (if in attendance);
- relaying instructions from the control room to the studio floor;
- keeping the director and producer informed of action off-camera;
- assisting in the planning and preparation of productions;
- overseeing the work of other departments, such as lighting and props;
- rehearsing live shows;
- giving cues and time counts to presenters, actors or guests;
- organising runners to make the best use of studio time;
- looking ahead in the programme schedule to anticipate any changes to the set or to see what props are required later in the show;
- briefing and looking after those involved in the programme;

- managing the audience, explaining safety requirements, show timings and explaining what will happen during filming and when the programme will be aired;
- referring to floor plans;
- dealing with any technical problems or crises;
- controlling the studio and halting production if necessary;
- liaising with public relations staff to agree who will be interviewed, for example at sports matches;
- passing information and progress reports from live events to studio presenters;
- adhering to health and safety regulations, *e.g.* keeping 'safe areas' and fire exits clear of equipment.

Salary and Conditions

- Range of typical starting salaries: £14,000 - £20,000 (salary data collected Mar 07).
- Range of typical salaries at senior level/with experience (*e.g.* after 10 - 15 years in the role): upwards of £25,000 (salary data collected Mar 07).
- Freelance salaries can be paid at an hourly, daily or weekly rate though this will vary according to location, company, experience, duration of contract and demand. A freelance floor manager may earn approximately £150 per eight-hour day (salary data collected Mar 07).
- Working hours can be long and irregular with evening and weekend work not unusual. It is not uncommon to work a 14-hour day. Hours are usually dictated by studio booking times and a floor manager is expected to stay until the job is done.
- A typical day may involve starting at 1.00pm and filming three episodes of a game show, having an hour's break, then filming another two in the evening. Alternatively, you could work ten days in a row. Two very long days may be followed by a day off.
- When working freelance, you will be expected to work the hours demanded by the production company.
- The work is mainly studio-based, but floor managers may

also work on location, particularly when covering sporting events.

- Self-employment/freelance work is commonly possible. Freelance work is now the norm across the range of television companies, from the BBC to small independents.
- At present, women are under represented in this field, possibly due to the unsocial hours associated with the job.
- Jobs with independent production companies and facilities houses are mainly in London and the South East. Whilst it is fair to say that many BBC and Independent Television (ITV) jobs are also based in the capital, there are also opportunities in the UK's larger cities.
- The work can be pressurised, particularly when working to tight production schedules and strict studio booking times.
- Dress is usually very casual, but a smart appearance may be required when working on outside broadcasts, *e.g.* sporting events.
- Outside broadcasts and location shoots involve working away from home on a regular basis or for fairly long periods of time, either in the UK or abroad.

Entry Requirements

Although this area of work is open to all graduates and Diplomates, the following degree and HND subjects may increase your chances:

- media studies;
- drama/theatre studies;
- photography/film/television.

Entry without a degree or HND is common as most floor managers have worked their way up to this position.

Pre-entry experience is essential. Potential floor managers may have theatre experience but are more likely to have worked in television and gained experience as a runner, trainee floor manager, or possibly in a technical sound or lighting role. In order to realistically compete for jobs, several years of broadcasting experience is necessary.

Potential candidates will need to show evidence of the following:

- the ability to foresee, solve and avoid problems under pressure;
- a friendly disposition and an air of calm authority;
- excellent communication skills to receive, interpret and convey information accurately and concisely;
- interpersonal skills, in order to quickly judge how to get the best out of a variety of people;
- IT skills.

A driving licence is an asset, as are foreign language skills if you intend to work abroad.

To gain entry to this field, you will find it helpful to read the media press, in particular Broadcast magazine and The Guardian (Mondays). It is also worthwhile trying to find unpaid work with a production company or in local television to gain experience. Telephone and arrange to meet producers, directors or other appropriate individuals; potential contacts can be found by looking at programme credits. Be prepared to network, make contacts and promote yourself. All these activities can help you get a foot in the door to secure your first paid job in the media.

Training opportunities within television companies are linked to operational needs and whilst companies, including the BBC, may aim for annual recruitment, this cannot be guaranteed. The BBC runs a number of training schemes including the ever-popular production trainee scheme, which emphasises the move towards multimedia. All BBC training opportunities and jobs open to new entrants are advertised in the national press and on their website. A summary also appears on CEEFAX page 696. Posts are advertised in the BBC staff magazine Ariel, available via subscription; many are filled by qualified staff internally.

Some independent television companies have graduate opportunities, which operate on an individual company basis. These are likely to be advertised on their websites, in the local press or in The Guardian and Broadcast magazine.

The development of satellite and cable television has created more opportunities throughout the industry as a whole, but current trends in programming mean there is less demand for floor managers. When opportunities arise, appointments are made for each production on a freelance basis. Freelance floor managers may spend periods of time out of work. Direct entry is rare and you should be prepared to take an administrative post within television to gain knowledge of the industry.

The broadcasting sector has a history of initiatives to promote careers in the industry to under-represented groups, in particular ethnic minorities. The BBC has made a strong commitment to a policy of equality and diversity, which covers all aspects of its business, including recruitment.

It is illegal for employers to discriminate against candidates on the grounds of age, gender, race, disability, sexual orientation or religious faith. You may be interested in further information about work experience and further study.

Training

There is no professional qualification for floor managers. Training for the job is usually gained by working through the ranks and this applies to all broadcasting organisations.

The British Film Institute (BFI) runs a database of courses (available on their website) to help freelancers and would-be entrants to identify appropriate courses.

Skillset (Sector Skills Council for the Audio Visual Industries) supports a number of advertised new entrant training courses, including one based in Wales through Cyfle and one based in Scotland through Scottish Screen. Along with other industry partners, Skillset part funds a national, new entrant, technical training scheme organised by FT2 - Film & Television Freelance Training. Trainees combine short courses with work experience and assessment to gain a qualification in one of 15 technical areas, including camera and sound.

The Broadcasting Entertainment Cinematographic and Theatre Union (BECTU) also run training programmes for those involved in media and broadcasting.

Career Development

Most people in this career will have gained substantial experience before entry, either in a technical role, such as sound or lighting, or as a runner and/or assistant floor manager. Having experience in a technical role can secure more work as the roles can sometimes be performed simultaneously, helping to reduce production crew costs. This practice is becoming more common.

Assistant floor managers work with the floor manager, who will delegate tasks to them. They may be in charge of props for the show, or look after the audience whilst the floor manager looks after the presenters and guests. Experience in an assistant role allows you to make an impression in order to progress to floor manager.

It is possible to specialise: there are some floor managers who prefer to work in sport; others enjoy children's entertainment; some are especially skilled at outside broadcasts. A reputation for excellence within your specialism can lead to higher fees and more work. Advancement to producer or director is possible via an assistant role.

As with initial contracts, opportunities for promotion and progression can be boosted by networking (many jobs are found through word of mouth). Whatever your role, whether at the lower or higher end of the ladder, it is vital to make a good impression. Excellent interpersonal and networking skills will help you gain recommendations for work, whether trying to get initial experience in the media or wishing to advance through the ranks.

Location Manager

Job Description and Activities: Location managers are responsible for all the practical arrangements involved with shooting programmes, photographs and productions outside the studio. Productions are made in a wide range of locations; location managers need to research, identify and organise appropriate sites.

As well as arranging and negotiating site use, the role usually involves managing sites throughout the shooting process. This involves working to strict budgetary and time limits and maintaining a high standard of health and safety and security. The demands of organising crews and dealing with a range of people - from television producers to the police- make this an intense and varied role.

Typical Work Activities: A location manager's role follows a sequence of activities from the pre-planning to completion stages of a production.

Typical activities include:

- assessing scripts or story boards and breaking them down into locations and a schedule;
- meeting with the director and designer to discuss projects;
- collating ideas and undertaking research using resources such as the internet, specialist location libraries, local and regional film commissions/agencies;
- visiting and photographing locations appropriate to budget to assess suitability;
- making preliminary enquiries regarding access, parking and location use;
- liaising with the director to discuss and show ideas and photographs;
- collating practical information on potential locations, such as hotels for accommodating the crew and cast. In the case of photography shoots, the location manager often books the hotel and travel arrangements as well;
- liaising with key members of the production team to assess visual and technical specifications;
- negotiating access and drawing up a contract with location owners;
- researching locations thoroughly to ensure no disruptive works or events are likely to take place during the shoot;
- organising permissions for access, for example with local authorities and the police;
- scheduling crew arrival dates and times and keeping all parties informed on site;

- organising the technical specification for equipment, power sources and accommodation for crew on site;
- ensuring health and safety and security requirements are met at all times;
- distributing maps, directions, parking plans and all relevant support information to all services and crew;
- arranging schedules for the day with the assistant director to ensure continuity;
- managing the location on the day and resolving practical or people-related problems as they arise;
- supervising location support staff throughout the process;
- being in constant attendance to ensure all aspects run smoothly including the final clearing up and thanking of site owners.

Salary and Conditions

- Rates vary with experience, but location assistants starting out can expect to be paid £100 per day on a shoot (salary data collected Feb. 06).
- For location managers, commercial rates are the highest at £329 per day on non-shoot days and £380 per day during filming, but they rarely last more than a couple of days. Dramas and feature films pay slightly lower rates of £1,000 - £1500 per week, but offer the security of longer contracts (salary data collected Feb. 06).
- Most location managers work as freelancers and are paid on a contract basis. The Broadcasting Entertainment Cinematographic and Theatre Union (BECTU) recommends minimum rates for working in location management.
- Location managers working on photographic ('stills') shoots work with smaller crews but also take on the role of producer, therefore their rates are higher. Photographic shoots are, however, less governed by unions so there is greater variation in the rates paid.
- Filming days demand that the location manager is the first person to arrive and the last person to leave. Hours are, therefore, always likely to be irregular.

- The initial scouting stage requires maximum viewings per day in the shortest period of time.
- A lot of the work is based outdoors and it is important to be able to adapt to and be comfortable with working in all kinds of environments and weather conditions.
- Work levels vary seasonally, with winter traditionally being quiet and summer the busiest period.
- Self-employment is common. Given the constant presence required on set, part-time work is rare.
- Work is only available in restricted locations.
- There are currently more men than women in the profession.
- Work is usually given on the basis of recognition or recommendation. Practitioners need to maintain a network and build on their experience and reputation.
- Work settings are highly pressurised. Location managers need to foresee any likely problems and respond quickly as they arise.
- The nature of employment in the profession may lead to periodic relocation and financial insecurity.
- Due to the nature of the role, driving to other locations and working away from home is a frequent part of the job. There may be opportunities abroad for experienced and established location managers.

Entry Requirements

Although this area of work is open to all graduates, the following subjects may increase your chances at foundation degree, HND or degree level:

- communication and media studies;
- photography/film/television.

Entry without a degree, HND or foundation degree is commonly possible, but all applicants should be able to demonstrate knowledge and commitment to the media industry. Doing a course that involves film/media production experience may be useful, but it is important to ensure that courses offer appropriate training. Skillset Careers operates a freephone information line with details of courses and funding sources. The Skillset (Sector Skills Council for the Audio Visual Industries)/British Film Institute (BFI) online database also provides details of media courses and course providers.

Pre-entry experience is likely to be required and it is advisable to have some understanding and knowledge of media production.

Potential candidates will need to show evidence of the following skills:

- the ability to work with a diverse range of people in the planning stages;
- adaptability - in order to deal with external influences when delivering the required environment for the actual shoot;
- a diplomatic approach - for encouraging or persuading people as the situation demands;
- good organisational, planning and administrative skills;
- excellent communication skills;
- a strong knowledge of the local region and a passable knowledge of architectural styles;
- basic knowledge of health and safety regulations and an understanding of the requirements of each of the film unit departments;
- the ability to problem-solve and think laterally;
- artistic/creative awareness and an ability to take photographs;
- stamina and the flexibility to work long hours under pressure.

Try to get some work experience whilst still studying or get involved with film/video/photography activities whilst at university. At the early stage, gaining experience within production support is more likely than finding specific location management support experience. Skillset provides details about the new entrant training scheme that can provide routes into media, as well as the opportunity to make industry contacts.

Because vacancies are not advertised it is important to look creatively for a hands-on location assistant or scout opportunity as a way in. Your skills-based CV needs to reach as many production companies as possible. Established freelance location managers also take on assistants. Film and screen commissions in major cities around the UK hold 'availability' databases of freelancers and there are also websites to subscribe to for those seeking opportunities in all aspects of production. Remember that a CV alone is unlikely to get you a job, so always follow-up with a phone call or visit.

From 1st October 2006 it will be illegal to discriminate against candidates on age grounds, but in practice age may continue to be used in selection criteria by some employers.

Training

There are limited formal training opportunities relating to location management. It is mainly the responsibility of individuals to take the initiative in identifying and following up relevant training. Skillset (Sector Skills Council for the Audio Visual Industries) offers a range of National Occupational Standards relevant to professionals already working in this area. Within standards for film and TV production, the following units are covered:

- researching and assessing locations;
- preparing locations for use;
- managing locations.

Further details of units are available through the Skillset website. Short courses in location management are also available. Check the British Film Institute (BFI)/Skillset database for up-to-date details. Courses may be available to freelance media professionals at a subsidised rate through Skillset.

Much of the work is knowledge-based and there are many issues surrounding health and safety with which short course attendance can assist. Public liability and legal contractual matters are other aspects to keep up with and working with local authorities and the police requires knowledge of procedures and bye-laws.

Some courses in production management may be useful to location managers as some of the skills used in both these fields can overlap. Maintaining and developing photographic and video skills could also be useful. Location managers working on 'stills' shoots generally train with one or two photographers over a period of time to gain experience of producing stills shoots and knowledge of the technical requirements of photographers. The Guild of Location Managers (GLM), a London-based non-profit organisation recognised by the UK Film Council, also provides training events for members as well as opportunities to network and share good practice.

Career Development

Developing a career in location management takes time, as gaining work often depends on industry contacts. Getting known to production companies and working to a flexible but professional standard is a key part of early career progression. With experience, it is possible to build a career in a specific area, such as drama or commercials.

In the area of moving-image location work, it is common for current students or recent graduates to gain some experience in the media industries as a runner, assistant director or camera person in production, or specifically in location running. A common career progression route is for a location runner to move on to location assistant, location scout, or, in larger productions, unit manager and eventually location manager. You need to show a willingness to get involved, be prepared to work hard and undertake basic tasks and demonstrate problem-solving skills.

Career development for freelancers usually takes the form of progressing from small productions to larger and more ambitious projects. Because projects can vary from one-day shoots for a pop video or commercial advertisement to a major feature film or television drama over several weeks or months, this aspect of work offers great scope for the development of a location management career.

Location managers may choose to set up their own companies or location agency, independently or with other professionals. Others move into working for location companies. It is also possible to progress into working as a producer or director. There are a limited number of opportunities to gain an in-house post in location, production, or unit management. New opportunities within regional film commissions, working in roles such as film officer, are also developing.

Programme Researcher

Job Description and Activities: A programme researcher provides support to the producer and production team. Researchers collect, verify and prepare information for film, television and radio productions, either working on a wide variety of programmes or within one subject area.

The work, which is very different from academic research, involves organising, planning and researching everything that will happen during the programme: who will be interviewed; where; will the film crew fit; does the budget stretch? The researcher will contribute ideas, contacts and sources to the process.

The job can be seen as an apprenticeship for the producer role and a chance for ambitious recruits to show their potential.

Typical Work Activities: The variety of the work carried out by researchers depends on individual producers and the production companies that employ them.

In radio, broadcasters do a lot of their own programme research, assisted by the producers. In television and film, researchers may be involved in a wide variety of activities and the role may be roughly divided into two: factual research (checking all the information used in making a film, *e.g.* period costume and architecture) and picture research (examining archives for film, video and photographic material to be used in documentaries).

Typical work activities include:

- meeting with producers, directors, presenters and writers to discuss the research needs of a programme;
- generating new programme ideas;
- sourcing and researching facts, figures and information

using the internet, film and tape archives, specialist collections, picture libraries, museums and government departments;
- conveying findings accurately to others in report form and briefings;
- updating scripts and editing news reports;
- researching and booking appropriate people and locations;
- booking resources, facilities and freelance staff;
- providing administrative support, such as typing, answering the phone and dealing with contracts;
- briefing scriptwriters and presenters on topics;
- sourcing copyright for literary and music sources and gaining clearance for any materials used;
- negotiating broadcasting rights;
- tracking down film, archive and video tape;
- finding interviewees and conducting initial interviews;
- finding members of the public for a vox pop response to current events;
- directing a small shoot and doing straightforward editing.

Salary and Conditions

- A typical starting salary for researchers with little experience would be £22,000 in London, or £18,500 outside the capital, rising to approximately £24,500 in London with a couple of years' experience (salary data collected July 06). You may well have to work for minimal payment or for free before getting a fully paid job.
- Experienced researchers can earn up to £32,500 in London, or £29,000 outside London and with specialist skills, such as subtitling, as much as £50,000, depending on the size of the company and its location.
- Salaries vary depending on employers, location, experience and the responsibilities of the job, which often makes salaries negotiable. Freelance rates vary widely and are calculated at a daily rate between £150 and £400 (salary data collected July 06).

- Employment is generally precarious. Staff jobs are extremely hard to come by and researchers are generally taken on for specific projects or programmes (often lasting no more than two or three months). In order to secure regular employment, freelancers need to build up a reputation. Large corporations, such as the BBC, employ some researchers on permanent contracts.
- Unsocial working hours are a common feature and researchers may work up to seven days a week for long periods. Work on live programmes is more predictable.
- Researchers' work takes place in a variety of settings, ranging from typing in an office to interviewing people in the street. Documentary researchers may sometimes work undercover.
- Almost three-quarters of all researchers are women. Science and news/current affairs programmes tend to have a higher percentage of men.
- Jobs are mostly restricted to London and other major cities with broadcasting bases, such as Manchester.
- The work is stressful and demanding and requires a very high level of commitment. The work culture is generally informal but you may feel pressured with tight deadlines to meet.
- Researchers may travel a great deal, occasionally overseas, depending on the research project.

Entry Requirements

This area of work is open to all graduates and work experience and contacts may count for more than your degree subject. Nevertheless, a degree in one of the following subjects may increase your chances:

- public relations;
- English and literary studies;
- journalism;
- broadcasting and media studies;
- history.

Although this area of work is open to all Diplomates, the following subjects may increase your chances:

- business-related studies;
- broadcasting and media studies;
- legal studies;
- journalism.

Graduates tend to be preferred but relevant work experience, personal qualities, confidence and evidence of skills can compensate. Specialist knowledge and research experience may be required for specific subject areas or documentaries. For general areas, a knowledge of current affairs and the media is useful, plus evidence of lateral thinking.

A pre-entry postgraduate qualification is not essential, although a practical journalism or media course may help.

Many graduate researchers have previously worked in newspapers or radio (mainly as journalists) or gained experience in entry-level jobs in television, often unpaid. Opportunities for work experience do exist and there are new entrant training schemes available. Information about these can be found on the Skillset (Sector Skills Council for the Audio Visual Industries) website. FT2 - Film & Television Freelance Training run an Independent Companies Research Training Scheme. The BBC offers work experience opportunities nationally.

Competition for all advertised vacancies is fierce, so pre-entry work experience is vital and you need determination to succeed. Try getting summer work experience in a research role with the local or regional press, community radio, student union publications, archives and picture libraries. Contacts in the industry are often the means to a first position and you must be prepared to network. Be as well prepared as possible before you approach people: keep copies of everything you have contributed to, from newspaper articles to television programmes and stay in touch with what is going on in the industry. Follow news and current affairs programmes with a critical approach.

Researchers must be multi-skilleded, resourceful and able to generate new ideas and have an instinct for a good story.

Excellent written communication and outstanding interpersonal skills are essential qualities, along with organisational ability. Confidence, patience and motivation are also important. Reseachers must be able to work under pressure to meet changing deadlines within budgetary constraints. To be successful in securing freelance work, researchers also need to be skilled in self-management and self-promotion. IT and research skills, a knowledge of legal and ethical principles in relation to the media and copyright and a driving licence are all essential.

From 1 October 2006 it is illegal to discriminate against candidates on age grounds but, in practice, age may continue to be used in selection criteria by some employers.

Training

Training is gained by experience on the job. There are short training courses available in-house or externally. Training opportunities within broadcasting companies are linked to operational needs and whilst companies, including the BBC, may aim for annual recruitment, this cannot be guaranteed. The BBC runs a number of training schemes, including weekly modules which are advertised on BBC Training and Development.

The Skillset (Sector Skills Council for the Audio Visual Industries) Freelance Training Fund supports some advertised training courses. Along with other industry partners, it part-funds a national new-entrant, technical training scheme organised by FT2 - Film & Television Freelance Training, who also run a researchers' training scheme for independent production companies. Trainees work towards NVQ3 Production Research.

In Scotland, Scottish Screen provides training for the Scottish broadcast and film industry, including a new entrants' scheme. The Research Centre for Television and Interactivity in Glasgow delivers training programmes aimed mainly at researchers and lists opportunities for work placements with independent production companies. All the above schemes attract hundreds of applicants.

Skillset and the British Film Institute (BFI) develop courses and run a database to help freelancers and would-be entrants to identify appropriate courses. The Producers Alliance for Cinema and Television (PACT), the UK trade association that represents and promotes the commercial interests of independent feature film, television, animation and interactive media companies, also provides courses for members and a guide to gaining work experience in the media.

The broadcasting sector has a history of initiatives to promote careers in the industry to under-represented groups, particularly ethnic minorities. The BBC has published a set of core values, including diversity, which covers all aspects of its business, including recruitment.

Career Development

There is no fixed career ladder, but the nature of the job makes it an excellent starting point for an ambitious entrant.

Career progression is achieved by working on a variety of programmes, films and stations. Researchers in local radio may move into the national network, while those in television may go on to work on high-profile current events programmes or specialise in a particular area, such as music research or stills research. On a larger production there may be opportunities for experienced researchers to supervise a team of researchers and to maintain a high level of contact with the producer and director, in effect moving into a senior researcher role.

Most researchers continue to work on short, freelance contracts, eventually becoming producers or directors. Being a researcher is a great way to get a good view of what other roles exist within the industry.

Researchers are becoming fewer in some areas of broadcasting, mainly due to the introduction of assistant producers. However, it has been recognised in some areas that a researcher's skills still have an important role to play and this may mean that researchers will be more specialised in future. Currently, researchers are becoming more hands-on, involved in shooting, sound recording and even directing, alongside traditional research and increasing responsibility in programme making. The BBC runs a three-week course to train researchers to become assistant producers. Some move into other media roles, such as journalism or other areas of production. Competition is fierce for all promotional positions.

To progress in this rapidly changing industry, you need to be pro-active and willing to learn new skills, meet new people, make new contacts and, above all, work hard to show a firm commitment to your job. See the careers section of the Skillset (Sector Skills Council for the Audio Visual Industries) website, which provides careers information about the media industry.

Radio Producer

Job Description and Activities: Radio producers are responsible for controlling the output of radio programmes. From generating ideas to editing (and sometimes even presenting), they are involved in the entire process of broadcasting content for radio. They manage small teams of broadcast assistants, studio engineers and DJs. Selecting music, scheduling, scriptwriting and researching are key aspects of the role.

Although producers usually specialise in one particular area of radio (music, features/documentaries, sports, drama or news), many of the responsibilities a producer will face are common to all areas. As well as fulfilling a creative role, producers may also be in charge of budgets, negotiating contracts and other business matters.

Typical Work Activities: Although specific responsibilities will vary according to type of programme and the station, typical work activities include:

- deciding on content and programme scheduling;
- controlling programme output/'desk-driving', approving final versions of recorded features;
- selecting music appropriate to the programme, the audience and the station;
- managing and training small creative teams, working with DJs and sound engineers;

- choosing, sourcing and researching guests and bands;
- generating ideas for programmes/features and pitching these to commissioning editors;
- researching material for programme content and writing interview questions;
- editing recorded material using digital equipment and understanding technical procedures;
- resolving scheduling issues which includes editing down materials recorded by colleagues;
- managing budgets;
- meeting with record company 'pluggers' and other industry professionals;
- some smaller local stations may require producers to double up as presenters;
- dealing with legal issues including negotiating contracts, completing documentation relating to the Performing Right Society (PRS) and guests' consent, ensuring the demands of relevant artists' unions are considered etc.;
- taking responsibility for the health and safety of colleagues and guests;
- responding to listeners' comments and questions;
- conducting interviews either in the studio or on location;
- if working in the production of radio commercials/adverts, liaising with local businesses and helping to create an audio identity for them, as well as casting actors for voice-overs.

Skillset (Sector Skills Council for the Audio Visual Industries) lists the national occupational standards for radio production, which provide more details for many of the key responsibilities of radio producers. The BBC Training and Development website, plus other BBC radio websites (Radio 1, 1xtra, 6 Music) also contain numerous profiles and 'day in the life' features, which offer good insights into the role of radio producers.

Salary and Conditions

- Range of typical starting salaries: £10,000 - £12,000 (salary data collected Dec. 05).

- Range of typical salaries at senior level/with experience (*e.g.*, after 10-15 years in the role): £30,000 - £80,000 for senior positions (salary data collected Dec. 05).
- Freelance salaries vary from £150 to £300 a day, depending on experience (salary data collected Dec. 05).
- Freelancers account for 19% of the workforce. Freelancing is becoming more popular as work is increasingly offered on a short-term contract basis.
- Working hours can be long and unpredictable and typically include unsocial hours.
- Producers are mainly office-based but may need to travel to conduct interviews or work on live concerts/festivals.
- The majority of opportunities are based in London but most major towns and cities now have local stations, whether BBC, commercial or community based. The BBC's Nations and Regions also produce networked programmes outside the capital.
- 43% of radio producers are women and 7.4% are from ethnic minorities. Across the media, organisations are addressing diversity issues. The advent of digital radio and expansion of community radio is also increasing representation as ethnic groups set up their own stations, such as Asian Sound Radio.
- The level of paperwork and management responsibility generally increase with seniority.
- Working to tight deadlines and generating new ideas can result in periods of great pressure, as can working on live programmes.
- Limited financial resources, particularly within non-commercial radio stations, can create creative and production challenges.
- The work provides the excitement and satisfaction of producing immediate and very public end products.
- This can be a very sociable and fairly informal working environment.
- Travel within a working day and absence from home at

night are occasionally necessary but overseas work or travel are uncommon.

Entry Requirements

Although this area of work is open to all graduates and Diplomates, the following subjects may increase your chances:

- broadcast journalism;
- journalism;
- media studies;
- drama/theatre studies.

An HND/foundation degree in Communication and Media Studies or an NVQ/SVQ in Broadcast Journalism Production are also relevant qualifications.

Postgraduate diplomas and MAs in radio production are available.

Live music producers may need a technical qualification and news production may require a journalism degree. Educational qualifications are not, however, necessary, as work experience and a demonstrable passion for radio are valued much more highly.

Experience is essential to the role of a radio producer and very few are younger than mid-20s. Potential candidates will need to show evidence of the following:

- excellent written and oral communication skills;
- an ability to work as a part of a team and also on own initiative;
- good organisational skills and an ability to cope under pressure;
- an awareness of current affairs, good general knowledge;
- good people skills and a sense of humour;
- creativity, quick thinking and ability to generate ideas.

Up-to-date technical skills are useful. A good radio voice is also very helpful, particularly in local radio where the producer may double as the presenter. Participation in drama, music, radio and journalistic activities at school, university or in the community can provide valuable experience.

Try to gain practical experience by volunteering for local, student, hospital or community radio and get to know as many people as possible whilst on placement - they may be able to offer additional opportunities once the placement ends. Use industry resources such as The Radio Directory and the The Production Guide to make contact with relevant organisations. Competition for placements is fierce so in order to secure work experience, gain an understanding of specific stations of interest and the industry as a whole. Know target audiences, playlists and a station's ethos. Have opinions and ideas and do not be afraid to express them. Be persistent, do not fear rejection and be prepared to do anything to get experience. Remember that even the most senior producers will probably have started as broadcast assistants or runners.

Organisations such as the Student Radio Association (SRA) and the Women's Radio Group can be helpful and may also provide industry contacts. The Radio Academy provides one-off radio 'masterclasses' at universities and higher education institutions around the country. These are aimed at students and others thinking about working in radio and offer an insight into working in the industry. Mediafly Broadcast Training Company also runs a wide range of courses at commercial stations across the country, aimed at those who want to break in to radio.

As is typical of the media industry, getting into radio can be difficult. Perseverance and determination are vital. The Radio Academy website has a useful audio guide to 'getting in' which can be downloaded. Amongst other things, it suggests considering commercial production (making adverts) as this area of radio production is less competitive and often more lucrative.

Although it is illegal to discriminate against candidates on age grounds, in practice age may continue to be used in selection criteria by some employers.

Training

Training is usually gained whilst working. With the emergence of multi-skilling across the media, producers are increasingly involved in all aspects of radio including presenting, editing and sound recording. Many producers learn these skills from experienced colleagues or by attending short in-house training courses. BBC Training and Development offer a number of short courses relevant to training and developing as a producer including radio producer foundation, live studio production, radio features and directing the presenter. The BBC also runs production training schemes through its new talent initiative.

It is important that producers keep up to date with technical and multimedia developments, especially following the expansion of digital radio. Skillset (Sector Skills Council for the Audio Visual Industries) and the British Film Institute (BFI) produce the Media Courses and Multimedia Courses Directory. This provides information and contact details of relevant training courses and providers. Courses are available on a short or longer term basis and cover technical production and broadcast skills.

Skillset provides subsidised training to freelance media professionals, with up to a 60% discount offered on some courses. The BBC has a system of 'attachments', through which individuals can gain experience in other jobs for up to six months. This is a common route for progression from broadcast assistant to producer.

Career Development

Progression within this career is usually self-driven. Many producers work on a freelance basis and move from one employer to another. It is possible to gain freelance work on a long-term basis. As many vacancies are never advertised, making contacts within the industry is essential. At the start of your career, particularly, think of creative ways to make links with potential employers and to gain relevant experience.

Generally, career development is achieved through moving programme or network. For example, a local radio producer with several years' experience may then apply for a post on national radio. Career progression is gained through working for a more prestigious network, programme or presenter. As they gain more experience, producers will also tend to focus on a specialist area of interest such as news, drama or documentaries. Various professional bodies hold annual awards for the radio industry. Gaining an industry-recognised accolade within their area of expertise will inevitably help to progress the career of a talented producer.

Some presenters, particularly if they are high-profile, will choose their own production team to stay with them for the duration of the contract. On news and current affairs or magazine-type programmes, where there is likely to be a team of producers, progression may be to a role at senior producer level and then to programme editor. Some may progress from senior producer or editor to a managerial role such as network controller.

Ongoing continuing professional development (CPD) is important in an industry such as radio where technology is constantly changing and in the media generally, where multi-skilling is more prevalent. Producers may undertake courses such as voice training, website editing, news writing, media law. Relevant professional bodies such as the BBC and the Commercial Radio Companies Association (CRCA) provide a range of development courses. The Radio Academy organises annual fast-track conferences aimed at professionals under 25, or in the first five years of their radio career, to help them clarify and plan their career development.

A small number of radio producers progress into teaching or lecturing in related subjects.

Television Production Assistant

Job Description and Activities: A television production assistant (PA) is a vital link in the production team. PAs assist the director or producer and are involved in all stages of the production process (from pre-production through to post-production and transmission) to help ensure production runs smoothly.

The role is technical, creative and administrative: PAs supervise setup and operation of production equipment, help plan programme format and research scripts, maintain production records and hire equipment. Unlike other roles in the industry, PAs are more generalist than specialist. They are given responsibility for a wide variety of tasks, which may be both menial and complex.

Typical Work Activities: Typical work activities include some or all of the following tasks:

- working closely with the producer, director and production team;
- liaising with writers, artists' agents, members of the public and publicity staff;
- coordinating and communicating production resources and facility arrangements in tandem with the production managers;
- attending and timing production rehearsals;
- attending and coordinating planning meetings;
- checking copyright and permission issues;
- ensuring royalties are paid for additional images, music or footage used;
- dealing with artists' payments and expenses;
- producing budgets, monitoring costs and controlling expenses;
- cueing prerecorded material;
- overseeing the timing during a shoot or show;
- ensuring continuity, both on location and in the studio;
- dealing with production enquiries from members of the public;
- keeping accurate shot lists, especially for drama productions;
- typing up camera scripts and shot cards;
- producing timing schedules, shot lists and logs for post-production;
- calling shots;
- liaising with the camera and sound crew during studio recordings;
- booking artists and performers;
- organising the production and distribution of scripts;

- booking catering, accommodation, equipment and flights for performers and crew;
- managing contracts with external organisations;
- conducting research;
- completing all necessary paperwork in relation to the above tasks.

Salary and Conditions

- Starting salaries for television production assistants (PAs) are about £14,000 - £18,000 per annum (salary data collected Dec. 06).
- An experienced production assistant can expect to earn between £20,000 and £25,000 per annum (salary data collected Dec. 06).
- A weekly freelance guideline rate of £481 has been outlined by the Broadcasting Entertainment Cinematographic and Theatre Union (BECTU) and the Producers Alliance for Cinema and Television (PACT), but top freelancers can negotiate their own salaries.
- The hours are mainly irregular and very long: most PAs work shifts, early mornings, late evenings and weekends, depending on production requirements. PAs are first to arrive and last to leave. Due to the demanding and unpredictable nature of the work, it is often difficult to make plans in advance, which can have lifestyle implications. Travel adds to the working day.
- Shoots can take place in a range of settings: indoors in offices and studios; outdoors on location in all weather conditions. The work may involve standing and waiting around for long periods of time.
- Freelance work is increasingly likely for experienced PAs, particularly in the independent sector. Work is based on short-term contracts for the duration of the assignment.
- You need to become multi-skilled in order to be able to work successfully in a range of environments. As a freelancer, those extra skills will increase the amount and range of work open to you. To be successful in securing

freelance work, you will also need to be highly organised and skilled in your own self-management and promotion.

- Career breaks are possible, but time away can often result in missed opportunities.
- Jobs with independent production companies and facilities houses are mainly in London and the South-East. Although many BBC and Independent Television (ITV) jobs are also based in London, there are growing opportunities in the UK's larger cities, *e.g.* Manchester, for BBC work.
- The majority of PAs are women.
- Travel within a working day is common. Outside broadcasts (OBs) and location shoots may involve working away from home on a regular basis or for fairly long periods of time, either in the UK or abroad.

Entry Requirements

This area of work is open to all graduates and Diplomates. People in the industry often believe it is more important to have a qualification in a discipline outside the media area to demonstrate knowledge of different subjects, with relevant media training gained on the job. The following degree/HND subjects may increase your chances of success:

- business-related studies;
- engineering;
- English and literary studies;
- political and social sciences.

Entry without a degree or HND is commonly possible.

In this profession, it is far more important to have work experience, enthusiasm and contacts than qualifications. An interest in and knowledge of the industry, ability to network and promote yourself well and eagerness to work for free, will help significantly.

Although by no means essential, a postgraduate course can help increase your practical skills. For details of courses, see the Prospects Postgraduate Directory. With media qualifications, it is always important to ask about accreditation by industry bodies and opportunities for placements and using equipment.

Media experience is crucial. You may already have gained some experience from your course, university television unit or film-making society. Volunteering on a local community film project or at your local hospital radio station, entering media competitions, applying for awards and building up a portfolio of your work, will all help.

Candidates will need to show evidence of the following:

- excellent communication and interpersonal skills;
- ability to remain calm and level-headed under pressure;
- sound administrative and organisational skills;
- fast, accurate word processing skills;
- good level of numeracy;
- enthusiasm, motivation and a pro-active manner;
- ability to work effectively as part of a team and on your own initiative;
- stamina and persistence;
- initiative, flexibility and adaptability;
- common sense and problem-solving skills;
- the ability to prioritise and cope with last-minute changes, *e.g.* to scripts, whilst under pressure.

Making your CV as impressive and diverse as possible will give you an advantage: make sure you tell prospective employers if you have a driving licence and your own transport; knowledge of different cultures; ability to speak different languages; contacts in other industries and countries; etc. Having the skills and experiences that make you stand out from other candidates, commitment, passion and drive is what the industry demands. Candidates with a background in journalism, research, business, accountancy, law, engineering, management, politics, etc. are viewed favourably, as their knowledge of other areas can be highly relevant and useful.

Media directories, such as The Knowledge and the PACT Directory of Independent Producers, can be useful for addresses, named contacts and information on productions. Find out what is going on in the industry by reading the media press, in particular Broadcast now and The Guardian on a Monday.

Contact production companies, independent film makers, or local TV or radio stations, for paid or unpaid work opportunities. Some companies will offer unpaid work experience opportunities. The BBC offers a limited number of work experience placements, for which competition is fierce.

It is now illegal to discriminate against candidates on age grounds but, in practice, age may continue to be used in selection criteria by some employers.

Many factors, such as the need to travel frequently, the unstructured nature of recruitment in many areas and the often unsocial hours, may make television production a more difficult area for mature applicants to enter.

Training

Television production assistants (PAs) receive the majority of their training on the job by shadowing an experienced PA. However, a number of training organisations offer additional training and short courses for media professionals:

- Skillset (Sector Skills Council for the Audio Visual Industries) has a pool of money to subsidise training for freelancers through their freelance training fund. They also offer a range of nationally-recognised industry qualifications (NVQs) and professional standards for a whole range of media careers, including production.
- FT2 - Film & Television Freelance Training offers training for new entrants in production careers, including production assistants. Training is for a period of up to two years with production assistants working towards an NVQ qualification.
- Cyfle, the national training provider for the television, film and interactive media industry in Wales, offers a range of production-based courses.
- In Scotland, Scottish Screen provides training for new entrants in areas such as creative and financial skills and the production process.

Career Development

There is no structured route for career development within the industry. Success often comes through seizing opportunities, making a positive impression, knowing the right people, making your own luck and being in the right place at the right time. Career development is linked to proactivity and balancing workload with the development of new skills and you are only as good as your last piece of work.

The traditional BBC route from secretary to programme-maker is less popular, with the majority of new entrants beginning their career with an independent company and progressing from there. Having acquired knowledge of a variety of broadcasting and production techniques from a range of different programme areas, a number of possible career areas are available.

Production assistants (PAs) can progress to roles such as senior production assistant or production manager, where the focus is on financial management and handling budgets, though senior production posts are rarely advertised. Other positions include assistant director, director, floor manager, unit manager, location manager and vision mixer.

Many PAs tend to stay within their area of specialisation, where they feel their skills are most suited to the type of production they are working on. However, it is possible to move from TV into film, radio, commercials and community television. With further training, specialisation is possible in areas such as music and continuity.

Television/Film/Video Producer

Job Description and Activities: Producers are the main players in the television, film and video industries. The initial idea for a project often comes from a producer, who will oversee each project from conception to completion and may also be involved in the marketing and distribution processes.

Producers work closely with directors and the other production staff on the shoot. Increasingly, they need to have directing skills themselves. They attract the money to fund each project and are responsible for keeping production within the allocated budget. Creative input varies, but producers have the ultimate say on the final product.

Typical Work Activities: Producers are responsible for facilitating a project from beginning to end. They are involved in every stage of the television programme, film or video, overseeing the project from start to finish, both in a studio and on location.

Essentially team leaders, they are supported by production assistants, coordinators and managers, depending on the size of the project.

Typical work activities include:

- raising funding;
- reading, researching and assessing ideas and finished scripts;
- commissioning writers;
- securing the rights to novels, plays or screenplays;
- building and developing a network of contacts;
- liaising and discussing projects with financial backers - projects can vary from a small, corporate video costing £30,000 to a Hollywood feature film of more than £100million;
- using computer software packages for screen-writing, budgeting and scheduling;
- hiring key staff, including a director and a crew to shoot films or videos;
- controlling the budget and allocating resources;
- pulling together all the strands of creative and practical talent involved in the project to create a team;
- organising shooting schedules;
- troubleshooting;
- supervising the progress of the project from production to post production;
- holding regular meetings with the director to discuss characters and scenes;

- acting as a sounding board for the director;
- bringing the finished production in on budget.

In theory, the producer deals with all the practical and political aspects of keeping a project running smoothly, so that the director and the rest of the team can concentrate on the creative angles.

Salary and Conditions

- Range of typical starting salaries: £15,000 - £25,000.
- Range of salaries with experience: £30,000 - £75,000 (All salary data collected Oct. 06, Skillset Film Workforce Survey 2005).
- Experienced staff can earn more by freelancing.
- Salaries can vary enormously depending on the size of the company and the size and scale of the project.
- There are currently fewer salaried, permanent jobs with companies available, which can lead to financial insecurity.
- Work involves regular unsocial hours at weekends and in the evenings. Long hours and time spent in meetings or on location are the norm.
- The working environment can be varied and producers can be based in an office, studio or on location.
- Self-employment and freelance work are common with work frequently offered on a contract basis. The freelance nature of the work may cause some employment insecurity.
- Career breaks may create difficulties due to the competitive nature of the industry and the need to network and keep up to date with industry changes.
- The ratio of male to female producers is becoming more equal.
- A great many of the jobs are in London, with many post-production and facilities houses based in Soho. Outside the capital, most production companies are in large cities such as Manchester, Birmingham, Cardiff, Edinburgh and Glasgow. You could work on location anywhere in the country.

- You need to be highly motivated by success and pressure as this is a job with the potential for an enormous amount of stress. Flexibility and mobility are extremely important, as is the ability to handle the pressure of financial responsibility.
- Travel during the working day is frequent. Absence from home at night is also common.
- Overseas work or travel can occur, but is occasional.

Entry Requirements

Although this area of work is open to all graduates and Diplomates, the following subjects at degree or HND level may increase your chances:

- communication and media studies;
- photography/film/television;
- information technology/multimedia;
- broadcasting.

Entry without a degree or HND is commonly possible, but most producers are educated to degree level.

Postgraduate qualifications are not required for entry into the profession. However, courses containing practical work experience in production may increase your chances of success in a notoriously competitive environment. Be aware that entry on to these courses is also competitive and most require some previous experience in order for you to demonstrate your practical skills and evidence of your work.

Look for courses that provide cutting-edge technical resources, a reasonable final production budget and contacts within the industry. The Media Courses and Multimedia Courses Directory on the British Film Institute (BFI) website provides details of a range of courses.

This is a job that requires experience. Even first-time producers will have a significant track record in the industry, perhaps as an assistant producer or in research, marketing and scriptwriting. Producers are expected to have several years' experience and a thorough understanding of all programme-making techniques, including directing and editing skills.

Potential candidates will also need to show evidence of the following:

- confidence in your own ability;
- strong communication and people skills;
- strong time and resource management skills;
- creative ability;
- the ability to cope under pressure;
- a strong head for figures;
- leadership skills.

Competition is fierce. Job vacancies are rarely advertised, therefore developing networks of contacts is essential. Use creative job-hunting methods, such as approaching production and post-production companies speculatively. Be prepared to follow up letters and CVs in person by knocking on doors. Research the industry and individual production companies thoroughly. Keep abreast of current trends.

Focus your job search initially on runner positions. This is the area of work that recent graduates are most likely to find a job in. Running provides some experience and a certain amount of contacts to help get a first job or training place.

Provide up-to-date evidence of what you can offer (*e.g.* a showreel, video, portfolio or script) gained through involvement with a university film society or community film project.

Gain work experience or take a weekend course whilst still studying to improve your chances of entry.

In the early stages of your career you may have to be prepared to accept very low salaries and, if necessary, to work part time in the industry and part time in another area of employment to make ends meet.

Training

The structure of the television, film and video industries has changed rapidly in the past decade and programme/film makers are having to react to these changes. New developments and changes in working practices have created more mobility and increased entry into the industry, but have also resulted in more job insecurity. Producers, for example, are starting to take a more directorial role in programme making. Staff need to be flexible, increasingly multi-skilled and able to move across traditional jobs. It is advisable, therefore, to develop as many skills in as many different environments as is possible.

Training is provided mainly on the job by employers and a range of short courses for those working in the profession is available.

Skillset (Sector Skills Council for the Audio Visual Industries) is the government and industry-funded organisation responsible for ensuring that workers in the audio visual industries are appropriately trained. In conjunction with industry employers and training providers, it runs free and subsidised training programmes including the Audio Visual Industries Induction Programme (a 'New Entrants' programme) for those with a few months' experience. Its website also has links to non-Skillset funded training programmes run by broadcast and independent production companies.

FT2 - Film & Television Freelance Training provides training for people seeking to establish a freelance career in production and technical areas of the UK film and television industry. Information on training schemes can be found on their website.

Some independent television companies have graduate training schemes which operate on an individual company basis. These are likely to be advertised on their websites, in the local and national press and in Broadcast magazine.

Career Development

Programme makers and producers working in television, film and video tend to work as self-employed freelancers on fixed, often short-term, contracts. More often than not, the length of the contract will depend on the length of the production or programme series.

Skilled staff often work across the television, film and video industries. Job titles can be similar, although this is not always the case and the range of activities and responsibility will depend on the size of the production. For these reasons, there is often no formal promotion ladder for producers and opportunities often arise on an 'as and when basis'. However, from this role it is possible to progress to running your own studio or to working as an executive producer, taking responsibility for several projects.

After the producer, the director is the most important person involved in making a programme/film. Substantial experience of the industry is required for this role.

Broadcast Engineer (Operational)

Job Description and Activities: A broadcast engineer installs, maintains, modifies, operates and repairs broadcast equipment and systems, including the latest multimedia technology.

Working alongside others in the technical department, broadcast engineers use a wide range of equipment and systems to ensure that programmes are transmitted across television and radio networks at the correct times and to the highest standards of technical quality.

The work can be based in a variety of locations and situations for television and radio. Many programmes are broadcast from studios, but work can also include outside broadcasts (OBs), which involves transmitting sound and images from different locations back to a main studio.

Typical Work Activities: The nature of the work will vary according to location and type of media, but tasks typically involve:

- designing and setting up audio and video circuits;
- manufacturing and repairing multimedia hardware, software and other broadcast technology systems;
- utilising knowledge of analogue and digital systems;
- installing, testing and maintaining technical facilities;
- setting up and monitoring audio and visual links with a variety of different units;
- maintaining specialist equipment for video and film production, broadcast and satellite transmission and interactive media;

- analysing and rectifying technical faults;
- identifying and implementing alternative ways of meeting requirements to cover equipment failures, with minimum loss of service;
- investigating new techniques and equipment;
- custom-making electronic systems for programmes;
- setting up and operating links for outside broadcasts (OBs);
- building knowledge and utilising an awareness of health and safety in the workplace;
- interpreting instructions and requests from others working on programmes;
- communicating effectively with own team and other project members;
- networking and establishing and maintaining industry contacts.

Salary and Conditions

- Range of typical starting salaries: £13,000 - £16,000 (salary data collected Oct. 05).
- Range of typical salaries at senior level/with experience (*e.g.*, after 10-15 years in the role): £30,000 upwards (salary data collected Oct. 05).
- Working hours can be long and irregular. Because studios need to be booked in advance, you will often be working within allocated slots. If things do not go to schedule, *e.g.* because of technical or operational difficulties, employees are expected to remain until the job is done. Shifts are common and include weekends, evenings or nights. You may also be required to work long hours at short notice, particularly for news programmes.
- The environment can vary from comfortable and warm in enclosed studios, to extreme conditions on location. Locations can be abroad and may occasionally involve working in dangerous conditions, for example, a war zone.
- Work patterns may involve relatively quiet periods

followed by intense activity. Stability and security no longer apply to this industry. Contracts may be renewable, fixed-term or freelance, usually without paid holiday or sick leave.

- Self-employment is unlikely, due to the highly specialist nature of the work in a fast-changing technological environment. However, increasing numbers of staff are becoming freelance. To be successful in securing freelance work, you will need to be highly organised and skilled in your own self-management and promotion, multi-skilled (able to use a wide range of equipment, thus saving costs for the employer) and willing to go wherever the work is.
- Career breaks are possible, although this depends on the employer. Some companies require you to have worked with them for a particular length of time before you can take a break.
- Jobs are quite widely available as television and radio stations are found in most areas of the UK. Jobs with the independent production companies and facilities houses are mainly in London and the South East. Leading employers have large bases in London, although there are also opportunities in other large cities.
- Most employers have active equal opportunities policies.
- There is generally high job satisfaction in the industry.
- The working environment is often informal.
- The work can be both physically demanding and pressurised and the long hours can be very disruptive to social and family life.
- Location work and outside broadcasts (OBs) involve working away from home on a regular basis or for fairly long periods and may also include working abroad.

Entry Requirements

Most broadcast engineers are taken on as trainees. The majority of new entrants are graduates, but entry as a trainee is possible with a BTEC/HNC/HND/foundation degree/degree in the following subjects:

- electrical engineering;
- electronic engineering;
- broadcast engineering.

Entry is also possible for graduates from non-relevant disciplines. In this instance, an active interest in and aptitude for technology is paramount.

Some companies may take on trainees with a minimum of an Advanced VCE (vocational certificate of education) in engineering or equivalent. An access qualification may also be accepted for entry to certain courses. If you are experienced in a related field, you may be able to gain recognition of skills through accredited prior learning (APL), but check with individual colleges and universities for exact requirements. If you are already working within broadcasting, *e.g.* as a runner, you may be able to move into this role via internal training schemes. It is also possible to progress to this level through technician entry and part-time qualifications.

Postgraduate qualifications are not required but can help you gain experience of the industry.

Pre-entry experience, usually unpaid work experience with a production company or in local television, is important.

Potential candidates will need to show evidence of the following:

- experience in electronic engineering and using communication equipment;
- sufficient colour vision and hearing;
- the ability to apply analogue and digital theory and work from diagrammatic information;
- excellent IT skills;
- the ability to work well in teams;
- effective people skills;
- the capacity to solve technical problems in a creative way.

Be prepared to write, phone and arrange to meet producers and directors and other appropriate contacts. Use media directories, such as The Knowledge and the PACT Directory of Independent Producers, for addresses, named contacts and information on productions. Although it is important for you to show your enthusiasm, employers will be more impressed by your knowledge, insight or experience of the industry.

It is advisable to prepare thoroughly before approaching people for pre-entry work experience. Reading publications like Broadcast and The Guardian (media section on Mondays) can help you learn more about the industry. See the BBC Work Experience website for details about work experience opportunities.

Although job prospects for experienced, well-qualified people can be good, for the less experienced, job-hunting can be very difficult. The BBC is virtually the only employer with a graduate entry scheme.

The broadcasting sector has a number of initiatives to promote careers in the industry to under-represented groups, in particular ethnic minorities. The BBC has made a strong commitment to a policy of equality and diversity, which covers all aspects of its business, including recruitment. However, many factors, such as the need to travel frequently, the unstructured nature of recruitment and the often unsocial hours, make it a difficult area for some applicants to enter.

Training

Training is delivered through a combination of work placements and specialist technical courses. Most training meets the requirements of the Institution of Engineering and Technology (IET) for chartered engineer (CEng) status.

Training schemes are available, in both radio and television, on a national and regional level. These are run by various organisations and also by some of the major broadcasters. The BBC runs a number of training schemes, including the production trainee scheme, which emphasises the move towards multimedia.

The British Film Institute (BFI) maintains a database of courses (available on their website) to help freelancers and would-be entrants to identify appropriate courses. Skillset (Sector Skills Council for the Audio Visual Industries) supports a number of advertised new entrant training courses, including one based in Wales. Along with other industry partners, it part-funds a national new entrant technical training scheme organised by FT2-Film & Television Freelance Training. Trainees are paid a monthly grant for two years and can specialise in one of 15 technical areas, including camera and sound. See the Skillset website for further details. Scottish Screen provides training for the broadcast and film industry in Scotland. Broadcast engineers are often required to undertake further training in the use of new equipment. This is usually organised by employers.

Career Development

Graduate training schemes are the ideal way to enter the industry, as they allow participants to gain an insight into the different specialisms within broadcasting (and the variety of roles available within these different specialisms).

As a broadcast engineer you will have the opportunity to specialise in a particular system or technology. You may also take responsibility for upgrading and modifying specialist software. After you have completed your initial training and gained a suitable amount of experience, it is possible to move into a supervisory post. Promotion is based on merit.

The BBC offers secondments, which enable existing members of staff to widen their experience.

This is a competitive field. The recruitment of broadcasting engineers for short or fixed-term projects often takes place on the basis of reputation (smaller companies especially will often approach experienced freelancers), so developing this will increase your chances of securing work and thus being able to develop your career further.

Within some companies, following several years' experience, it may be possible to progress from broadcast engineer into management roles within the industry.

Film/Video Editor

Job Description and Activities: A film or video editor is responsible for assembling the final product as a sequence consisting of shots from the raw camera footage, dialogue, sound effects and graphics. This is a key role in the post-production process and the editor's skill determines the quality and delivery of the final product. Digital technology is increasingly the key medium for editing. Based in the post-production editing suite, the editor works closely with the director to meet his or her requirements. The majority of film/ video editors are employed on a freelance basis, working on short-term contracts for post-production studios, television companies and corporate employers.

Typical Work Activities: Feature films and some broadcast drama productions still tend to use the traditional manual method of cutting film and arranging the shots into the required sequence, but this is increasingly being replaced by the use of digital technology and specialist computer software, which has been developed to enable the high-quality digitisation of sound and pictures. The widespread availability of streaming media over the internet has led to a huge increase in digital film-making. Depending on the product, an editor may work with or without being overseen by the director. In some cases- mainly involving fiction films-the editor may be there merely to operate the machine. In other situations the editor may have creative freedom.

The process involves:

- receiving a brief and maybe an outline of footage and/or a shot list, or screenplay;
- assembling all raw footage, with the camera shots either recorded or manually transferred onto high-format video tape in preparation for inputting into the computer;
- inputting uncut rushes and sound and synchronising and storing them into files on computer;
- digitally cutting the files to determine the sequence of the film and determining what is usable;
- creating a 'rough cut' of the programme/film and determining the exact cutting for the next and final stages;
- reordering and tweaking the content to ensure the logical sequencing and smooth running of the film/video.

The final stage of the process requires the skills of the online editor, who is responsible for the creation and delivery of the final product. Adding special effects software and grading/colouring the finished film or programme is the online editor's function in producing and perfecting the final product.

Additional work activities may include:

- overseeing the quality and progress of audio and vision engineering and editing;
- consulting with the director, producer and/or client throughout the post-production process;
- familiarising oneself with the style of specific directors;
- experimenting with styles and techniques;
- selecting the most effective shot of a scene in terms of drama, story relevance or continuity;
- if freelancing: negotiating rates of pay and project content and managing business affairs.

Salary and Conditions

- Range of typical starting salaries: £18,000 - £25,000, for those employed by a television or post-production studio (salary data collected Nov. 06). This is not typically an entry level/graduate entry job; entrants start at a much lower-paid level (around the national minimum wage), working as runners and then assistant/trainee editors before reaching this level and salary.
- Range of salaries with three to five years' experience: £20,000 - £35,000 (salary data collected Nov. 06).
- Range of typical salaries at senior levels: £37,000 - £70,000 upwards (salary data collected Nov. 06).
- For the majority of editors, *i.e.* those working freelance, work is paid on a contract basis. Rates advised by the Broadcasting Entertainment Cinematographic and Theatre Union (BECTU) can be found on their website.
- Hours vary depending on workload. When working in-house for a company with a steady flow of work, hours are typically nine to five. When there are deadlines to

meet, long hours and weekend working may be required. Dedicated freelance editors may spend longer than is required on a job to achieve the best possible finished edit.

- Freelance work is likely to involve an intensive work pattern on projects, but there may also be periods of inactivity between projects. Freelance editors often compete for work or may be involved with several productions, both large and small, at any given time and this can be very demanding.
- Work is conducted alone or as part of a small team, essentially behind closed doors. An editor may work with a sound effects editor, music editor and assistant editors on a large project. The role may be pressured and gruelling, for example when working intensively to strict deadlines on limited studio time.
- The workplace rarely changes - editors spend most of their time in editing suites, which are mostly small but comfortable environments. Freelance editors with their own equipment may work from home.
- Slightly more men than women work as editors.
- Whilst the majority of television and film editing work in the UK is London-based, post-production and facilities houses and independent production companies can be found in most cities.
- Freelancers may have to travel to different editing suites, but these are unlikely to be distant venues or involve working away from home. There may be opportunities abroad for experienced and established editors.

Entry Requirements

Although this area of work is open to all graduates and Diplomates, the following subjects may increase your chances:

- communication and media studies;
- photography/film/television;
- fine art/visual art;
- information technology/multimedia.

Entry without a degree or HND is commonly possible but all applicants must show commitment and determination to enter the industry. Pre-entry postgraduate courses offering film/media production experience may be advantageous.

Pre-entry experience is essential and you will need to show evidence of having worked on film/video production or post-production within or outside your degree, preferably via an up-to-date and well-prepared showreel. Film/video editing is not a starting role in the industry and it is common for current students or recent graduates to gain some experience by starting as a Runner, broadcasting/film/video.

For direct entry, in addition to experience, you must be able to demonstrate your skill with appropriate editing software packages. Specific training and experience in the AVID, Lightworks or Final Cut Pro packages are essential. Courses cater for various levels of expertise and can be costly, but should provide you with specific industry-required skills. You should be selective about the courses you choose to ensure they fully match your career and training aims. If you have experience of the very latest technology, it may reduce the competition you face. General computer literacy and an aptitude for working with digital equipment to achieve results are also important.

In addition, the following personal qualities are essential:

- a keen eye for detail and a critical mind;
- creativity;
- the ability to listen to others and to work well as part of a team;
- a high level of self-motivation, commitment and dedication;
- organisational skills and self/time management skills;
- communication skills, both written and oral.

A passionate interest in film/video editing and the ability to be creative are essential, as well as being highly technically skilled in order to construct the product. You need to be extremely determined to succeed in editing, so you will have to show a willingness to get involved and be prepared to do the most basic of tasks. Getting to know the precision and intensity of this area of work will help you decide if it is for you. This experience will give you some contacts, which may lead to a first job or training opportunity in editing.

Job vacancies are rarely advertised and competition is fierce even for entry-level jobs. Use creative job seeking methods such as sending your skills-based CV to every production company and post-production house possible. Get to know people in the industry and make and maintain good working relationships.

Visit the Skillset Careers website for further information and advice on entry into the industry, including information on the new entrants schemes, which provide long-term training in a range of professional areas in the industry.

Although it is now illegal to discriminate against candidates on age grounds, in practice, age may continue to be used in selection criteria by some employers.

Training

Learning whilst working within the industry is the key way to develop the relevant skills. A combination of learning by observing experienced professionals and experimenting by developing your own work is the common way for editors to develop the required technical and creative skills. Actually working at a computer, editing, is the best way to improve skills. Studying films, videos and advertisements you like and working out why you like them, is one way of learning more about the craft.

On-the-job training usually involves updating skills through software providers or by attending short courses. The Media Courses and Multimedia Courses Directory, which is produced by Skillset (Sector Skills Council for the Audio Visual Industries) and the British Film Institute (BFI) provides details of a range of short and long courses in film, television, video and radio across England, Northern Ireland, Scotland and Wales.

Courses to help improve and expand skills may offer additional training in project management, non-linear editing and craft editing, or in additional programmes such as Adobe Premier Pro, Pinnacle Edition or Sony Vegas.

Skillset Careers can provide a significant reduction in training fees for established freelancers on a range of courses. The Broadcasting Entertainment Cinematographic and Theatre Union (BECTU) also has a firm commitment to lifelong learning and offers a range of courses.

Additional training can be undertaken in the special effects field and this may enhance career opportunities and development. Freelancers in the early stages of their career, particularly outside London, may need to extend their skills into camera or sound work in order to keep themselves employed and to maintain a network of contacts.

Career Development

A pro-active approach and a willingness to start at the bottom are essential for developing and progressing a career in this fast-changing industry. Be prepared to learn new skills, meet new people, make new contacts, keep up to date with changes in the industry, especially new technologies and, above all, show a firm commitment to your job. It is essential to establish a good reputation and develop networking skills in order to succeed in this area.

Because of the nature of the industry, gaining a first entry role in London (as a runner, for example) can benefit career development. Although the number of opportunities in regional areas is increasing, flexibility as to geographical location is an advantage, especially at the early stages of a career. Aspiring editors could work unpaid for short film companies or get involved with student film-making in order to gain experience and build up a showreel.

In post-production or broadcasting companies, progression may be from assistant editor to senior editor. Larger employers, such as the BBC, provide well-structured career paths. Experienced in-house editors may ultimately move to management roles or to working as directors. These roles demand additional skills and, in order to progress, it may be advisable to attend management training courses.

For freelancers, career development takes the form of progressing from small productions to larger and more ambitious or prestigious projects. Whilst relevant qualifications may be of benefit, career development is based more on evidence, experience and practical involvement within the industry and on developing a strong network of contacts.

Lighting Technician

Job Description and Activities: Lighting technicians set up and operate lighting equipment under the supervision of a lighting director or lighting camera operator in television, or a gaffer or director of photography in film, high-budget television drama and commercials.

At entry level, job titles include (apprentice) lighting technician, lighting electrician or lighting assistant. In film, more experienced technicians can specialise as a moving light operator, practical light operator, genny operator, console operator, or take a supervisory post as 'best boy'.

The lighting team's work is crucial to any performance or programme. Lighting creates the right atmosphere to evoke an audience's response and demands high-level technical and creative skills.

Typical Work Activities: Depending on the production you are working on and your particular experience, you may be involved in all or some of the activities outlined below:

- liaising with the director and/or other staff to interpret their creative vision into the lighting design;
- managing the lighting budget;
- advising on the purchase/hire of suitable equipment;
- visiting and assessing locations for technical purposes;
- conducting risk assessments for health and safety purposes;
- establishing lighting requirements;
- plotting the lighting;
- deciding on crew numbers and equipment needed;
- employing the crew and hiring equipment;
- coordinating the equipment and the technical crew;
- training other crew members as required;

- assembling all the lighting and filter equipment needed;
- ensuring all lighting equipment is in working order;
- organising scaffolding and cranes, if required;
- pre-rigging the lighting;
- ensuring all cables and wires are safely concealed;
- loading automated colour change systems;
- programming and operating lighting consoles;
- supervising the focusing of lighting at rehearsals;
- operating and maintaining equipment during the shoot;
- changing lighting between shots, as necessary;
- de-rigging all equipment at the end of the broadcast/ production;
- ensuring all equipment is stored/transported back safely from location;
- reviewing footage shots with the director;
- liaising with the floor manager, producer and sound technician throughout the project.

Salary and Conditions

- Range of typical starting salaries: £10,000 - £16,000 (salary data collected Jan. 07).
- Range of typical freelance salaries with 10-15 years' experience: lighting cameraperson £721 per week; lighting director £638 per week; assistant technician £420 per week (Broadcasting Entertainment Cinematographic and Theatre Union (BECTU) minimum rates Jan. 07).
- Many lighting technicians are freelance and earnings can vary enormously, depending on the jobs undertaken and the availability of work.
- Hours are invariably long and unsocial.
- Work settings will vary: you could be in a television studio, which can get stuffy and oppressive; on a film set; on location in buildings not designed for an influx of high-tech lighting equipment; or on outside broadcasts, where you are at the mercy of the weather.
- A great deal of heavy lifting is required.

- Working at heights is common, for example on walkways above the studio floor, on ladders, scaffolding or on cranes.
- Protective clothing, including hard hats, safety boots and overalls, is often required.
- This is a male-dominated field and women are currently under-represented in this area of work.
- Most employment is in London and the South East, due to the concentration of broadcast production there, although regional employment in broadcasting is possible. There is an increasing number of production companies settling in the North West (particularly Manchester and Liverpool).
- Working freelance impacts on your ability to plan holidays in advance, take career breaks and undergo training.
- Some find freelance work stressful due to the uncertainty of finding work and an irregular income.
- Stress can be high at more senior levels as mistakes are expensive and careers may depend on your technical and creative abilities.
- Long periods away from home on location are common, particularly in television and film.

Entry Requirements

Although a degree is not necessary for this role, degree subjects such as electrical engineering or physics may be useful for the technical side. The following specialist degree/HND courses may also improve your chances:

- lighting design;
- lighting technology;
- sound, light and live event technology;
- theatre arts, lighting and sound operation.

An alternative entry route is to become a camera operator. There are no formal entry requirements but a degree or HND in photography and/or video or film may improve your chances.

Most new entrants are qualified electricians who have obtained skills through vocational training such as City & Guilds courses. SVQs (Scottish Vocational Qualifications) are available in lighting at levels 2 and 3 (live performance). Specialist courses are also offered by the Association of British Theatre Technicians (ABTT). Skillset (Sector Skills Council for the Audio Visual Industries) is currently working on the development and piloting of new models of qualification (to replace vocational qualifications). It is intended that a network of screen academies will be approved as centres of excellence for training and education in film. For up-to-date information visit the Skillset website.

Relevant pre-entry experience, paid or voluntary, is essential. Many degree holders look for a role as a technician to get the necessary work experience in order to progress. Experience may be gained with amateur dramatic companies or drama societies at university or college. Understanding lighting for the stage will give you a good grounding in the technical aspects of the job.

Potential candidates will need to show evidence of the following:

- excellent colour vision;
- sound technical knowledge;
- creative flair;
- the ability to work as part of a team;
- good communication skills;
- problem-solving ability;
- attention to detail;
- patience;
- sensitivity to the needs of actors and other professionals on set;
- awareness of health and safety issues at all times;
- a good level of physical fitness.

Freelancers must also have good networking skills, have a willingness to deal with financial matters, such as tax and invoicing and be customer focused.

The BBC offers various training schemes throughout the year. These regularly include technology, engineering and studio schemes, including training with lighting. They are very competitive as they represent possibly the only formal industry training available. The BBC also runs work experience schemes that regularly involve working in studios, including experience with lighting.

It is also worth seeking out amateur video makers and postgraduate film students and offering to help light their projects. It may also be possible to get unpaid work experience with a professional lighting director.

Although it is now illegal to discriminate against candidates on age grounds, in practice age may continue to be used in selection criteria by some employers.

Training

Most developmental training is on the job. Lighting skills are usually picked up by observing, questioning and working under the supervision of a lighting director or director of photography. Once working in lighting, getting training can be a problem as you are most likely to be working freelance and will, therefore, have to cover the cost and time of attending courses yourself.

There are some specialist courses in lighting design available, as well as technical courses offered by the Association of British Theatre Technicians (ABTT) and Skillset (Sector Skills Council for the Audio Visual Industries). New training schemes may be set up for new entrants in the future. Check the Skillset website for further details of developments in this area.

Professional organisations, such as the Society of Television Lighting Directors, offer their members opportunities for professional updating through events such as talks, visits and exhibitions and articles in their journal. Student membership is available.

Additionally, lighting technicians tend to be naturally inclined towards experimenting with new techniques (often in their own time). This can result in 'ad hoc' training and the benefits may be shared among immediate colleagues and contacts. This emphasises the importance of building a good network.

Career Development

Depending on the way you develop your skills and the experience you build up, progression is possible through roles such as 'best boy', rigging gaffer or gaffer. Typically, after ten years' or more experience and possibly having gained further qualifications, you could progress to lighting director or director of photography in film or broadcasting. Progression is frequently faster into lighting design roles in theatre, events, festivals or live shows and this is a growth area for work.

Most lighting technicians eventually specialise in a particular type of work. In television, this could be live shows or outside broadcasts. Film and high-budget productions in television drama, commercials and music videos are considered the most prestigious work and are also the best paid. Corporate video is another possibility.

Specialist lighting equipment hire companies employ freelance lighting personnel. It may sometimes be possible to move into permanent management roles with them.

Some lighting technicians move into sound operations, or combine sound and lighting expertise. Others move into special effects or production design. Event organisation, which would involve organising large events, including all the staging and safety aspects, is a further possibility.

Freelance technicians sometimes choose to supplement their income by training others via recognised course providers. This may be most likely where the technician has a particular set of skills or experience to impart.

Other freelance technicians offer their services to the photographic industry in addition to broadcasting, film and video.

A move into a broadcast engineering role offers a broader range of career options, but would depend on having the right mix of experience, skills and qualifications. The BBC regularly offers trainee schemes. Entry requirements vary, although qualifications in engineering, science or technology subjects are usually required.

Sound Technician

Job Description and Activities: Sound technicians assemble, operate and maintain technical equipment to amplify, enhance, record, mix or reproduce sound for:

- films;
- television programmes;
- live performances.

They interpret production requirements and work with a range of equipment used for entertainment, commercial and industrial purposes.

Based within a studio or on location, they interpret the director's wishes to help achieve the desired end result. Tasks include: setting up, testing and operating equipment in accordance with the acoustics of the area; selecting, placing and adjusting microphones; monitoring audio signals to detect quality deviations or malfunctions; servicing, maintaining and repairing sound equipment; and introducing prerecorded special effects.

Typical Work Activities: There are a range of related roles in sound production. These include sound designer, production sound mixer, sound supervisor, boom operator, sound assistant, sound editor, dialogue editor, foley editor and foley artist (sound effects).

Typical work activities tend to include:

- assessing the acoustics of an area and setting up equipment in accordance with this assessment;
- working closely with the sound team, including the sound designer and supervisor;
- applying technical knowledge of sound recording equipment in a number of different environments;
- ensuring health and safety standards for the recording environment are met;
- maintaining computer literacy to utilise new and developing technology;
- designing sound equipment (in some roles);

- assembling, rigging and operating technical equipment for amplification, recording and mixing sound, *e.g.* cables and microphones;
- adding sound effects;
- recording sound - this may be in a studio or on location, working to a script or unscripted;
- anticipating and reacting to various problems as they occur;
- maintaining an understanding of and empathy with, creativity in the appropriate environment, *e.g.* music studio, film or TV location, radio studio;
- if self-employed or freelance, applying business skills and financial management to manage own business.

Salary and Conditions

- Typical starting salary: £16,000 in television and radio, or £20 to £25 per hour for freelancers (salary data collected Aug. 05).
- Typical salary with experience, *e.g.* after 10-15 years in the role: £30,000 to £35,000 (including a 20% unpredictability allowance for short notice changes to working hours in some roles) or £25 - £35 per hour freelance. Individual negotiation above these rates of up to over £1,000 a day may be possible for some sound technicians with very established reputations (salary data collected Aug. 05).
- Pay rates and conditions of employment vary. The Broadcasting Entertainment Cinematographic and Theatre Union (BECTU) has consulted its members on pay rates and conditions of employment. See the BECTU website for further details.
- Working hours typically include regular unsocial hours. There is no regular work pattern and working hours are long, including evenings, night shoots and weekends. Sound technicians may be required to record a television or radio interview for a breaking story, travel to and from an out-of-studio location, or, in a recording studio, work

with an artist through the night to ensure 'creative flow' is not interrupted.

- The work involves being on your feet most of the time, working as part of a team alongside artists, production staff and the public.
- Self-employment/freelance work is common. Work is increasingly on fixed-term contracts. Employers, such as the BBC, take on many freelancers to cover peaks of work.
- Jobs are in restricted locations with a concentration in London, which currently houses 85% of the UK's production base, or major studios in Glasgow, Manchester, Leeds and Birmingham, or on location worldwide.
- Currently, 9% of those working in sound are female but this is set to increase. Of the total workforce, 4.7% are from ethnic minorities, an increase on previous years and 1% has a disability (source: Skillset (Sector Skills Council for the Audio Visual Industries) employment census, 2004.)
- A normal social life can be difficult as a result of the irregular hours and required absence from home. Dedication and stamina are needed. Working to tight production deadlines can be stressful.
- Travel within a working day and absence from home at night are frequent. Overseas work or travel are occasional.

Entry Requirements

There are no specific qualifications required for this role but an understanding of the physical properties of sound is necessary, particularly in order to grasp the technical aspects of the job. The following degree/HND subjects may increase your chances:

- sound technology;
- audio engineering;
- acoustics;
- music recording;
- music technology;

- maths;
- physics;
- electronic engineering.

Technical aptitude, a passion for sound and relevant experience are essential and as important as academic qualifications.

Entry without a degree or HND is commonly possible. A good general education is desirable. GCSEs or A-levels in maths and physics and qualifications in electronics will help.

A pre-entry postgraduate qualification is not needed, although appropriate courses with relevant training may improve your chances.

Work experience, relevant placements or voluntary work are almost essential to secure a first post. Experience in theatre or the music industry can be a useful background. Practical experience can be gained by working in hospital or community radio. Experience of working with equipment manufacturers and hire companies can also provide useful training. Domestic equipment is increasingly accessible and sophisticated, providing opportunities to learn and experiment.

Potential candidates will need to show evidence of the following:

- excellent hearing skills;
- scrupulous attention to detail;
- general technical ability;
- quick reactions.

Do not rely on advertised vacancies - you will need to make your own contacts and apply directly. Stay in contact with people you have met or worked with before. Keeping an ear to the ground and reading the trade press (where some jobs are still advertised) is a good way of anticipating where jobs are likely to come up. Diary services and agencies can save a freelance worker considerable time and effort. Contact them directly for details of the services they offer and the fees charged (they are a valuable resource for production companies and broadcasters, who contact them for CVs when vacancies arise).

Attending media events, to network with people in the industry and make contacts, is also advisable.

Training

The practical side of training for this role is often developed post-graduation or in work experience placements. This is due to the lack of facilities in academic institutions. Although specialist courses are increasing at degree and HND level, other shorter courses are also available.

For instance, The National Film and Television School offers a one-year diploma in sound recording, a diploma in sound recording for film and TV and an MA in post-production sound.

Industry-led new entrant training schemes run by FT2 - Film & Television Freelance Training, Cyfle (Wales) and Scottish Screen provide a mixture of attachments and formal training. Competition for places is fierce.

Broadcasters also run trainee schemes. The regional training partners of Skillset (Sector Skills Council for the Audio Visual Industries) offer a range of new entrant, freelance and attachment training programmes.

Other more specific and postgraduate courses are also available for those who wish to specialise in a certain area or update their knowledge. These include:

- Digital Sound Recording and Stereo Sound Mixing;
- Post-Production for Sound Recordists;
- Digital Audio for Sound Recordists;
- New Technologies in Sound Recording;
- MA Animation and Sound Design;
- MA Post Production - Sound Design.

The media industry is constantly changing and developing, creating new opportunities in a variety areas. Once you are in the industry you will need to maintain an interest in upgrading your skills to fill skills gaps by committing to a programme of continuing professional development (CPD), either through a structured scheme or by identifying and tailoring your own programme.

Career Development

Sound personnel usually start in a trainee or assistant role and work their way up through on-the-job training and shadowing more experienced personnel. A typical route in is by working as a runner or secretary at a facilities house that specialises in audio post-production.

Digital technology has brought some changes to jobs in sound, particularly in post-production and there has been some blurring of roles as a result of multi-skilling. However, most roles remain fairly traditional. Career routes include the following positions:

- Production sound - sound supervisor; production mixer/sound recordist; boom operator; sound assistant; sound technician.
- Post-production sound - sound editor; dialogue editor; music editor; re-recording mixer/dubbing mixer; foley editor (post-synchronised sound effects); foley artist (sound effects).
- General sound - sound designer/sound director; studio manager.

As an example of career progression, in the BBC there are three grades for sound technicians: junior, middle and senior. Promotion beyond this means moving into management, away from the studios.

To progress in the media industry it is vital to keep abreast of developments. Skills shortages occur for different reasons: not enough new people enter the industry to take the place of retired technicians; the demand for certain equipment knowledge, or types of work, sometimes exceeds the current practitioners trained in these fields (particularly in new media and new technology). Skillset (Sector Skills Council for the Audio Visual Industries) works with various groups and organisations to develop strategies to address these areas of skills shortage.

Television Camera Operator

Job Description and Activities: A television camera operator works with digital, electronic and film cameras in multi and single camera operational conditions, producing pictures for directors by combining the use of complex technology with creative visual skills.

The work is based in two settings:

- in a studio, where the camera operator usually follows a camera script, which gives the order of shots practised at rehearsal and is cued by the director during recording- the skill lies in interpreting what the director wants and acting quickly and effectively to achieve it;
- on location, where there is likely to be more opportunity for creativity through suggesting shots to the director.

Typical Work Activities: A camera operator usually works under the direction of a director or director of photography and is sometimes supported by a camera assistant (or a focus puller/ clapper loader, although with the advent of digital and electronic cameras these functions are in decline).

Typical work activities include:

- assembling, preparing and setting up equipment prior to filming, which can include tripods, monitors, lighting, cables and leads and headphones;
- offering advice on how to best shoot a scene, explaining the visual impact created by the angle of particular shots;
- planning shots - when filming an expensive drama scene, such as an explosion, there is only one chance to get things right so shots need to be meticulously planned beforehand;
- practising required positions for prearranged shots;
- studying scripts;
- finding solutions to technical or other practical problems (in outside broadcasts, for example, the natural light conditions need to be taken into account when setting up shots), being prepared to innovate and experiment with ideas;
- taking instructions from the director or the director of photography;
- working quickly, especially as timing is such an important factor;

- taking sole responsibility in situations where there is only one camera operator involved in the filming;
- keeping up-to-date with filming methods and equipment;
- repairing equipment;
- demonstrating good awareness of health and safety issues.

Part of the role involves interacting and maintaining good working relationships with other members of the camera crew, including:

- sound recorders;
- lighting technicians;
- actors.

Salary and Conditions

- Typical starting salary for newly trained camera operators: £13,500 (salary data collected Sept. 05).
- Typical salary range for camera operators with experience (*e.g.*, after 10-15 years in the role); £22,000 - £30,000 (salary data collected Sept. 05).
- Freelance rates (for a forty hour week): camera operator - £621; senior lighting/camera operator - £702 (salary data collected Sept. 05).
- Working hours are unsocial and include evening, weekend and night shoots. A standard shooting day usually lasts ten hours or more.
- Work is in either a studio or on location (in all weather conditions), mostly as part of a team.
- Self-employment is commonly possible as work is increasingly freelance on fixed-term contracts.
- Work tends to be concentrated in areas with major studios, such as London, Birmingham, Glasgow, Leeds and Manchester. Short-term contracts are common, particularly at the start of a career whilst a network of industry contacts is established.
- The number of female camera operators is increasing slowly. Of staff on permanent contracts, 25% of respondents to the 2004 Skillset (Sector Skills Council for

the Audio Visual Industries) industry census were women; ethnic minorities make up 11% of permanent employees and 1.2% of freelancers; less than 1% of the camera workforce is registered disabled.

- This profession requires dedication and stamina. The work can be fairly physically demanding as you will be required to stand for long periods of time and carry heavy equipment. It can be stressful working to tight deadlines. It can also be frustrating having to wait long periods between shots or to repeat the same shot many times if the director is not happy.
- Travel in the UK or overseas is common for news and location filming.

Entry Requirements

Although this profession is open to all graduates and Diplomates, the following subjects offer a useful background:

- media studies;
- performing arts;
- photography/film/television;
- media production.

Other relevant subjects include lighting, optics and cinematography.

Technical skills and appropriate experience are far more important than formal qualifications. Employers seek candidates with a well-developed interest in photography, along with related experience, evidenced via film stills or a collection of photographs.

Entry without a degree or HND is commonly possible.

A pre-entry postgraduate qualification is not required.

Potential candidates will need to show evidence of the following:

- a good theoretical and technical knowledge of cameras;
- an interest in lighting, video, film or theatre;
- excellent hand-eye coordination;
- good hearing and colour vision;

- knowledge of editing;
- patience;
- attention to detail;
- knowledge of sound engineering.

Additional useful skills include a driving licence and competence in IT. Many freelance operators own their equipment and therefore need an understanding of its maintenance and at least basic emergency repair.

For work experience, contact production companies and facility houses and investigate structured schemes, such as those offered by BBC Work Experience and Skillset (Sector Skills Council for the Audio Visual Industries).

Show enthusiasm and read about related areas of sound, lighting, optics and new developments in broadcasting, such as high definition.

Competition is severe. Vacancies are not necessarily advertised so you will need to network, make your own contacts and apply direct. If called for an interview, expect to be asked about your theoretical and technical knowledge, as well as your creative ideas.

From 1 October 2006 it will be illegal to discriminate against candidates on age grounds but, in practice, age may continue to be used in selection criteria by some employers. In practice, entry tends to be for younger candidates prepared to work up the ladder from junior positions.

Training

A small number of new entrant training schemes do exist, but training is predominantly on the job with entrants starting at assistant level observing experienced crew members and gradually gaining experience.

FT2 - Film & Television Freelance Training runs the New Entrant Technical Training Scheme, which offers the opportunity to train as a camera assistant/clapper loader. Similar schemes are offered in Scotland by Scottish Screen and in Wales by Cyfle. BBC Jobs also regularly offers training schemes.

In addition, the BBC Training Centre offers a range of short courses, as do the BKSTS (British Kinematic, Sound and Television Society): The Moving Image Society. Also Skillset (Sector Skills Council for the Audio Visual Industries) offers professional training specifically for freelancers.

Some television companies set up their own in-house training programmes as and when they need staff in technical roles. Such schemes are likely to be advertised on an ad-hoc basis rather than offering annual opportunities.

All camera operators should take responsibility for ensuring they keep up to date with changing technology and techniques in the field.

Career Development

The main career development path is to start in a junior position, such as a runner, technical operator or camera assistant and progress from here. With experience and depending on openings within the organisation, the natural progression is into the position of camera operator and, after many years' experience, to lighting camera operator and director of photography. The more senior roles allow more creative input and demand leadership skills.

Advancement within the profession can depend on a number of factors, such as:

- developing excellent relationships with directors of photography;
- keeping up to date with new technologies and techniques;
- earning the respect of a camera crew;
- demonstrating high level technical and artistic skills.

With experience, camera operators can build up a list of credits, which can lead to further opportunities and offers of work.

The trend towards freelance working has led to a less structured career path, with camera operators having to take responsibility for maintaining their own skills, employability and personal development. However, once experienced, there are currently good employment opportunities (camera operation is listed by Skillset (Sector Skills Council for the Audio Visual Industries as a shortage skills area).

Broadcast Presenter

Job Description and Activities: Broadcast presenters work in television and radio and are the public 'face' of any broadcast show. Their job is to entertain and inform the viewer or listener. They work in all areas of broadcasting, including national, regional, satellite or cable television and radio.

The exact nature of the role will vary depending on the type of programme being broadcast, *e.g.* news, current affairs, sport, gameshow, chatshow, music, or gardening. Essentially, though, a broadcast presenter will introduce and host the programme and create links between items, often introducing and interviewing guests, as well as interacting with the audience.

Typical Work Activities: Typical work activities will vary according to the type of programme and broadcast medium.

Prior to the broadcast, presenters may be involved in:

- researching topics and background information;
- planning shows;
- writing scripts and sometimes learning these off by heart;
- selecting music;
- rehearsing the show;
- discussing the programme with the director/producer;
- liaising with other members of the team, *e.g.* the producer and technical staff.

During the actual show, a presenter may be involved in:

- introducing programmes;
- playing music;
- interviewing guests, either in the studio or over the telephone;
- reviewing papers, books, films and music;
- providing links between programmes;
- reading from a script or autocue, or improvising;
- reading short news, traffic or weather bulletins.

In addition, radio presenters on music shows usually 'drive' the desk and operate some of the technical equipment for recording and playback. This usually involves using computers, often with touch screens, to cue up and play music and jingles.

Salary and Conditions

- Work conditions vary enormously, depending on the broadcast medium and type of programme involved: the working conditions of a presenter on a small local radio station with a show in the middle of the night will not bear any resemblance to those of a high profile celebrity with a prime-time television show. Most presenters, particularly those on national radio and television, will employ an agent to negotiate working terms and conditions on their behalf.
- Starting salaries in broadcasting generally, for example as a researcher or engineer, can be as a low as £10,000 (salary data collected Jan. 06).
- Salaries for presenters with significant experience can rise to £30,000 - £50,000. Very successful/celebrity presenters can earn much higher salaries of over £100,000 (salary data collected Jan. 06).
- Salaries are normally calculated per show. A well-known radio presenter on national radio could expect to earn a lot more money for a two-hour show, than a local radio presenter would for a four-hour show.
- Generally speaking, television pays more than radio but, again, this will depend on the type of programme and the profile of the presenter.
- Hours of work will, inevitably, depend on the timing of the programme and whether it is live or prerecorded. In all cases, the presenter will put in considerably more hours than those that are actually broadcast: prior to the show, presenters spend several hours in preparation, *e.g.* meeting with their producer, researching, writing scripts and rehearsing; after the show, the presenter will review the broadcast with the producer, begin advance planning for the next show and may also be engaged in other activities, *e.g.* answering listener or viewer letters.

- The work is largely based in a radio or television studio, which is usually comfortable, but outside broadcasts will involve working in all weather conditions.
- Most presenters are self-employed and on a fixed-term contract to deliver a certain number of programmes.
- Much of the national broadcast industry is centred on London, although there are other regional opportunities available.
- Presenters have a public image to maintain and, as a result, must be prepared for some loss of privacy.
- Travel during the working day will vary according to the type of programme. Radio roadshows, for example, will involve a significant amount of travel with presenters working away from home for extended periods of time.

Entry Requirements

Although this area of work is open to all graduates and Diplomates, the following degree/HND/foundation degree subjects may improve your chances:

- media/communication studies;
- journalism;
- performing arts;
- media performance;
- music technology.

Entry without a degree/HND/foundation degree is possible.

Postgraduate study is not essential for general broadcasting positions, although, if you have an unrelated first degree, it can be useful, not only to learn and develop practical and technical skills, but also in order to make contacts. To become a news/ current affairs presenter you will usually need a journalism qualification. Expertise and further study in politics, finance or economics is usually sought for current affairs broadcasting.

Pre-entry work experience is essential, be it through on-campus media activities and events such as the student newspaper or radio station, or via vacation work as a runner with local hospital radio and television stations.

Potential candidates will need to show evidence of the following:

- confidence and the ability to sell yourself;
- flexibility;
- the ability to take the initiative;
- excellent communication skills;
- the ability to work as part of a team;
- creativity and problem-solving skills.

Entry requirements will vary according to the type of programme and broadcast medium. There is no one fixed route into this profession:

- in television: many news presenters will have worked as news gatherers in local radio or in newspaper journalism; presenters in light entertainment shows may have come from an acting background;
- in radio (music-based programmes): presenters may have had performance careers themselves, worked as a self-employed club DJ, or begun their careers as producers or broadcast assistants.

This is a highly competitive area to break into and requires persistence, perseverance and a certain degree of luck. As a new graduate, you may have to enter the profession in a related role, for example as a runner on a television show or a broadcast assistant/researcher on radio and work your way up.

Try to gain as much experience as possible and start early - it is vital to get a foot in the door and make as many contacts as possible. BBC Work Experience offers placements (unpaid), including a four-week placement in their radio newsroom, which involves experience of recording a broadcast. Competition for these placements is fierce. Another way to gain related experience is to pay a fee and have your details posted on websites such as Start in TV and envenio. These websites are searched by those in the media industry looking for extras and quiz contestants.

Although it is illegal to discriminate against candidates on age grounds, in practice age may continue to be used in selection criteria by some employers.

Training

Training is not likely to be very formalised and most presenters are expected to be fully trained, with prior knowledge of what the role involves, before starting the job. Any training offered will normally involve familiarisation with specific systems and formats being used for individual programmes.

If you are hoping to become a presenter and already fulfilling a supporting role in the studio, such as broadcast assistant or production assistant, you should take every opportunity to watch and copy what the presenters around you are doing and learn by example.

If the role, as in radio, requires the use of technical equipment, such as microphones or recording equipment, or to work or 'drive' the desk, then training for this will normally be provided on the job. However, because most presenters produce their own demo tapes, a certain level of technical knowledge will be expected.

Organisations such as the Broadcasting Entertainment Cinematographic and Theatre Union (BECTU), Skillset (Sector Skills Council for the Audio Visual Industries), Commercial Radio Companies Association and the Broadcast Journalism Training Council run a variety of training programmes for those involved in media and broadcasting.

Career Development

Career development can be difficult to define.

Many presenters start their careers in local radio or in minor support roles on television. Most will try to develop their careers by moving to more prestigious programmes or more mainstream time slots, or by being the support presenter to the lead role. Presenters who start out in local stations will hope to move to national radio or television.

This is a highly competitive area but it is not the type of career where qualifications will make a major difference. What might be more important is to have a pro-active agent and to grasp all opportunities to develop as they arrive. For more specialist programmes, such as current affairs, widening your profile can help with career development, for example by writing for a broadsheet newspaper or journal.

The most successful presenters will usually have a portfolio career, presenting on more than one show or station and perhaps also appearing on both television and radio.

The Skillset Careers website offers practical advice on how to get on in the media industry and how you can further your career through training and professional development.

Commissioning Editor

Job Description and Activities: Commissioning editors identify and assess the publishing market, develop and support projects and authors, maintain a publishing programme and contribute to marketing and sales activities. In essence, their role is to develop a publisher's book list.

The role is most associated with book publishing. In magazine publishing, they commission writers to produce articles and features. In academic journal publishing, contributions are obtained through an external editor.

This is a middle to senior level post requiring suitable experience and ability. An initial entrant is likely to be recruited to a more junior position, which may then lead on to a career as a commissioning editor.

Typical Work Activities: Commissioning editors are involved with a book at every stage of its production. They are the key link between the manuscript and the published work.

To develop their publisher's book list, commissioning editors research their field to learn about trends and gaps in the market. For this purpose, they:

- attend book fairs;
- study catalogues and book lists;
- draw up surveys to be able to identify demand.

Typical work activities involve:

- building up a publisher's book list (*e.g.*, consumer books, fiction, nonfiction, by genre);
- managing the list in the current market and identifying future markets and new products;

- researching market trends;
- identifying authors;
- assessing proposals for new books;
- developing and supporting projects and authors;
- reading and evaluating manuscripts offered by authors and agents;
- issuing contracts to authors and agents;
- maintaining a book publishing programme;
- dealing with administration, finance, budgets and strategy;
- liaising with other publishing functions and roles (in-house and external readers and referees);
- contributing to marketing and sales activities.

The job may also involve some repetitive tasks, especially in junior positions.

Salary and Conditions

- Range of typical starting salaries: £16,300 - £18,172 (salary data collected Nov. 05).
- Average salary: £27,436 (salary data collected Nov. 05).
- Range of typical salaries at senior level/with experience (*e.g.*, after 10-15 years in the role): £34,000 - £40,000 (salary data collected Nov. 05). Salaries at senior level are competitive and may be negotiable.
- Benefits can include a car, health insurance and pension, although this is dependent upon the size and type of publisher and previous experience.
- Working hours typically include extra hours, although not normally weekends, except when travelling or attending meetings/conferences.
- Work is mainly office-based with some outside visits to authors and to conferences or book fairs.
- Working practices are increasingly dependent on the internet and web-based technologies.
- Self-employment/freelance work is sometimes possible for those with experience and contacts in publishing. The

Society for Editors and Proofreaders (SfEP) provides support and advice in this field.

- Most opportunities are in London (fewer in the centre) and, increasingly, in the South East. Oxford, Cambridge and Edinburgh are also important centres.
- The majority of commissioning editors are female.
- The work involves the pressures of managing a team, dealing with financial budgets and working within tight deadlines.
- There is close liaison with editorial, marketing and design colleagues and literary agents.
- Travel within a working day and absence from home at night are occasional.
- Overseas work or travel may be required by some publishers.

Entry Requirements

This area of work is open to all graduates, although academic and scientific publishers may prefer graduates with specific subject expertise. A degree in publishing may increase your chances.

Entry with an HND only is not normally sufficient.

A pre-entry postgraduate qualification is not a requirement, although an MA in Publishing may improve your chances.

Commissioning editors are usually graduates with a number of years' experience in publishing. Traditionally, a new entrant begins as an editorial assistant and then works their way up through desk editor (copy-editing, proofreading and writing book cover texts) and eventually to commissioning editor. However, there are exceptions:

- some enter from a publishing, sales and marketing, or contracts and rights background;
- in academic publishing, academics with specialist subject knowledge may be recruited directly into a commissioning editorship;
- in magazine publishing, a magazine journalist can progress to commissioning editor.

Relevant pre-entry work experience - voluntary, temporary or otherwise - is strongly recommended. In some cases, general office experience would be considered valuable. Potential candidates will need to show evidence of the following:

- enthusiasm and flair;
- business acumen;
- interpersonal skills;
- self-motivation;
- flexibility;
- competence in IT.

Getting a first job in the industry is difficult and requires real determination. Experience of writing or editing a college magazine is useful. Learn as much as possible about publishing from people in the industry and read trade magazines such as The Bookseller and Publishing News Online. Your Future in Magazines, which covers careers in magazine publishing, including editorial and writing, sales, production and marketing, may also be useful.

Many publishing jobs are never formally advertised. People are recruited to trainee positions through contacts (which you can develop by visiting book fairs, work shadowing and talking to people working in publishing), from specialist training courses or because they have made direct contact at the right time.

Speculative applications have a greater chance of success if you have already made contact with someone in the firm, including junior personnel, *e.g.* recent graduates from your own institution who can explain the business and the way of working to you.

Jobs that are advertised are usually done so shortly before they have to be filled. Many employers choose to advertise in the specialist press, rather than the dailies, in the hope that the this will attract only a small number of suitable applicants.

You may need to consider part-time or temporary work. This will demonstrate your commitment and show that you are serious about your career. A surprising number of publishing careers start in this way and lead to permanent jobs.

Publishers may be willing to take on students for work experience during vacations. This offers an excellent opportunity to make contacts. Applications for work experience should be taken as seriously as a job application (read the advice given on the website of the The Periodical Publishers Association (PPA)).

Training

In both book and magazine publishing, few structured graduate training schemes exist, although publishing companies are keen to employ graduates. Training is mainly on the job, supported by short courses run by organisations such as the Publishing Training Centre and the Periodicals Training Council (PTC).

Larger organisations often take a more structured approach to training and have more substantial training budgets. Increasingly, all professionals take responsibility for their own continuing professional development (CPD) in order to keep up to date with developments in their area of publishing.

The Publishing Training Centre runs a whole range of relevant short courses in:

- electronic publishing;
- computer skills;
- production
- marketing;
- rights and contracts;
- picture research.

It also offers five distance-learning courses in basic proofreading, copy-editing, editorial project management, effective copywriting and picture research. The Periodical Publishers Association (PPA) offers the Diploma in Publishing and a number of relevant certificate courses in different aspects of magazine publishing, marketing and management.

Career Development

A commissioning editor post is not normally achievable without at least five years' experience. New entrants start in junior roles.

Job titles in publishing houses vary considerably and this can be confusing to new entrants. The most important thing to consider is whether you want to join a large or a small organisation as this may determine opportunities for progression. A small publishing house may offer early exposure across a range of editing, production, marketing and business management areas, while larger companies may offer the opportunity to specialise earlier with more opportunity for promotion.

Progression is usually through the ranks. Once appointed, entrants have to prove their worth and capabilities in order to gain promotion. A clear career structure exists in larger publishers from junior editorial level to senior commissioning editor. Promotion, however, is not automatic and is very competitive.

Breadth and variety of experience in one or more organisations will increase chances for enhancing future employment. Whilst not the only marker of success, generally commissioning editors are assessed on results, *i.e.* how much profit is brought in by their books.

Successful commissioning editors can progress to become publishers with control over the whole editorial function, or move sideways and look after another part of the list.

3

Career in Advertisement

Advertising is the means of informing as well as influencing the general public to buy products or services through visual or oral messages. A product or service is advertised to create an awareness in the minds of potential buyers. Some of the commonly used media for advertising are TV, radio, websites, newspapers, magazines, billboards, hoardings etc. As a result of economic liberalization and the changing social trends advertising industry has shown rapid growth in the last decade.

Advertising is one of the aspects of mass communication. Advertising is actually brand-building through effective communication and is essentially a service industry. It helps to create demand, promote marketing system and boost economic growth. Thus advertising forms the basis of marketing.

Advertising plays a significant role in today's highly competitive world. A career in advertisement is quite glamourous and at the same time challenging with more and more agencies opening up every day. Whether it's brands, companies, personalities or even voluntary or religious organizations, all of them use some form of advertising in order to be able to communicate with the target audience. The salary structure in advertising is quite high and if you have the knack for it one can reach the top. It is an ideal profession for a creative individual who can handle work-pressure.

Today, new areas are emerging within advertising like event management, image management, internet marketing etc. Event management wherein events are marketed, Image management wherein a particular profile of an individual or an organisation is projected. Internet marketing has also brought about a lot of changes in advertising as Internet means that one is catering to a select group of audience rather than a mass audience.

Remuneration: Job positions and earnings in an agency vary with its size and turnover. Accredited agencies have a large set up while small agencies may have just a handful of employees looking after all the various jobs. The earnings range from 7,000 for production mangers to 8,000 for copy writers up to 35,000 for General Managers plus perks.

Eligibility & Course Areas: Educational: Most advertising agencies recruit candidates with a formal management or advertising/mass communication qualification. Preference is given for MBA's for posts in the market research, client servicing and media planning departments. In the creative department, on the other hand, a general BA with a command of the language of communication plus knowledge of designing packages like Photoshop, coral draw or fine arts is the requirement.

There are also specialised courses in advertising/mass communication at diploma level and post graduate level for which basic qualification is graduation. However, advertising is also offered as a subject for the graduate degree course in mass communication studies at certain institutions for which minimum qualification is 10+2. In addition there are also certificate courses for which 10+2 is enough.

Personal attributes: Basic qualities like creativity and flair for writing or ability to translate ideas into a visual format are required for making a successful career in this field. They should have insight into the interests of people from all walks of life, ability to work as part of team, mental and physical toughness to be able to withstand high pressure and criticism, must be sociable and have calm temperament. Market and media researchers should have an analytical and logical brain. Those in creative field should possess artistic abilities to make the ad appealing to the masses.

Job Prospects & Career Options

Job Prospects : Career opportunities in advertising include openings in private advertising agencies; advertising department in private or public sector companies; in advertising sections of newspapers, journals, magazines; commercial section of radio or television; market research organisations etc. One can also do freelancing.

Career Options: Advertising field offers a range of lucrative, interesting careers. The job in this field is categorised into two, executive and creative. Executive side include Client Servicing, Market Research and Media Research. Creative side consist of copywriters, scriptwriters, visualisers, photographers and typographers.

The executive department understand client needs, find new business and retain existing business, selects the appropriate media, analyses timing and placement of advertisements and negotiate the financial aspects of the deal. Creative department creates the advertisement copy. They verbalises and visualises the specific need of the client.

As ad films are also a part of film making career options of film are related to this field.

Executive Department

Client Servicing: The Client Servicing department is the link between the client and the agency. It is an important part of any advertising firm like what the heart is to the body. This department is responsible for meeting prospective clients and getting business for the company. It involves a study of the client, the product and the market; an analysis of consumer behaviour and marketing; a knowledge of all available media and their cost effectiveness and a strategic plan to be presented to the client. Those in client servicing must therefore interact with clients, gather information, oversee research where necessary, gauge consumer attitudes and based on this, work along with the various departments of the agency to formulate the most appropriate and effective advertising strategy within the specified budget.

To be an effective client-servicing person, the candidate has to have a thorough knowledge of the client's business and also know his weak points so that, through advertising and communications, the gap can be minimised.

An accounts executive who works in the client servicing department takes care of all the monitory dealings. He should know the most effective way to advertise clients product or service *i.e.* the media and their cost effectiveness. Account executives should also have an idea about market research and target audiences.

Market Research: Every good ad plans, start with research. This is the department which surveys the market and analyses and studies consumer behaviour about a product or service. They are involved with collection of data- information about the consumer, the market, existing competition and so on. The research studies provide basic information to the manufacturer, for planning a new product.

If you are a MBA or hold a degree in statistics/operations research, you can go for market researching jobs.

Media Planning/Research: Responsibility of media planning department starts at the point when the ad is complete. Media Department is responsible for the planning, scheduling, booking and purchase of space and time (in newspapers, magazines, radio and TV and outdoor hoardings). The media department must therefore devise the most effective use for an advertising budget to effectively and economically transmit a campaign message to the target audience. This department consists of the following:

Media Planners who decide the different media where the ads would be featured in order to get maximum viewership.

Media Buyer has to negotiate to buy space in the Press, or time on electronic media at the best rates for which he has to understand the buying as well as selling trends.

Creative Department : The Creative department designs and conceptualizes the advertisement. This consist of copywriting department and art department. Copywriting department works on text for the ad and themes for campaign. Art department visualises the campaign.

Copywriters: The Copywriter evolves a theme for the campaign and provides the text for advertisements. He is responsible for making the ad look attractive and delivering the message to the point. They work out the campaign slogan, jingles, scripts and promotional literature of the product or service as well as proposals, concept notes and film treatments. They are also expected to edit all textual matter for factual, syntax and typesetting discrepancies before it goes into production. Some times specialists called Typographers are appointed for making the format of textual matter who give advise on fonts, lettering etc.

Copywriters need to have a flair for writing backed up by the knowledge of advertising and oral communication skills, to become successful. They also need to have skill in analysing clients' needs and research skills for finding out about the products and services they are helping to sell. Problem-solving and time-management skills are important.

Visualisers: The Visualisers work on the visual concepts and decide how the ad shall eventually look. They do the overall layout of message including graphics, sketching etc.

Must be Artistic: A degree/diploma in commercial arts or fine arts as well as the knowledge of designing software like Photoshop, Pagemaker, Corel Draw etc. are often the required qualifications.

Photographers: Photographers should have an idea about angles and lighting effects. Good technical ability and knowledge of cameras and lenses is essential.

Advertising is a major career in Western countries. It is a new and fast growing career in all developing countries including India. The special importance of advertising as a profession is that it has room for so many different kinds of talents.

Once advertising simply meant a good- looking model and a clever head line. Business today is new and complex. The old methods will no longer work. Today more and more products are competing in the market. A whole new set of problems has been created by foreign brands. An entirely new concept of advertising is replacing the old. Clients have become very concerned about the brand image of their products.

Advertising plays a critical role in marketing a product. The success and survival of a product depend to a large extent on its advertising. Advertising is very powerful and it is very costly too. A full page ad in a newspaper like the Times of India may cost Rs.14 lakhs and a 30 second display on Doordarshan's national net work may be about 4.5 lakhs. Advertising is a big business. There is much more to advertising than a cute picture or a catchy slogan. It may take months of hard work for a professional team to set forth the right advertising strategy for a product.

Career Options: Advertising as a profession is a general term, which includes numerous professions. There are several kinds of advertising jobs in a wide variety of areas. Career options are plenty with Advertising Agencies. In advertising agencies, you will find creative people, researchers, production specialists, media experts, management people, account planners and so on. These various functions call for different types of talents, skills and training. Similarly, job opportunities are there with the advertising departments of Companies, with the media, in Public Relations, TV Software Production etc.

Advertising Agencies: You can find a job as a Copy Writer, Art Director/Visualiser, Account Executive/Account Manager, or as Account Planner

Market Research: You can have a career in Market Research. Researchers work on questionnaire design, interviews, sampling techniques and statistical analysis to arrive at meaningful results. Large companies have market research departments. But the job of a researcher in an advertising agency is somewhat different. Here the research is aimed at formulating advertising strategies, evaluating the effectiveness of advertisements etc.

The Media: The media includes the press, the TV, radio, exhibitions and anything, which can be used to carry an advertising message. It may be the side of a bus or a flying balloon. Media professionals ensure that the advertisement gets the best coverage at the lowest cost. Newspapers, magazines, TV and radio sell advertising space or time. This is a growing area for talented professionals.

Govt. Departments: Central and state governments have departments for advertising and publicity.

Working Freelance: It is quite common for advertising people to do freelance work for several agencies. You can work freelance full time or part time and can earn good money

Own Agency: Many advertising professionals start their own agencies. It does not require much capital to start a non-INS accredited agency. Small agencies like these are now spreading all over India and doing quite well.

Advertising Jobs

India is considered to be a great source for creativity; its people are sought after by everyone abroad and they command a lot of respect in the International Advertising Community. The country is now on the international map. The global impact of the Indian aptitude with respect to the advertising Industry is not only being noticed but appreciated worldwide.

The advertising in India is quite superior and the local talent boasts of high production values with interesting ideas and concepts, thus, making it a desirable hub for International Recruiters.

The Advertising Career: There are numerous career options available in the advertising world. In a typical Ad-agency, there are various job options, like, an advertising manager, who administers creative, in-house accounts and Media services departments. Then there is an account executive who manages the account services department in advertising agencies, determines the need for advertising and maintains the accounts of clients. Another vital department in the advertising world is 'The creative services department' which is responsible for developing the subject matter and presentation of the advertisements. There is a creative director who oversees the copy chief, art director, copywriters and associated staff. Then there exists a media department which is headed by a media director who organize planning groups that select the communication media, like, radio, television, newspapers, magazines, Internet, or outdoor signs in order to disseminate the ads.

Other Advertising Career Opportunities: There are many professions, trades and art forms that are closely connected with the advertising industry. You may find one of them suits your talents best, or, they could open the door to a career in an agency.

These include career options as, Printer, Photographer, Illustrator, Commercials Director, Public Relations, Direct Marketing, Designer, Sales Promotion, Set Designer, Make-up Artist, Commercials Producer, Model, voice-over, Sound Engineer, Typographer, Stylist, Brand/Product Manager, Market Research Analyst.

Job Scenario: The world has woken up to the fact that India is a big market. We have seen every possible global brand available in India. With respect to the advertising industry, it is maximizing this new opportunity. An opportunity to work on global brands is helping the local talents think and stay ahead with the rest of the world. In this knowledge driven industry, its the Indian Advertising Industry's ideas and accepted wisdom, which has shaped winning strategies and scripted many success stories.

The job applicants face a more stable environment but a highly competitive market. Projections for the coming years suggest an average growth of over 30% for marketing research analysts, advertising managers and visual artists. Nevertheless, the International Recruiters will continue to be highly selective. The most motivated, energetic, well-organized candidates with top-notch analytic and communication skills will land the best jobs.

The Recruiters look for the following attributes:

The Must Have's

- Creativity, high motivation, resistant to stress, flexibility and decisiveness.
- Ability to communicate persuasively, both orally and in writing.
- (with other managers, staff and the public)
- Tact and good judgment.
- Exceptional ability to establish and maintain effective personal relationships.

- (with supervisory and professional staff members and client firms)

Eligibility: Though there exists a wide assortment of educational backgrounds which are applicable for accessing the avenues of advertising, but most of the employers favour candidates with a broad liberal arts background plus experience in related occupations. A bachelor's degree in sociology, psychology, literature, journalism, or philosophy, among other subjects, is more acceptable. However, requirements vary, depending upon the kind of job.

For management positions in advertising, some recruiters also look for a Postgraduate Degree in advertising or journalism. The course of study should include marketing, consumer behaviour, market research, sales, communication methods, technology and visual arts.

Like other industries, advertising industry worldwide has toed the line where they look for Indian workforce for outsourcing bulk of their work.

Advertising and Marketing Communications

There is perhaps, no other business that so greatly influences our daily lives. Our choices regarding the type of cars we drive, the beer we drink, or the clothes we wear, are largely influenced by advertising.

The Work: As a career, advertising offers a unique blend of opportunities. In few other industries will you find a more eclectic group of individuals — all under one roof! The main areas of operation are client servicing, media planning, creative and research.

Client Servicing: The front face of the agency, Client Servicing, represents the agency to the client and the client within the agency. After receiving a detailed brief from the client, the Account Executive and Account Planner chalk out a strategy based on the brand's positioning, its USP and its communication objective.

While the better agencies require an MBA, some others will be satisfied with a Degree/Diploma in marketing or mass communication.

Accounts Planning: This is a senior-level position in the Servicing Department. It involves evolving the overall strategic plan including the budget, selecting the right media and zeroing-in on the communication message after interacting with the client and internally with the creative team, the media planning department and if necessary, the market research agency. The various elements of the communication package are integrated into a logical whole in the context of the brand and its desired positioning in the market.

Media Planning: Media Planners help ad agencies choose the best outlet or medium to reach the customer they want. They plan, schedule, book and purchase space in the print media (newspapers, magazines) or outdoors (billboards, kiosks and bus panels) and time (TV & radio, internet). The media planning exercise may also involve conducting some targeted brand or need-specific research to assess recall and viewership/ readership of a campaign.

Typically, media planners have a background in Maths and Statistics, an MBA (from MICA or a good B-school) or an MBE and are good with computers and number-crunching using sophisticated software.

The Creative Department: The creative department's task is to harness the right words, the most appropriate and arresting visuals — anything and everything that will grab the attention and prompt a sale.

The creative team in an agency can be further divided into two sections: Copy and Creative.

Copy Department: After the AE briefs the creative team, the Copywriter gets down to the task of putting across the message in words — headline, followed by the body copy in the case of a press ad, a dialogue or jingle for a radio spot, or a detailed story board in the case of a TV commercial.

A good copywriter must be able to think laterally and originally each time, to corelate masses of data and research findings so as to present the conclusions in language that is lucid and convincing. Besides a way with words, you need infinite patience to chisel and craft words into a subtly compelling sales pitch, until you've got it just right. And above all, you need to be highly creative and versatile. However unlike poetry or short story writing, copywriting is not creativity for creativity's sake. The famous ad guru, David Ogilvy, puts it very succinctly, "If it doesn't sell, it isn't creative."

Most copywriters start out as copy trainees after taking a copy test administered by the agency and proceed to write their way to the advertising hall of fame.

The Art Department: Takes care of the overall "look and feel" of the campaign starting with a "scribble" or rough sketch which accommodates the various components *i.e.* headline, visual, picture, text, logo, etc. in a balanced format within the given space.

Selecting the size and type of the font (lettering), the photographic treatment and the overall treatment of the TV commercial is the purview of the visualisers and art directors who man (and woman) the art department.

While a high level of originality and creative talent form the mainstay, a BFA or degree in applied art or graphic design with knowledge of computer graphics/multimedia is mandatory.

Market Research: The Research department tries to measure the effectiveness of the ad campaign. It Is research that provides the media planner and creatives a scientific and measurable basis to sharp-focus their strategy. These professionals are from a variety of disciplines, but share a common comfort level with mathematical or statistical modelling, sampling techniques and psychographics.

What it Takes?: Advertising demands a high level of creativity, imagination and innovative thinking from every person working in this profession. Writers and artists need to develop a portfolio of their best work.

This might include work from art school, or as a result of freelance assignments. Although no specific academic degree is required by most agencies, a commercial or graphic arts course from a reputed college of art coupled with some knowledge of multimedia and computer graphics is essential for those pitching for a spot in the art department.

Account Executives on the other hand, usually have a business degree in marketing, or mass communication or specifically in advertising.

What you'll Make?: In this industry rewards are directly commensurate with the initiative you display, the effort you put in and the results you achieve. If you are ambitious and hard working, you can quickly move up the ladder. Starting with Rs.3,500 or thereabouts as a fresh wet-behind-the-ears trainee, you can easily gross ten times as much five years down the line if you've got what it takes.

Where to Train?: Very few colleges offer specialisation in advertising at the bachelor's level. However, elements of advertising such as media planning and client servicing are covered in Mass Communication courses offered at both the undergraduate and postgraduate level.

- Indian Institute of Mass Communication, Aruna Asaf Ali Marg, JNU, New Campus, New Delhi 110067 (UT)
- MS University of Baroda, Fatehganj, Vadodara 390002. (Guj)
- Mudra Institute of Communications (MICA), Shela, Ahmedabad 380007 (Guj)
- Narsee Monjee Institute of Management Studies, V.L. Mehta Road, Vile Parle (West), Mumbai-400056. (Mah)
- National Institute of Advertising, Deen Dayal Upadhyay Marg, New Delhi 110002 (UT).
- National Institute of Design (NID), Paldi, Ahmedabad 380007 (Guj)
- Sir J.J. Institute of Applied Art, Dr. D.N. Road, Mumbai 400001
- University of Delhi, College of Art, Tilak Marg, New Delhi 110002

Advertising Sales Agents

Significant Points: Overall earnings are higher than average but can vary considerably because they are usually based on a salary plus performance-based commissions and bonuses. Pressure to meet monthly sales quotas can be stressful.

Nature of the Work: Advertising sales agents—often referred to as *account executives* or *advertising sales representatives*—sell or solicit advertising, including graphic art, advertising space in publications, custom-made signs, or television and radio advertising time.

More than half of all advertising sales agents work in the information sector, mostly for media firms, including television and radio broadcasters, print and Internet publishers and cable programme distributors. Other agents work for firms engaged in direct mail advertising or display and outdoor advertising, such as billboards and signs. Because most revenue for magazines, newspapers, directories and broadcasters is generated from advertising, advertising sales agents play an important role in their success.

Outside sales agents call on clients and prospects at their place of business. They may have an appointment, or they may practice "cold calling," arriving without an appointment. *Inside sales agents* work on their employer's premises and handle sales to customers who walk in or telephone the firm to inquire about advertising.

Some also may make telephone sales calls—calling prospects, attempting to sell the media firm's advertising space or time and arranging follow-up appointments between interested prospects and outside sales agents. Advertising sales agents should not be confused with *telemarketers,* whose duties are limited solely to soliciting orders for goods or services over the telephone and who work primarily in call centres that provide telemarketing services on contract.

Within the advertising and related services industry, media representative firms sell advertising space or time for media owners, including print and Internet publishers, radio and television stations and cable systems. Media representative firms maintain offices in major cities and employ their own teams of advertising sales agents.

These agents work exclusively with the executives at advertising agencies, called media buyers, who purchase advertising space for their clients. Media representative firms may represent any number of publications and radio or television stations, selling space to advertising agencies with clients who want to initiate a national advertising campaign or place advertisements outside their local market.

Sales agents employed in media representation normally do not cultivate new advertisers but maintain contacts with existing advertisers through the advertising agencies. A local television or radio station or publication would have a national sales manager to promote its best interests and coordinate the efforts of all the media representative firms on its behalf.

Local sales agents are employed by local publications or radio and television stations and are responsible for sales in a local territory. For these sales agents, obtaining new accounts is an important part of the job and they may spend much of their time travelling to and visiting prospective advertisers and current clients.

During a sales call, they discuss the client's advertising needs and suggest how their products and services can meet those needs. A critical part of building a relationship with a client is to find out as much as possible about the client and its products. Sales agents inquire about the client's current customers, prospective customers and the geographic area of the target market.

During the first meeting with a client, sales agents gather background information and explain how specific types of advertising will help promote a client's products or services most effectively. Next, the advertising sales agent prepares an advertising proposal to present to the client. This entails determining the advertising medium to be used, preparing sample advertisements and providing clients with estimates of the cost of the proposal. Consolidation in the media industries has brought the sale of different types of advertising under one roof. Sales are increasingly made of integrated packages that include advertisements to be placed in print, online and with a broadcast subsidiary.

After a contract has been established, advertising sales agents serve as the main contact between the client and the firm. They handle communication between the parties and assist the client in developing sample artwork or radio and television spots. They also arrange for commercial taping sessions and may accompany clients to the sessions.

Beyond selling, advertising sales agents have other duties as well. They analyze sales statistics, prepare reports and handle the scheduling of their appointments and work hours. They read about new and existing products and monitor the sales, prices and products of their competitors. In many firms, the advertising sales agent handles the drafting of contracts specifying the advertising work to be performed and its cost, as well as the billing and record-keeping for their customers' accounts—which may include customer service responsibilities such as answering questions or addressing any problems the client may have with the proposal. Sales agents also are responsible for developing sales tools, promotional plans and media kits, which they use to help make the sale.

Working Conditions: Selling can be stressful work because income and job security depend directly on the agent's ability to maintain and expand clientele. Companies generally set monthly sales quotas and place considerable pressure on advertising sales agents to meet those quotas. The added stress of rejection places more pressure on the agent.

Many advertising sales agents work more than 40 hours per week. Although the hours are long and often irregular, most have the freedom to determine their own schedule. The Internet and other electronic tools allow agents to do more work from home or while on the road, enabling them to send messages and documents to clients and coworkers, keep up with industry news and access databases that help them target potential customers. Advertising sales agents use e-mail to conduct much of the business with their clients. Use of e-mail has considerably shortened the time it takes to negotiate a sale and place the ad. Sales agents may accomplish more in less time, but many work more hours than in the past, spending additional time on follow-up and service calls.

Training, Other Qualifications and Advancement: Some employers prefer applicants with a college degree, particularly for sales positions that require meeting with clients.

Courses in marketing, leadership, communication, business and advertising are helpful. For those who sell over the telephone or who have a proven record of successfully selling other products, a high school degree may be sufficient. After gaining entry into the occupation, successful sales experience becomes more important than education when looking for a position. In general, smaller companies are more willing to hire unproven individuals.

Personality traits are equally important as academic background. Because they represent their employers to the executives of client organizations, advertising sales agents must have excellent interpersonal and written communication skills. Employers look for applicants who possess a pleasant personality, honesty and a neat professional appearance. Self-motivation, organization, persistence, independence and the ability to multitask are required because advertising sales agents set their own schedules and perform their duties without much supervision.

Training takes place mainly on the job. In most cases, an experienced sales manager instructs a newly hired advertising sales agent who lacks sales experience. In this one-on-one environment, the supervisor typically coaches the new hire and observes as she makes sales calls and contacts clients. The supervisor then advises the new hire on ways to improve. To conduct more specialized training—for example, in selling to a particular market segment, such as real estate professionals or automotive dealers—the employer may bring in a consultant.

Advancement in the occupation means taking on bigger, more important clients. Agents with proven leadership ability and a strong sales record may advance to supervisory and managerial positions such as sales supervisor, sales manager, or vice president of sales.

Frequent contact with managers of other departments and people in other firms provides sales agents with leads about job openings, enhancing advancement opportunities. In small firms, where the number of supervisory and management positions is limited, advancement may come slowly. Promotion may occur more quickly in large firms.

Employment: Advertising sales agents held over 154,000 jobs in 2004. Workers were concentrated in three industries: More than 3 in 10 jobs were in newspaper, periodical, book and directory publishers; 3 in 10 in advertising and related services; and 2 in 10 in radio and television broadcasting. A relatively small number of jobs were found in specialized design services, including industrial and graphic designers; printing and related support activities; computer systems design and related services; business support services; and cable and other programme distribution.

Employment was spread around the country, but jobs in larger, well-known publications or radio and television stations were concentrated in big cities. Media representative firms also were concentrated in large cities with many advertising agencies.

Part-time employment of advertising sales agents was most common in advertising and related services and less common in publishing and radio and television broadcasting. Self-employment also was more common in advertising and related services. Overall, relatively few advertising sales agents were self-employed.

Job Outlook: Employment of advertising sales agents is expected to grow about as fast as the average for all occupations through the year 2014 because of growth in population and advertising revenue. Rising demand for advertising sales agents also will stem from fast growth in cable systems and from the expansion of firms into the growing Hispanic market.

The industries employing advertising sales agents experienced considerable consolidation in recent years and that trend is expected to continue over the next decade, although at a slower pace. This consolidation is not expected to affect employment of advertising sales agents significantly because prospective clients still will require sales agents to create and demonstrate advertising proposals.

Technology has made advertising sales agents more productive, allowing them to take on additional duties and improve the quality of the services they provide, without substantially lessening overall demand. Productivity gains have occurred mostly in the accounting, proposal creation and customer service responsibilities of sales agents, allowing them to provide improved services.

In addition to the job openings generated by employment growth, openings will occur each year because of the need to replace sales representatives who transfer to other occupations or leave the labour force. Each year, many advertising sales agents discover they are unable to earn enough money and leave the occupation. As a result, job opportunities should be good, especially for those with a college degree or a proven sales record.

Advertising revenues are sensitive to economic downturns, which cause the industries and companies that advertise to reduce both the frequency of campaigns and the overall level of spending on advertising. Advertising sales agents must work hard to get the most out of every dollar spent on advertising under these conditions. Therefore, the number of job opportunities for advertising sales agents fluctuates with the business cycle.

Earnings: Most employers pay a combination of salaries, commissions and bonuses. Commissions are usually based on the amount of sales, whereas bonuses may depend on individual performance, on the performance of all sales workers in the group or district, or on the company's performance. For agents covering multiple areas or regions, commissions also may be based on the difficulty in making a sale in that particular area. Sales revenue is affected by the economic conditions and business expectations facing the industries that tend to advertise. Earnings from commissions are likely to be high when these industries are doing well, low when companies decide not to advertise as frequently.

Median annual earnings for all advertising sales agents were $40,300 including commissions, in May 2004. The middle 50 percent earned between $27,740 and $59,880 a year. The lowest 10 percent earned less than $20,210 and the highest 10 percent earned more than $89,720 a year. Median annual earnings for sales agents in May 2004 in the industries employing the largest numbers of them were as follows:

Advertising and related services	$44,900
Radio and television broadcasting	38,980
Newspaper, periodical, book and directory publishers	35,090

In addition to their earnings, advertising sales agents usually are reimbursed for expenses such as transportation costs, meals, hotels and entertaining customers. They often receive benefits such as health and life insurance, pension plans, vacation and sick leave, personal use of a company car and frequent flier mileage. Some companies offer incentives such as free vacation trips or gifts for outstanding sales workers.

Advertising and Public Relations Services

Significant Points: Competition for many jobs will be keen because the glamour of the industry traditionally attracts many more jobseekers than there are job openings.

California and New York together account for about 1 in 5 firms and more than 1 in 4 workers in the industry.

Layoffs are common when accounts are lost, major clients cut budgets, or agencies merge.

Nature of the Industry: Firms in the advertising and public relations services industry prepare advertisements for other companies and organizations and design campaigns to promote the interests and image of their clients. This industry also includes media representatives-firms that sell advertising space for publications, radio, television and the Internet; display advertisers-businesses engaged in creating and designing public display ads for use in shopping malls, on billboards, or in similar media; and direct mail advertisers. A firm that purchases advertising time (or space) from media outlets, thereafter reselling it to advertising agencies or individual companies directly, is considered a media buying agency. Divisions of companies that produce and place their own advertising are not considered part of this industry.

In 2004, there were about 47,000 advertising and public relations services establishments in the United States. About 4 out of 10 write copy and prepare artwork, graphics and other creative work and then place the resulting ads on television, radio, or the Internet or in periodicals, newspapers, or other advertising media. Within the industry, only these full-service establishments are known as advertising agencies. About 1 in 6 were public relations firms. Many of the largest agencies are international, with a substantial proportion of their revenue coming from abroad.

Most advertising firms specialize in a particular market niche. Some companies produce and solicit outdoor advertising, such as billboards and electric displays. Others place ads in buses, subways, taxis, airports and bus terminals. A small number of firms produce aerial advertising, while others distribute circulars, handbills and free samples.

Groups within agencies have been created to serve their clients' electronic advertising needs on the Internet. Online advertisements link users to a company's or product's Web site, where information such as new product announcements, contests and product catalogues appears and from which purchases may be made.

Some firms are not involved in the creation of ads at all; instead, they sell advertising time or space on radio and television stations or in publications. Because these firms do not produce advertising, their staffs are mostly sales workers.

Companies often look to advertising as a way of boosting sales by increasing the public's exposure to a product or service. Most companies do not have the staff with the necessary skills or experience to create effective advertisements; furthermore, many advertising campaigns are temporary, so employers would have difficulty maintaining their own advertising staff.

Instead, companies commonly solicit bids from ad agencies to develop advertising for them. Next, ad agencies offering their services to the company often make presentations. After winning an account, various departments within an agency-such as creative, production, media and research-work together to meet the client's goal of increasing sales.

Widespread public relations .services firms can influence how businesses, governments and institutions make decisions. Often working behind the scenes, these firms have a variety of functions. In general, firms in public relations services advise and implement public exposure strategies. For example, a public relations firm might issue a press release that is printed in newspapers across the country. Firms in public relations services offer one or more resources that clients cannot provide themselves.

Usually this resource is expertise in the form of knowledge, experience, special skills, or creativity; but sometimes the resource is time or personnel that the client cannot spare. Clients of public relations firms include all types of businesses, institutions, trades and public interest groups and even high-profile individuals. Clients are large and small for-profit firms in the private sector; State, local, or Federal Governments; hospitals, universities, unions and trade groups; and foreign governments or businesses.

Public relations firms help secure favourable public exposure for their clients, advise them in the case of a sudden public crisis and design strategies to help them attain a certain public image. Toward these ends, public relations firms analyze public or internal sentiment about clients; establish relationships with the media; write speeches and coach clients for interviews; issue press releases; and organize client-sponsored publicity events, such as contests, concerts, exhibits, symposia and sporting and charity events.

Lobbying firms, a special type of public relations firm, differ somewhat. Instead of attempting to secure favourable public opinion about their clients, they attempt to influence legislators in favour of their clients' special interests. Lobbyists often work for large businesses, industry trade organizations, unions, or public interest groups.

In an effort to attract and maintain clients, advertising and public relations services agencies are diversifying their services, offering advertising as well as public relations, sales, marketing and interactive media services. Advertising and public relations services firms have found that highly creative work is particularly suitable for their services, resulting in a better product and increasing their clients' profitability.

Working Conditions: Most employees in advertising and public relations services work in comfortable offices operating in a teamwork environment; however, long hours, including evenings and weekends, are common. There are fewer opportunities for part-time work than in many other industries; in 2004, 14 percent of advertising and public relations employees worked part time, compared with 16 percent of all workers.

Work in advertising and public relations is fast-paced and exciting, but it also can be stressful. Being creative on a tight schedule can be emotionally draining. Some workers, such as lobbyists, consultants and public relations writers, frequently must meet deadlines and consequently may work long hours at times. Workers whose services are billed hourly, such as advertising consultants and public relations specialists, are often under pressure to manage their time carefully. In addition, frequent meetings with clients and media representatives may involve substantial travel.

Most firms encourage employees to attend employer-paid time-management classes, which help reduce the stress sometimes associated with working under strict time constraints. Also, with today's hectic lifestyle, many firms in this industry offer or provide health facilities or clubs to help employees maintain good health. In 2004, workers in the industry averaged 33.8 hours per week, a little higher than the national average of 33.7.

Employment: The advertising and public relations services industry employed 425,000 workers in 2004. An additional 61,000 workers were self-employed.

Although advertising and public relations services firms are located throughout the country, they are concentrated in the largest States and cities. California and New York together account for about 1 in 5 firms and more than 1 in 4 workers in the industry. Firms vary in size, ranging from one-person shops to international agencies employing thousands of workers. However, 68 percent of all advertising and public relations establishments employ fewer than 5 employees.

The small size of the average advertising and public relations services firm demonstrates the opportunities for self-employment. It is relatively easy to open a small agency; in fact, many successful agencies began as one-person or two-person operations.

About 76 percent of advertising and public relations employees are 25 to 54 years of age. Very few advertising and public relations services workers are below the age of 20, which reflects the need for post-secondary training or work experience.

Occupations in the Industry: Training, Other Qualifications and Advancement Management, business and financial workers; professionals and related workers; and sales and related workers account for more than 6 out of every 10 jobs in the industry table. Employees have varied responsibilities in agencies with only a few workers and the specific job duties of each worker often are difficult to distinguish. Workers in relatively large firms specialize more, so the distinctions among occupations are more apparent.

Within advertising and public relations, the account management department links the agency and the client-it represents the agency to the client, as well as the client to the agency. Account management brings business to the agency and ultimately is responsible for the quality of the advertisement or public relations campaign. Account management workers carefully monitor the activities of the other areas to ensure that everything runs smoothly. Account managers and their assistants analyze competitive activity and consumer trends, report client billing, forecast agency income and combine the talents of the creative, media and research areas. The creative director oversees the copy chief, art director and their respective staffs. The media director oversees planning groups that select the communication media-for example, radio, television, newspapers, magazines, Internet, or outdoor signs-to be used to promote the organization, issue, product, or service.

In public relations firms, public relations managers direct publicity programmes to a targeted public. They often specialize in a specific area, such as crisis management-or in a specific industry, such as health care. They use every available communication medium in their effort to maintain the support of the specific group upon whom their organization's success depends, such as consumers, stockholders, or the general public. For example, public relations managers may clarify or justify the firm's point of view on health or environmental issues to community or special interest groups.

Public relations specialists handle organizational functions such as media, community, consumer and governmental relations; political campaigns; interest-group representation; conflict mediation; or employee and investor relations. They prepare press releases and contact people in the media who might print or broadcast their material. Many radio or television special reports, newspaper stories and magazine articles start on the desks of public relations specialists.

Working with an idea that account management obtains from the client, the creative department brings the idea to life. For example, an ad agency's staff works together to transform a blank piece of paper into an advertisement. As the idea takes shape, copywriters and their assistants write the words of ads-both the written part of print ads as well as the scripts of radio and television spots.

Art directors and their assistants develop the visual concepts and designs of advertisements. They prepare pasteups and layouts for print ads and television storyboards, cartoon-style summaries of how an advertisement will appear. They also oversee the filming of television commercials and photo sessions. Graphic designers use a variety of print, electronic and film media to create designs that meet clients' commercial needs. Using computer software, they develop the overall layout and design of print ads for magazines, newspapers, journals, corporate reports and other publications.

They also may produce promotional displays and marketing brochures for products and services, design distinctive company logos for products and businesses and develop signs and environmental graphics-aesthetically pleasing signs that deliver a message, such as a sunset to advertise a beach resort. An increasing number of graphic designers develop material to appear on the Internet.

Workers in the research department try to understand the desires, motivations and ideals of consumers, in order to produce and place the most effective advertising or public relations campaign in the most effective media. Research executives compile data, monitor the progress of internal and external research, develop research tools and interpret and provide explanations of the data gathered.

Research executives often specialize in specific research areas and perform supervisory duties. Market research analysts are concerned with the potential sales of a product or service. They analyze statistical data on past sales to predict future sales. They provide a company's management with information needed to make decisions on the promotion, distribution, design and pricing of products or services.

Media planners gather information on the public's viewing and reading habits and evaluate editorial content and programming to determine the potential use of media such as newspapers, magazines, radio, television, or the Internet. The media staff calculates the numbers and types of people reached by different media and how often they are reached. Media buyers track the media space and times available for purchase, negotiate and purchase time and space for ads and make sure ads appear exactly as scheduled.

Additionally, they calculate rates, usage and budgets. Advertising sales agents sell air time on radio and television and page space in print media. They generally work in firms representing radio stations, television stations and publications. Demonstrators promote sales of a product to consumers, while product promoters try to induce retail stores to sell particular products and market them effectively. Product demonstration is an effective technique used by both to introduce new products or promote sales of old products because it allows face-to-face interaction with potential customers.

Office and administrative support occupations accounted for 28 percent of jobs in 2004. Positions ranged from secretaries and administrative assistants to financial clerks. The occupational composition of this group varies widely among agencies. The remaining jobs in the industry were in service, construction and extraction, production, transportation and installation, maintenance and repair occupations.

Employment of Wage and Salary Workers in Advertising and Public Relations Services by Occupation, 2004 and Projected Change, 2004-14. (Employment in Thousands)

Occupation	*Employment, 2004*		*Percent change, 2004-14*
	Number	*Percent*	*Percent*
Total, all occupations	425	100.0	22.4
Management, business and financial occupations	66	15.6	29.1
General and operations managers	15	3.5	25.8
Advertising and promotions managers	8	1.8	30.8
Marketing managers	4	0.9	35.1
Sales managers	3	0.8	27.9
Public relations managers	4	0.9	36.6
Purchasing agents, except wholesale, retail and farm products	4	0.9	27.1
Accountants and auditors	6	1.4	27.1
Professional and related occupations	105	24.6	33.0
Computer programmers	5	1.1	3.7
Market research analysts	4	0.9	27.1
Art directors	10	2.3	27.1
Multimedia artists and animators	6	1.4	39.8
Graphic designers	22	5.2	38.9
Merchandise displayers and window trimmers	4	0.9	26.2
Public relations specialists	22	5.2	39.8
Editors	3	0.8	27.1
Writers and authors	8	1.8	21.0
Sales and related occupations	95	22.4	24.0
Supervisors, sales workers	6	1.5	17.5
Advertising sales agents	43	10.2	27.2
Sales representatives, services, all other	8	2.0	27.1
Sales representatives, wholesale and manufacturing	10	2.4	27.1
Demonstrators and product promoters	19	4.4	22.4
Telemarketers	5	1.2	-1.0
Office and administrative support occupations	118	27.8	8.3
First-line supervisors/managers of office and administrative support workers	8	1.8	15.2
Bookkeeping, accounting and auditing clerks	11	2.6	14.4
Customer service representatives	14	3.3	30.1
Receptionists and information clerks	5	1.2	21.1
Production, planning and expediting clerks	6	1.5	25.8
Shipping, receiving and traffic clerks	4	1.0	15.1

Contd...

Occupation	*Employment, 2004 Number*	*Percent change, 2004-14*	*Percent*
Secretaries and administrative assistants	18	4.3	14.9
Mail clerks and mail machine operators, except postal service	16	3.7	-34.9
Office clerks, general	13	3.1	13.1
Production occupations	17	4.0	19.6
Printers	8	1.8	18.1
Transportation and material moving occupations	13	3.1	22.0
Labourers and material movers, hand	9	2.1	19.6

Note: May not add to totals due to omission of occupations with small employment

Training and Advancement: Most entry-level professional and managerial positions in advertising and public relations services require a bachelor's degree, preferably with broad liberal arts exposure.

Beginners in advertising usually enter the industry in the account management or media department. Occasionally, entry-level positions are available in the market research or creative departments of an agency, but these positions usually require some experience. Completing an advertising-related internship while in school provides an advantage when applying for an entry-level position; in fact, internships are becoming a necessary step to obtaining permanent employment. In addition to an internship, courses in marketing, psychology, accounting, statistics and creative design can help prepare potential entrants for careers in this field.

Assistant account executive positions-the entry-level account management occupation in most firms-require a bachelor's degree in marketing or advertising, although some firms require a master's degree in business administration.

Bachelor's degrees are not required for entry-level positions in the creative department. Assistant art directors usually need at least a 2-year degree from an art or design school. Although assistant copywriters do not need a degree, obtaining one helps to develop the superior communication skills and abilities required for this job.

Assistant media planner or assistant media buyer also are good entry-level positions, but almost always require a bachelor's degree, preferably with a major in marketing or advertising. Experienced applicants who possess at least a master's degree usually fill research positions. Often, they have a background in marketing or statistics and years of experience. Requirements for support services and administrative positions depend on the job and vary from firm to firm.

In public relations, employers prefer applicants with degrees in communications, journalism, English, or business. Some 4-year colleges and universities have begun to offer a concentration in public relations. Because there is keen competition for entry-level public relations jobs, workers are encouraged to gain experience through internships, co-op programmes, or one of the formal public relations programmes offered across the country.

However, these programmes are not available everywhere, so most public relations workers get the bulk of their training on the job. At some firms, this training consists of formal classroom education but, in most cases, workers train under the guidance of senior account executives or other experienced workers, gradually familiarizing themselves with public relations work. Entry-level workers often start as research or account assistants and may be promoted to account executive, account supervisor, vice president and executive vice president.

A voluntary accreditation programme for public relations specialists is offered by the Public Relations Society of America. The programme is a recognized mark of competency in the profession and requires that workers have been employed in the field for several years.

Employees in advertising and public relations services should have good people skills, common sense, creativity, communication skills and problem-solving ability. Foreign language skills have always been important for those wanting to work abroad for domestic firms or to represent foreign firms domestically. However, these skills are increasingly vital to reach linguistic minorities in U.S. cities, such as Los Angeles,

New York, Miami, Houston and Phoenix. New media, such as the Internet, are creating opportunities to market products, but also are increasing the need for additional training for those already employed. Keeping pace with technology is fundamental to success in the industry. In addition, advertisers must keep in tune with the changing values, cultures and fashions of the Nation.

Success in increasingly responsible staff assignments usually leads to advancement to supervisory positions. As workers climb the organizational ladder, broad vision and planning skills become extremely important. Another way to get to the top in this industry is to open one's own firm. In spite of the difficulty and high failure rate, many find starting their own business to be personally and financially rewarding. Among the self-employed, advancement takes the form of increasing the size and strength of the company.

Outlook: Competition for many jobs will be keen because the glamour of the advertising and public relations services industry traditionally attracts many more jobseekers than there are job openings. Employment in the industry is projected to grow 22 percent over the 2004-14 period, compared with 14 percent for all industries combined.

New jobs will be created as the economy expands and generates more products and services to advertise. Increased demand for advertising and public relations services also will stem from growth in the number and types of media outlets used to reach consumers, creating opportunities for people skilled in preparing material for presentation on the Internet.

On the other hand, employment growth may be tempered by the increased use of more efficient non-print media advertising, such as Internet or radio, which could replace some workers.

Employment also may be adversely affected if legislation, aimed at protecting public health and safety, further restricts advertising for specific products such as alcoholic beverages and tobacco. In addition to new jobs created over the 2004-14 period, job openings also will arise as workers transfer to other industries or leave the workforce.

Layoffs are common in advertising and public relations services firms when accounts are lost, major clients cut budgets, or agencies merge.

Earning: In 2004, non-supervisory workers in advertising and public relations services averaged $633 a week-significantly higher than the $529 a week for all non-supervisory workers in private industry. Earnings of workers in selected occupations in advertising and public relations services appear in table.

Median Hourly Earnings of the Largest Occupations in Advertising and Public Relations Services

Occupation	*Advertising and public relations services*	*All industries*
General and operations managers	$55.06	$37.22
Public relations specialists	24.25	21.07
Advertising sales agents	21.59	19.37
Graphic designers	19.23	18.28
Executive secretaries and administrative assistants	17.65	16.81
Bookkeeping, accounting and auditing clerks	15.15	13.74
Customer service representatives	14.47	12.99
Office clerks, general	11.18	10.95
Mail clerks and mail machine operators, except postal service	9.76	10.76
Demonstrators and product promoters	8.42	9.95

In addition to a straight salary, many workers receive additional compensation, such as profit sharing, stock ownership, or performance-based bonuses.

Only 2 percent of workers in advertising and public relations services belong to unions or are covered by union contracts, compared with about 14 percent of workers in all industries combined.

Advertising Executive

There are many different specialisms within the world of advertising, including:

- Account Executives (also known as an account handlers), who are the link between the agency and the client, preparing pitches or presentations to win new business as well as servicing the needs of existing clients. To do this, they plan, organise and monitor advertising campaigns. Once they have received the brief from a client they discuss with other agency staff what steps to take. Account executives need to be familiar with the client's product, business culture and the competition. Typically, they handle three to four accounts at once.

- Advertising Creatives in an advertising agency generally work in a team with an art director. They start as a copywriter, eventually going on to be a director. The scope of their work depends on the size of the agency and its clients. They may write slogans for posters and advertisements, text for leaflets and brochures and scripts or jingles for TV and radio.

The account executive and the client would normally decide the campaign's core message. The copywriter would then find the most effective way of communicating it, receiving a brief from the account management team, giving background information about the client, its products and the target audience. Along with the art director, they consider the brief, rejecting some ideas and developing others.

Entry Level: There are no set qualifications, but advertising is fiercely competitive and most entrants have at least A levels/ H grades. A degree or HND is often required by large agencies, while smaller agencies also look for relevant work experience. For an account executive, a degree in marketing could be particularly valuable. You could also study on a postgraduate course.

There is no upper age limit for starting in this work, but in practice 80 per cent of advertising agency staff are under 40.

Making the Grade: Most advertising executives train on the job, including shadowing experienced staff. Some agencies offer an induction programme and larger agencies tend to have structured training programmes with placements in different departments.

Account executives may enrol on a course run by the Institute of Practitioners in Advertising (IPA), or take qualifications with the Communication Advertising and Marketing Education Foundation (CAM).

The Creative Circle and the Design and Art Directors Association offer a range of seminars and workshops for practising creative staff. It is also possible to take qualifications with CAM and the IPA.

Career progression in advertising is based on experience and ability but gaining relevant qualifications is an advantage. Experienced advertising staff often set up small advertising agencies of their own.

Personal Qualities: As an account executive, you would need a real flair for business, a smart appearance and a professional manner. You must be an effective team leader and you must be skilled at handling budgets.

As a creative, you would need excellent creative writing skills, especially the ability to express a message clearly, briefly and persuasively. You would also have to be commercially aware, with an understanding of your market and the ability to work well under pressure.

Looking Ahead: Advertising is a very popular career and applicants outnumber vacancies by ten to one. There is a tendency for creative and commercial functions to merge, so you would improve your prospects if you can combine imaginative flair with sound business sense. Agencies differ in size and speciality and executives often seek promotion by moving between agencies. With sufficient experience, you could start your own business.

4

Career in Public Relations

In the last decade, Public Relations (PR) has gained popularity and importance. The speed of communication and the bewildering change and progress in various fields has resulted in the rise of PR as a profession.

PR has a key role to play in informing the public about an organization and converting ignorance into knowledge and understanding. Generating public interest and turning hostility into acceptance in some cases is also the job of a PR manager. PR analyzes the effects of organizational policies and the reactions of the public. The public is a very important part of an organization and is essential for its survival and success.

The basic components of public relations, according to a monograph issued by the PRSA Foundation, include the following:

Counselling: This involves providing advice to management concerning policies, relationships and communications.

Research: Determining attitudes and behaviours of the public in order to plan public strategies.

Media Relations: Working with mass media in seeking publicity or responding to their interests in the organization.

Publicity: Disseminating planned messages through selected media to promote the organization's interests.

Employee/Member Relations: Responding to concerns, informing and motivating an organization's employees or members.

Community Relations: Planned activity with a community to maintain an environment that benefits both the organization and the community.

Public Affairs: Developing effective involvement in public policy and helping an organization adapt to public expectations. The term is also used by government agencies to describe their public relations activities and by many corporations as an umbrella term to describe multiple public relations activities.

Government Affairs: Relating directly with legislatures and regulatory agencies on behalf of the organization. Lobbying can be a part of the government affairs programme.

Issues Management: Identifying and addressing issues of public concern that affect the organization.

Financial Relations: Creating and maintaining investor confidence and building good relationships with the financial community. Also known as Investor Relations or Shareholder Relations.

Industry Relations: Relating with other firms in the industry of an organization and with trade associations.

Development/Fund-Raising: Demonstrating the need for development and encouraging the public to support an organization, primarily through financial contributions.

Special Events: Stimulating an interest in a person, product or organization by means of a focused "happening"; also, activities designed to interact with publics and listen to them.

Marketing Communications: Combination of activities designed to sell a product, service, or idea, including advertising, collateral materials, publicity, promotion, direct mail, trade shows and special events.

The Work: If you plan on entering this field, PR provides you with a wide range of work opportunities.

Corporations: You can work for departments who seek to protect and enhance a company's reputation. Providing information to the public as well as to special audiences such as stockholders, financial analysts and employees would be a part of your job.

Non-profit Organizations: Trade and environmental organizations, social and cultural groups, hospitals and health agencies also offer jobs to PR professionals. The job often involves fund-raising.

Entertainment, Sports and Travel: Practitioners in these areas are often concerned with publicity for individuals and promotion of events ranging from football games to motion pictures.

Government and the Military: This area includes promotion of political issues, sometimes through lobbying, work with politicians, dissemination of information about government activities to citizens and distribution of information about the armed forces.

Education: At the college level, you would primarily work with alumni, faculty and administration, students and the public to promote the school's image, recruit students and raise fund. Secondary schools often have specialists to handle community relations.

International Public Relations: The immense expansion of almost instantaneous global communications has opened an intriguing new area, especially for practitioners with language skills and familiarity with other cultures.

Personal Attributes: Ability with words, analytical skill, creative ability, an instinct for persuasion and the ability to make compelling and polished presentations are essential requirements if you are looking to become a PR professional. Common sense, first-class organizing ability, good judgement, objectivity, creativity, flexibility and the willingness to work long and inconvenient hours are also important attributes that you must posses.

Salary: Over the years, the status of PR professionals has changed and evolved. To keep pace with changes, businesses and journalists have begun to rely on PR professionals. Hence, depending on your qualification and experience, you can expect to be paid well. As a trainee, you can start with a salary of Rs.3000-Rs.7000. Eventually you can expect to be paid a salary between Rs.10000-Rs25000, depending on you individual performance.

In the government sector, you can expect to start with Rs.5000. After you are established in the profession, you can expect a salary of Rs.20000 or more. MNCs and private companies will pay you higher.

Public Relations

Public Relation is a management function that involves monitoring and evaluating public attitudes and maintaining mutual relations and understanding between an organisation and its public. Public could include shareholders, government, consumers, employees and the media.

It is the act of getting along with people we constantly come in touch with. PROs ensures internal cohesion in the company by maintaining a clear communications network between the management and employees. Its first objective is to improve channels of communication and to establish new ways of setting up a two-way flow of information and understanding.

Public relations as a separate career option has came into existence when lots of private or government companies and institution felt the need to market their product, service and facilities. Public image is important to all organisations and prominent personalities. The role of public relation specialist becomes pertinent in crisis situations when the correct and timely transmission of information can help save the face of the organisation.

In terms of career opportunities, Public relations is broadly practiced for product publicity, corporate publicity, to have better relations with the government, to publish corporate publications like newsletter, bulletins, magazines for employees etc.

Eligibility & Course Areas: Educational: Bachelors degree in any discipline preferably with social sciences, liberal arts and humanities is required to take up a course in this field. There are diploma as well as post graduate diploma courses in Public relations. Duration of most the courses is of one year. Apart from this there are also short term certificate courses. Most training programmes in Advertising also includes public relations. Some institutes have entrance exams while others prefer admission on merit basis.

These courses mainly cover areas like public relations principles and techniques, public relations management and administration, including organizational development, writing, emphasizing news releases, proposals, annual reports, scripts, speeches and related items, visual communications, including desktop publishing and computer graphics and research, emphasizing social science research and survey design and implementation.

Personal Attributes: One must have excellent communication skills, both spoken and written so has to express thoughts clearly and simply. An effective personality and the ability to get along with a wide range of people both inside and outside an organisation is necessary. Must be polite always as he has to work under pressure or provocation. An organising ability is required too, as one may have to organise press conferences, lectures, exhibitions and events. Must have self-confidence and farsightedness. He must be able to understand human psychology and take decisions apt to the situation. Analytical skills are required to interpret research information and plan activity.

Job Prospects & Career Options: Public relation officers can find employment in the corporate sector, public sector, government agencies, tourist agencies, hotels, banks and other financial institutions, private consultancy firms etc. Nowadays they can find work even with individuals like political figures, models and film stars who want their pictures, profiles and interviews published in magazines and need agents who can do the work for them so as to have a image in front of general public.

Public relations officers have to work within and outside the organisation. Within the concern they have to conduct management-employee meets, to inform organisations policies, activities and accomplishments. Outside he has to liaison with government departments, trade unions, press etc. whose cooperation is required for the smooth functioning and also have to manage complaints from the consumers, organise events like fairs, exhibitions etc.

The work involves keeping management aware of public attitudes and concerns of the many groups and organizations with which they must deal. In addition, public relations departments employ public relations specialists to write, research, prepare materials, maintain contacts and respond to inquiries.

Another important area of work in this field is to create public identity or an image for public figures like political parties, models and film stars. It include advising them on every aspect of personality, including dress code, behaviour, statement given in press, public appearances etc.

Lobbying, a new field in this career, involves bringing about the passage of laws favourable to the special interest group they represent like a company, industries, government etc. It is a strategy used to raise public consciousness and influence policy makers in areas like environment, human rights, education etc. This is an interesting area of work in public relation.

Remuneration: One can start with a salary of Rs 3,000 to Rs 6,000 a month, depending on the kind of organisation that one joins. Thereafter, it is up to one's performance. A senior PR professional may get Rs 10,000 to Rs 25,000.

Career in Public Relations

What is public relations?

Public relations is one of the latest management disciplines. In the layman's language, it means maintaining relations with the public. The job of a PR person is to work primarily towards establishing and improving mutual relationship, understanding and goodwill between his company or organisation and the clients and the customers, various other groups and the public at large. It is a planned and sustained programme conducted by an organisation's management.

It monitors awareness, opinions, attitudes and behaviour inside and outside the organisation. It analyses the impact of organisational policies, procedures and actions on various publics. It counsels the management on the establishment of new policies and programmes that are mutually beneficial to the organisation and its publics.

It establishes and maintains two-way communication between the organisation and its publics. In order to speak for and on behalf of the organisation, the PR person must know the organisation thoroughly. Thus it has become a top management function today identifying, establishing and maintaining mutually beneficial relationships between an organisation and the various publics on whom its success or failure depends.

An organisation is a group of persons coming together with a common purpose- to produce and sell certain products, services or ideas. It has to get the job done by a certain number of people with the support of many more people. These people who are the concern of the organisation are the 'publics' in the vocabulary of Public Relations. These 'publics' form an integral part of the body of the organisation and are very important factors for its existence.

Job Opportunities: Public Relations as a fast track career, has grown phenomenally recently. In an age when image consciousness holds the key to success, the scope and influence of public relations is constantly widening. With the growth of industry and business, the need for well trained, polished and hard-working PR personnel is growing day by day in every branch of industry, business and services run by the private, government and the public sector.

Different kinds of PR personnel are required to handle various groups and areas like workers and employees, shareholders, customers and clients, suppliers, legislators, government departments, financial institutions, banks and above all, the public at large. Experts in Public Relations have started predicting that by 21st century, PR will overtake Advertising as it is less expensive, capable of communicating directly to the clients and customers and more result oriented as its effect can be evaluated almost spontaneously.

How to Get into a Career in Public Relations?

Public relations is one of the most popular career choices today amongst graduates and this article explains what PR is and how to get into it.

What is public relations?

Public relations is about reputation - the result of what you do, what you say and what others say about you.

Public relations is the discipline, which looks after reputation with the aim of earning understanding and support and influencing opinion and behaviour. It is the planned and sustained effort to establish and maintain goodwill and mutual understanding between an organisation and its publics.

'Organisation' can be a government body, a business, a profession, a public service or a body concerned with health, culture, education - indeed any corporate of voluntary body large or small. 'Publics' are audiences that are important to the organisation. They include customers - existing and potential; employees and management; investors; media; government; suppliers; opinion-formers.

To be effective, an organisation needs to listen to the opinion of those with whom it deals and not solely provide information. Issuing a barrage of propaganda is not enough in today's open society. At its best, public relations not only tells an organisation's story to its publics, it also helps to shape the organisation and the way it works. The practitioner needs to find out the concerns and expectations of a company's publics and explain them to its management.

The annual income of PR consultancies in the UK is estimated at £300 million and the turnover of the industry is estimated at £1 billion. The number of people working in a public relations role in the UK is estimated at around 48,000. The rate of growth in the number of PR jobs at all levels has been higher that of any management function over the last fifteen years.

Building a Career in PR: Career development opportunities within the public relations industry are excellent but competition for job is fierce. Most entrants tend to be graduates, although there are some opportunities for persistent school leavers with relevant work experience.

The Chartered Institute of Public Relations (CIPR) is the main professional body for individuals within the PR industry and publishes a list of approved courses, which provide a good foundation for a career in PR. All of the approved courses include opportunities for work experience and all have good employment records in the industry.

Whilst studying, students on these courses can become student members of the Institute and start making their own contacts with PR practitioners.

There is no standard promotion pattern for the industry but a talented and industrious graduate might expect the following career development plan:

One to two years as a junior account executive

Two of three years as an account executive

Two to three years as a senior account executive or account manager before moving to associate or account director.

Day to Day in PR

Writing and editing - this could be shareholder reports, annual reports, press releases, film scripts, articles and features, speeches, booklets, newsletters.

Media relations - developing and maintaining a good working contact with the media.

Corporate identity - developing and maintaining an organisation's identify, presenting the company's name and reputation rather than its products.

Special events - news conferences, exhibitions, facility celebrations, open days, competitions and award programmes are all used to gain the attention of specific groups.

Research and evaluation - the first activity undertaken by a public relations practitioner is usually analysis and fact gathering.

Public Relations Officer

Public relations officers are concerned with an organisation's reputation. Their task is to build long-lasting relationships by establishing and maintaining mutual understanding and goodwill between an organisation and the public. The work involves providing the outside world with information about the organisation or its products through newspapers, magazines, promotional literature, radio, TV and websites.

Some public relations officers work in the public relations department of a large organisation, while others work for a consultancy, serving the needs of a number of different clients. In either case, the work is likely to include liaising with the media, organising and arranging news conferences, press launches, exhibitions and trade fairs, writing and producing leaflets, brochures, press releases, company newsletters and websites, setting up photographic sessions and speaking at presentations, news conferences and in radio or TV interviews.

Entry Level: Most people applying to work as public relations officers are graduates, although entry into this career is so competitive that it is beneficial to have both a postgraduate diploma and previous experience.

Relevant experience can be gained through placements on some first degree and postgraduate courses, or by doing voluntary work or holiday jobs. The Chartered Institute of Public Relations (CIPR) can provide a list of approved first degrees in PR, together with appropriate masters degrees and postgraduate diploma courses.

Making the Grade: Training is performed mainly on the job, but varies according to the size and type of employer. Some of the larger consultancies and companies have graduate training schemes.

You can study part-time, full-time or by distance learning for the Communication, Advertising and Marketing Education Foundation Advanced Certificate and Higher Diploma in Public Relations. You can also become a member of the CIPR and study for the CIPR Diploma.

Career progression for an in-house public relations officer could involve promotion to public relations manager, public relations director and head of corporate affairs.

Similarly, in a consultancy, you could progress from junior account executive to account executive, then to senior account executive/account manager and could reach the position of associate or account director.

You may have to move from one organisation to another to gain promotion and some public relations people move into related areas such as advertising, writing or marketing.

Personal Qualities: As a public relations officer, you would need excellent people skills. You must be able to write clearly and concisely, to communicate effectively at all levels and to work well under pressure, with tight deadlines.

You should be able to understand and interpret information, to adapt to situations as they arise and to organise and manage other people.

Looking Ahead: There are an estimated 25,000 people working in public relations, with around 56 per cent employed in-house by a wide range of organisations such as local authorities, the police, commercial companies, professional bodies and charities. The largest single in-house employer in public relations is the Government Information Service.

The remainder work in consultancies ranging from large multinational organisations, to small firms run by one or two people. There are many opportunities for freelance work. There are also opportunities to work in all major towns and cities and to work abroad. Public relations is a highly competitive career, with hundreds of applicants for each job.

Public Relations Specialists

Significant Points: Although employment is projected to grow faster than average, keen competition is expected for entry-level jobs.

Opportunities should be best for college graduates who combine a degree in public relations, journalism, or another communications-related field with a public relations internship or other related work experience. Creativity, initiative and the ability to communicate effectively are essential.

Nature of the Work: An organization's reputation, profitability and even its continued existence can depend on the degree to which its targeted "publics" support its goals and policies. Public relations specialists—also referred to as *communications specialists* and *media specialists*, among other titles—serve as advocates for businesses, non-profit associations, universities, hospitals and other organizations and build and maintain positive relationships with the public. As managers recognize the importance of good public relations to the success of their organizations, they increasingly rely on public relations specialists for advice on the strategy and policy of such programmes.

Public relations specialists handle organizational functions such as media, community, consumer, industry and governmental relations; political campaigns; interest-group representation; conflict mediation; and employee and investor relations. They do more than "tell the organization's story." They must understand the attitudes and concerns of community, consumer, employee and public interest groups and establish and maintain cooperative relationships with them and with representatives from print and broadcast journalism.

Public relations specialists draft press releases and contact people in the media who might print or broadcast their material. Many radio or television special reports, newspaper stories and magazine articles start at the desks of public relations specialists. Sometimes the subject is an organization and its policies toward its employees or its role in the community. Often the subject is a public issue, such as health, energy, or the environment and what an organization does to advance that issue.

Public relations specialists also arrange and conduct programmes to keep up contact between organization representatives and the public. For example, they set up speaking engagements and often prepare speeches for company officials. These media specialists represent employers at community projects; make film, slide, or other visual presentations at meetings and school assemblies; and plan conventions. In addition, they are responsible for preparing annual reports and writing proposals for various projects.

In government, public relations specialists—who may be called press secretaries, information officers, public affairs specialists, or communication specialists—keep the public informed about the activities of agencies and officials. For example, public affairs specialists in the U.S. Department of State keep the public informed of travel advisories and of U.S. positions on foreign issues. A press secretary for a member of Congress keeps constituents aware of the representative's accomplishments.

In large organizations, the key public relations executive, who often is a vice president, may develop overall plans and policies with other executives. In addition, public relations departments employ public relations specialists to write, research, prepare materials, maintain contacts and respond to inquiries.

People who handle publicity for an individual or who direct public relations for a small organization may deal with all aspects of the job. They contact people, plan and research and prepare materials for distribution. They also may handle advertising or sales promotion work to support marketing efforts.

Working Conditions: Some public relations specialists work a standard 35- to 40-hour week, but unpaid overtime is common. Occasionally, they must be at the job or on call around the clock, especially if there is an emergency or crisis. Public relations offices are busy places; work schedules can be irregular and frequently interrupted. Schedules often have to be rearranged so that workers can meet deadlines, deliver speeches, attend meetings and community activities and travel.

Training, Other Qualifications and Advancement: There are no defined standards for entry into a public relations career. A college degree combined with public relations experience, usually gained through an internship, is considered excellent preparation for public relations work; in fact, internships are becoming vital to obtaining employment. The ability to communicate effectively is essential. Many entry-level public relations specialists have a college major in public relations, journalism, advertising, or communication. Some firms seek college graduates who have worked in electronic or print journalism. Other employers seek applicants with demonstrated communication skills and training or experience in a field related to the firm's business—information technology, health, science, engineering, sales, or finance, for example.

Many colleges and universities offer bachelor's and post-secondary degrees in public relations, usually in a journalism or communications department. In addition, many other colleges offer at least one course in this field.

A common public relations sequence includes courses in public relations principles and techniques; public relations management and administration, including organizational development; writing, emphasizing news releases, proposals, annual reports, scripts, speeches and related items; visual communications, including desktop publishing and computer graphics; and research, emphasizing social science research and survey design and implementation. Courses in advertising, journalism, business administration, finance, political science, psychology, sociology and creative writing also are helpful. Specialties are offered in public relations for business, government and non-profit organizations.

Many colleges help students gain part-time internships in public relations that provide valuable experience and training. Membership in local chapters of the Public Relations Student Society of America (affiliated with the Public Relations Society of America) or in student chapters of the International Association of Business Communicators provides an opportunity for students to exchange views with public relations specialists and to make professional contacts that may help them find a job in the field.

A portfolio of published articles, television or radio programmes, slide presentations and other work is an asset in finding a job. Writing for a school publication or television or radio station provides valuable experience and material for one's portfolio.

Creativity, initiative, good judgment and the ability to communicate thoughts clearly and simply are essential in this occupation. Decision-making, problem-solving and research skills also are important. People who choose public relations as a career need an outgoing personality, self-confidence, an understanding of human psychology and an enthusiasm for motivating people. They should be competitive, yet able to function as part of a team and open to new ideas.

Some organizations, particularly those with large public relations staffs, have formal training programmes for new employees. In smaller organizations, new employees work under the guidance of experienced staff members. Beginners often maintain files of material about company activities, scan newspapers and magazines for appropriate articles to clip and assemble information for speeches and pamphlets.

They also may answer calls from the press and the public, work on invitation lists and details for press conferences, or escort visitors and clients. After gaining experience, they write news releases, speeches and articles for publication or plan and carry out public relations programmes. Public relations specialists in smaller firms usually get all-around experience, whereas those in larger firms tend to be more specialized.

The Universal Accreditation Board accredits public relations specialists who are members of the Public Relations Society of America and who participate in the Examination for Accreditation in Public Relations process. This process includes both a readiness review and an examination, which are designed for candidates who have at least 5 years of full-time work or teaching experience in public relations and who have earned a bachelor's degree in a communications-related field.

The readiness review includes a written submission by each candidate, a portfolio review and dialogue between the candidate and a three-member panel. Candidates who successfully advance through readiness review and pass the computer-based examination earn the Accredited in Public

Relations (APR) designation. The International Association of Business Communicators (IABC) also has an accreditation programme for professionals in the communications field, including public relations specialists.

Those who meet all the requirements of the programme earn the Accredited Business Communicator (ABC) designation. Candidates must have at least 5 years of experience and a bachelor's degree in a communications field and must pass written and oral examinations. They also must submit a portfolio of work samples demonstrating involvement in a range of communications projects and a thorough understanding of communications planning.

Employers may consider professional recognition through accreditation as a sign of competence in this field, which could be especially helpful in a competitive job market.

Promotion to supervisory jobs may come to public relations specialists who show that they can handle more demanding assignments. In public relations firms, a beginner might be hired as a research assistant or account coordinator and be promoted to account executive, senior account executive, account manager and eventually vice president. A similar career path is followed in corporate public relations, although the titles may differ. Some experienced public relations specialists start their own consulting firms.

Employment: Public relations specialists held about 188,000 jobs in 2004. Public relations specialists are concentrated in service-providing industries such as advertising and related services; health care and social assistance; educational services; and government. Others worked for communications firms, financial institutions and government agencies.

Public relations specialists are concentrated in large cities, where press services and other communications facilities are readily available and many businesses and trade associations have their headquarters. Many public relations consulting firms, for example, are in New York, Los Angeles, San Francisco, Chicago and Washington, DC. There is a trend, however, for public relations jobs to be dispersed throughout the Nation, closer to clients.

Job Outlook: Keen competition likely will continue for entry-level public relations jobs, as the number of qualified applicants is expected to exceed the number of job openings. Many people are attracted to this profession because of the high profile nature of the work. Opportunities should be best for college graduates who combine a degree in journalism, public relations, advertising, or another communications-related field with a public relations internship or other related work experience. Applicants without the appropriate educational background or work experience will face the toughest obstacles.

Employment of public relations specialists is expected to grow faster than average for all occupations through 2014. The need for good public relations in an increasingly competitive business environment should spur demand for public relations specialists in organizations of all types and sizes. The value of a company is measured not just by its balance sheet, but also by the strength of its relationships with those on whom it depends for its success. With the increasing demand for corporate accountability, more emphasis will be placed on improving the image of the client, as well as on building public confidence. Employment in public relations firms should grow as firms hire contractors to provide public relations services rather than support full-time staff. In addition to those arising from employment growth, job opportunities should result from the need to replace public relations specialists who leave the occupation.

Earnings: Median annual earnings for salaried public relations specialists were $43,830 in May 2004. The middle 50 percent earned between $32,970 and $59,360; the lowest 10 percent earned less than $25,750 and the top 10 percent earned more than $81,120. Median annual earnings in the industries employing the largest numbers of public relations specialists in May 2004 were:

Advertising and related services	$50,450
Management of companies and enterprises	47,330
Business, professional, labour, political and similar organizations	45,400
Local government	44,550
Colleges, universities and professional schools	39,610

Demonstrators, Product Promoters and Models

Significant Points: Job openings should be plentiful for demonstrators and product promoters, but keen competition is expected for modelling jobs.

Most jobs are part time or have variable work schedules and many jobs require frequent travel.

Formal training and education requirements are limited.

Nature of the Work: Demonstrators, product promoters and models create public interest in buying products such as clothing, cosmetics, food items and house-wares. The information they provide helps consumers make educated choices among the wide variety of products and services available.

Demonstrators and product promoters create public interest in buying a product by demonstrating it to prospective customers and answering their questions. They may sell the demonstrated merchandise, or gather names of prospects to contact at a later date or to pass on to a sales staff. *Demonstrators* promote sales of a product to consumers, while *product promoters* try to induce retail stores to sell particular products and market them effectively. Product demonstration is an effective technique used by both to introduce new products or promote sales of old products because it allows face-to-face interaction with potential customers.

Demonstrators and product promoters build current and future sales of both sophisticated and simple products, ranging from computer software to mops. They attract an audience by offering samples, administering contests, distributing prizes and using direct-mail advertising. They must greet and catch the attention of possible customers and quickly identify those who are interested and qualified. They inform and educate customers about the features of products and demonstrate their use with apparent ease to inspire confidence in the product and its manufacturer. They also distribute information, such as brochures and applications. Some demonstrations are intended to generate immediate sales through impulse buying, while others are considered an investment to generate future sales and increase brand awareness.

Demonstrations and product promotions are conducted in retail and grocery stores, shopping malls, trade shows and outdoor fairs. Locations are selected based on both the nature of the product and the type of audience. Demonstrations at large events may require teams of demonstrators to efficiently handle large crowds. Some demonstrators promote products on video-tape or on television programmes, such as "infomercials" or home shopping programmes.

Demonstrators and product promoters may prepare the content of a presentation and alter it to target a specific audience or to keep it current. They may participate in the design of an exhibit or customize exhibits for particular audiences. Results obtained by demonstrators and product promoters are analyzed and presentations are adjusted to make them more effective. Demonstrators and product promoters also may be involved in transporting, assembling and disassembling materials used in demonstrations.

A demonstrator's presentation may include visuals, models, case studies, testimonials, test results and surveys. The equipment used for a demonstration varies with the product being demonstrated. A food product demonstration might require the use of cooking utensils, while a software demonstration could require the use of a multimedia computer. Demonstrators must be familiar with the product to be able to relate detailed information to customers and to answer any questions that arise before, during, or after a demonstration. Therefore, they may research the product to be presented, the products of competitors and the interests and concerns of the target audience before conducting a demonstration. Demonstrations of complex products can require practice.

Models pose for photos or as subjects for paintings or sculptures. They display clothing, such as dresses, coats, underclothing, swim-wear and suits, for a variety of audiences and in various types of media. They model accessories, such as handbags, shoes and jewellery and promote beauty products, including fragrances and cosmetics. The most successful models, called super-models, hold celebrity status and often use their image to sell products such as books, calendars and fitness videos. In addition to modelling, they may appear in movies and television shows.

Models' clients use printed publications, live modelling and television to advertise and promote products and services. There are different categories of modelling jobs within these media and the nature of a model's work may vary with each. Most modelling jobs are for printed publications and models usually do a combination of editorial, commercial and catalogue work. Editorial print modelling uses still photographs of models for fashion magazine covers and to accompany feature articles, but does not include modelling for advertisements. Commercial print modelling includes work for advertisements in magazines and newspapers and for outdoor advertisements such as billboards. Catalogue models appear in department store and mail order catalogues.

During a photo shoot, a model poses to demonstrate the features of clothing and products. Models make small changes in posture and facial expression to capture the look desired by the client. As they shoot film, photographers instruct models to pose in certain positions and to interact with their physical surroundings. Models work closely with photographers, hair and clothing stylists, makeup artists and clients to produce the desired look and to finish the photo shoot on schedule. Stylists and makeup artists prepare the model for the photo shoot, provide touchups and change the look of models throughout the day. If stylists are not provided, models must apply their own makeup and bring their own clothing. Because the client spends time and money planning for and preparing an advertising campaign, the client usually is present to ensure that the work is satisfactory. The client also may offer suggestions.

Editorial printwork generally pays less than other types of modelling, but provides exposure for a model and can lead to commercial modelling opportunities. Often, beginning fashion models work in foreign countries where fashion magazines are more plentiful.

Live modelling is done in a variety of locations. Live models stand, turn and walk to demonstrate clothing to a variety of audiences. At fashion shows and in showrooms, garment buyers are the primary audience. Runway models display clothes that either are intended for direct sale to consumers or are the artistic expressions of the designer. High fashion, or haute couture, runway models confidently walk a narrow runway before an audience of photographers, journalists, designers and garment buyers. Live modelling also is done in apparel marts, department stores and fitting rooms of clothing designers. In retail establishments, models display clothing directly for shoppers and may be required to describe the features and price of the clothing. Other models pose for sketching artists, painters and sculptors.

Models may compete with actors and actresses for work in television and may even receive speaking parts. Television work includes commercials, cable television programmes and even game shows. However, competition for television work is intense because of the potential for high earnings and extensive exposure.

Because advertisers need to target very specific segments of the population, models may specialize in a certain area. Petite and plus-size fashions are modeled by women whose dress size is smaller or larger than that worn by the typical model. Models who are disabled may be used to model fashions or products for disabled consumers. "Parts" models have a body part, such as a hand or foot, that is particularly well-suited to model products such as fingernail polish or shoes.

Almost all models work through agents. Agents provide a link between models and clients. Clients pay models, while the agency receives a portion of the model's earnings for its services. Agents scout for new faces, advise and train new models and promote them to clients. A typical modelling job lasts only 1 day, so modelling agencies differ from other employment agencies in that they maintain an ongoing relationship with the model. Agents find and nurture relationships with clients, arrange auditions called "go-sees," and book shoots if a model is hired. They also provide bookkeeping and billing services to models and may offer them financial planning services. Relatively short careers and variable incomes make financial planning an important issue for many models.

With the help of agents, models spend a considerable amount of time promoting and developing themselves. Models assemble and maintain portfolios, print composite cards and travel to go-sees. A portfolio is a collection of a model's previous work that is carried to all go-sees and bookings. A composite card, or comp card, contains the best photographs from a model's portfolio, along with his or her measurements.

Models must gather information before a job. From an agent, they learn the pay, date, time and length of the shoot. Also, models need to ask if hair, makeup and clothing stylists will be provided. It is helpful to know what product is being promoted and what image they should project. Some models research the client and the product being modeled to prepare for a shoot. Models use a document called a voucher to record the rate of pay and the actual duration of the job. The voucher is used for billing purposes after both the client and model sign it. Once a job is completed, models must check in with their agency and plan for the next appointment.

Working Conditions: More than half of all demonstrators, product promoters and models work part time and about 1 in 4 have variable work schedules. Many positions last 6 months or less.

Demonstrators and product promoters may work long hours while standing or walking, with little opportunity to rest. Some of them travel frequently and night and weekend work often is required. The atmosphere of a crowded trade show or State fair is often hectic and demonstrators and product promoters may feel pressure to influence the greatest number of consumers possible in a very limited amount of time. However, many enjoy the opportunity to interact with a variety of people.

Models work under a variety of conditions, which can often be both difficult and glamorous. The coming season's fashions may be modeled in a comfortable, climate-controlled studio or in a cold, damp outdoor location. Schedules can be demanding and models must keep in constant touch with an agent so that they do not miss an opportunity for work. Being away from friends and family and needing to focus on the photographer's instructions despite constant interruption for touchups, clothing and set changes can be stressful. Yet, successful models interact with a variety of people and enjoy frequent travel. They may meet potential clients at several go-sees in one day and often travel to work in distant cities, foreign countries and exotic locations.

Training, Other Qualifications and Advancement: Formal training and education requirements are limited for demonstrators, product promoters and models. Training usually is moderate term, lasting a month or more. Post-secondary education, while helpful, usually is not required: only 1 in 5 of these workers has a bachelor's degree or higher.

Demonstrators and product promoters usually receive on-the-job training. Training is primarily product oriented because a demonstrator must be familiar with the product to demonstrate it properly. The length of training varies with the complexity of the product. Experience with the product or familiarity with similar products may be required for demonstration of complex products, such as computers. During the training process, demonstrators may be introduced to the manufacturer's corporate philosophy and preferred methods for dealing with customers.

Employers look for demonstrators and product promoters with good communication skills and a pleasant appearance and personality. Demonstrators and product promoters must be comfortable with public speaking. They should be able to entertain an audience and use humour, spontaneity and personal interest in the product as promotional tools. Foreign language skills are helpful.

While no formal training is required to begin a modelling career, models should be photogenic and have a basic knowledge of hair styling, makeup and clothing. Some local governments require models under the age of 18 to hold a work permit. An attractive physical appearance is necessary to become a successful model. A model should have flawless skin, healthy hair and attractive facial features. Specific requirements depend on the client, but most models must be within certain ranges for height, weight and dress or coat size in order to meet the practical needs of fashion designers, photographers and advertisers. Requirements may change slightly from time to time as our society's perceptions about physical beauty change; however, most fashion designers feel that their clothing looks its best on tall, thin models. Although physical requirements may be relaxed for some types of modelling jobs, opportunities are limited for those who do not meet these basic requirements.

Because a model's career depends on preservation of his or her physical characteristics, models must control their diet, exercise regularly and get enough sleep in order to stay healthy. Haircuts, pedicures and manicures are necessary work-related expenses for models.

In addition to being attractive, models must be photogenic. The ability to relate to the camera in order to capture the desired look on film is essential and agents test prospective models using snapshots or professional photographs. For photographic and runway work, models must be able to move gracefully and confidently. Training in acting, voice and dance is useful and allows a model to be considered for television work. Foreign language skills are useful because successful models travel frequently to foreign countries.

Because models must interact with a large number of people, personality plays an important role in success. Models must be professional, polite and prompt; every contact could lead to future employment. Organizational skills are necessary to manage personal lives, financial matters and busy work and travel schedules. Because competition for jobs is stiff and clients' needs are very specific, patience and persistence are essential.

Modelling schools provide training in posing, walking, makeup application and other basic tasks, but attending such schools does not necessarily lead to job opportunities. In fact, many agents prefer beginning models with little or no previous experience and discourage models from attending modelling schools and purchasing professional photographs. A model's selection of an agency is an important factor for advancement in the occupation. The better the reputation and skill of the agency, the more assignments a model is likely to get. Because clients prefer to work with agents, it is very difficult for a model to pursue a freelance career.

Agents continually scout for new faces and many of the top models are discovered in this way. Most agencies review snapshots or have "open calls", during which models are seen in person; this service usually is provided free of charge. Some agencies sponsor modelling contests and searches. Very few people who send in snapshots or attend open calls are offered contracts.

Agencies advise models on how to dress, wear makeup and conduct themselves properly during go-sees and bookings. Because models' advancement depends on their previous work, development of a good portfolio is key to getting assignments. Models accumulate and display current tear sheets—examples of a model's editorial print work—and photographs in the portfolio. The higher the quality and currency of the photos in the portfolio, the more likely it is that the model will find work.

Demonstrators and product promoters who perform well and show leadership ability may advance to other marketing and sales occupations or open their own businesses. Because modelling careers are relatively short, most models eventually transfer to other occupations.

Employment: Demonstrators, product promoters and models held about 120,000 jobs in 2004. Of these, models held only about 2,200 jobs in 2004. About 23 percent of all salaried jobs for demonstrators, product promoters and models were in retail trade, especially general merchandise stores and 14 percent were in administrative and support services—which includes employment services. Other jobs were found in advertising and related services.

Demonstrator and product promoter jobs may be found in communities throughout the Nation, but modelling jobs are concentrated in New York, Chicago, Miami and Los Angeles.

Job Outlook: Employment of demonstrators, product promoters and models is expected to grow about as fast as average for all occupations through 2014. Job growth should be driven by increases in the number and size of trade shows and greater use of these workers in department stores and various retail shops for in-store promotions. Additional job openings will arise from the need to replace demonstrators, product promoters and models that transfer to other occupations, retire, or stop working for other reasons.

Job openings should be plentiful for demonstrators and product promoters. Employers may have difficulty finding qualified demonstrators who are willing to fill part-time, short-term positions. Product demonstration is considered a very effective marketing tool. New jobs should arise as firms devote a greater percentage of marketing budgets to product demonstration.

On the other hand, modelling is considered a glamorous occupation, with limited formal entry requirements. Consequently, those who wish to pursue a modelling career can expect keen competition for jobs. The modelling profession typically attracts many more jobseekers than there are job openings available.

Only models who closely meet the unique requirements of the occupation will achieve regular employment. The increasing diversification of the general population should boost demand for models more representative of diverse racial and ethnic groups. Work for male models also should increase as society becomes more receptive to the marketing of men's fashions. Because fashions change frequently, demand for a model's look may fluctuate. Most models experience periods of unemployment.

Employment of demonstrators, product promoters and models is affected by downturns in the business cycle. Many firms tend to reduce advertising budgets during recessions.

Earnings: Demonstrators and product promoters had median hourly earnings of $9.95 in May 2004. The middle 50 percent earned between $8.18 and $13.29. The lowest 10 percent earned less than $7.25 and the highest 10 percent earned more than $20.08. Employers of demonstrators, product promoters and models generally pay for job-related travel expenses.

Median hourly earnings of models were $10.50 in May 2004. The middle 50 percent earned between $8.44 and $14.34.

The lowest 10 percent earned less than $7.16 and the highest 10 percent earned more than $17.17. Earnings vary for different types of modelling and depend on the experience and reputation of the model. Female models typically earn more than male models for similar work. Hourly earnings can be relatively high, particularly for super-models and others in high demand, but models may not have work every day and jobs may last only a few hours.

Models occasionally receive clothing or clothing discounts instead of, or in addition to, regular earnings. Almost all models work with agents and pay 15 to 20 percent of their earnings in return for an agent's services. Models who do not find immediate work may receive payments, called advances, from agents to cover promotional and living expenses. Models must provide their own health and retirement benefits.

Bibliography

Albarran, Alan B. and Gregory G. Pitts: *The Radio Broadcasting Industry*, Boston, Allyn and Bacon, 2001.

Albrecht, Ulrich: *A Short Research Guide on Arms and Armed Forces*, New York, Facts on File, 1980.

Alexander, James: *Internships in Communications, Ames*, Iowa State University Press, 1995.

Allman, Paul: *Careers in Video and Digital Video*, New York: Rosen, 2001.

Anders, Peter: *Envisioning Cyberspace*, New York, McGraw-Hill, 1999.

Arkin, William M.: *Research Guide to Current Military and Strategic Affairs*, Washington, Institute for Policy Studies, 1981.

Baehr, H. and Gary A.: *Turning In On: A Reader in Women and Media*, London, Arnold, 1996.

Ball, Victoria Kloss: *Opportunities in Interior Design and Decorating Careers*, Chicago, VGM Career Horizons, 2002.

Barnouw, Erik: *A Tower in Babel: the History of Broadcasting in the United States to 1933*, New York, Oxford University Press, 1966.

Baucom, Alfred H.: *Hospitality Design for the Graying Generation: Meeting the Needs of a Growing Market*, New York, Wiley, 1996.

Baxter, John: *Australian Cinema*, Sydney, Pacific Books, 1970.

Beaman, Jim: *Interviewing for Radio*, New York, Routledge, 2000.

Berkowitz, Ira: *Vault Career Guide to Advertising*, New York, Vault, 2004.

Bertrand, Ina and Diane Collins: *Government and Film in Australia*, Sydney, Currency Press, 1981.

Bliss, Edward and James L. Hoyt: *Writing News for Broadcast*, New York, Columbia University Press, 1994.

Boella, Michael John: *Principles of Hospitality Law*, London, Cassell, 1999.

Bone, Jan, & Ana Fernandez: *Opportunities in Film Careers*, New York, VGM Career Books, 2004.

Bowers, C. A.: *The Cultural Dimension of Educational Computing: Understanding the Non-neutrality of Technology*, New York, Teachers' College Press; 1988.

Boyd, Andrew: *Broadcast Journalism: Techniques of Radio and TV News*, Woburn, Focal Press, 2001.

Brown, Douglas Robert: *The Restaurant Managers Handbook: How to Set Up, Operate, and Manage a Financially Successful Restaurant.* Lauderhill, Atlantic Pub., 1991.

Brown, James and Quaal Ward: *Radio-Television-Cable Management*, New York, McGraw Hill, 1998.

Bryant, Jennings: *Television and the American Family*, Hillsdale, Lawrence Erlbaum, 1990.

Buckingham, David: *Young People and the Media*, New York, Manchester University Press, 1993.

Buckner, Robert W.: *Site Selection: New Advancements in Methods and Technology*, New York, Lebhar-Friedman Books, 1998.

Caldwell, J. T.: *Electronic Media and Technoculture*, New Brusnwick, Rutgers University Press, 2000.

Careers in Focus: *Photography*, New York, Ferguson, 2004.

Carmouche, Rita: *Behavioural Studies in Hospitality Management*, New York, Chapman & Hall, 1995.

Carroll, Victoria: *Writing News for Television*, Ames, Iowa State University Press, 1997.

Cassiday, Doris, and Bruce Cassiday: *Careers in the Beauty Industry*, New York, Franklin Watts, 1978.

Clark, Mona: *Interpersonal Skills for Hospitality Managers*, London, Chapman Hill, 1995.

Clark, Roy Peter: *A Journalist Teaches Young Writers*, Portsmouth, Heinemann, 1987.

Cockburn, C. and Ormrod, S.: *Gender and Technology in the Making*, London, Sage, 1993.

Cohler, David Keith: *Broadcast Newswriting*, Englewood Cliffs, Prentice Hall, 1990.

Cracknell, H. L.: *Escoffier: The Complete Guide to the Art of Modern Cookery*, New York, John Wiley, 1979.

Craig, James: *Graphic Design Career Guide*, New York, Watson-Guptill, 1992.

Crawford, Tad: *Starting Your Career As a Freelance Photographer*, New York, Allworth Press, 2003.

Crouse, Chuck: *Reporting for Radio*, Chicago, Bonus Books, 1998.

Davidson, M. J. and Cooper, C. L.: *Women and Information Technology*, New York, John Wiley & Sons, 1987.

Delaney, Chuck: *Photography Your Way*, New York, Allworth Press, 2005.

Dennis, Everette E. and Edward C. Pease: *Children and the Media*, New Brunswick, Transaction Publishers, 1996.

Diamond, S. Taylor's Way: *Women, Cultures and Technology*, New York: Routledge; 1997.

Donald, Ralph and Thomas Spann: *Fundamentals of Television Production*, Ames, Iowa State University Press, 2000.

Dornenburg, Andrew: *Culinary Artistry*, New York, John Wiley & Sons, 1996.

Douglas, George H.: *The Early Days of Radio Broadcasting*, Jefferson, NC: McFarland, 1987.

Easlea, B.: *Fathering the Unthinkable: Masculinity, Scientists and the Nuclear Arms Race*, London, Pluto Press, 1982.

Ellis, Elmo: *Opportunities in Broadcasting Careers*, Chicago, VGM Career Books, 2005.

Faulkner, W. and Arnold, E.: *Smothered by Invention: Technology in Women's Lives*, London, Pluto Press, 1985.

Fensch, Thomas: *Television News Anchors*, Jefferson, McFarland, 1993.

Field, Shelly: *Career Opportunities in Advertising and Public Relations*, New York, Ferguson, 2006.

Foster, Timothy R. V.: *How to Succeed As an Independent Consultant*, London: Kogan, Page, 2002.

Fox Keller, E.: *Reflections on Gender and Science*, New Haven, Yale University Press, 1985.

Gardner, Garth: *Careers in Computer Graphics and Animation*, Fairfax, GGC, 2001.

Gibbs, Jenny: *Interior Design*, New York, H. N. Abrams, 2005.

Go, Frank M.: *Human Resource Management in the Hospitality Industry*, New York, Wiley, 1996.

Goldfarb, Roz: *Careers by Design*, New York, Allworth Press, 2001.

Gordon, Sandra R.: *Great Jobs for Film Majors*, Chicago, VGM Career Books, 2004.

Graham, Duane: *The Remarkable Story of Otto Graham*, Wayne, Immortal Investments Publishing, 2004.

Green, E. and Adam, A. Virtual Gender: *Technology, Consumption, and Identity*, New York, Routledge, 2001.

Greenman, Robert: *The Adviser's Companion*, New York, Columbia Scholastic Press Association, 1991.

Griffiths, D.: *The Exclusion of Women from Technology*, London, Pluto Press, 1985.

Hall, Ken G.: *Australian Film: the Inside Story*, Sydney, Summit Books, 1980.

Hewitt, John: *Airwords: Writing for Broadcast News, Mountain View*, Oxford, Mayfield Pub. Company, 2002.

Higham, Robin: *A Guide to the Sources of United States Military History*, Hamden, Archon Books, 1975.

Hilliard, Robert L. and Michael C. Keith: *The Broadcast Century and Beyond*, Boston: Focal Press, 2001.

Hinkin, Timothy R.: *Cases in Hospitality Management: A Critical Incident Approach*, New York, Wiley, 1995.

Holloway, J. C. : *Towards a Core Curriculum for Tourism: A Discussion Paper*, London, The National Liaison Group for Higher Education in Tourism, 1995.

Horstede, G.: *Cultures and Organizations: Software of the Mind*, London, McGraw-Hill Book Company, 1991.

Hungerland, Buff: *Marketing Your Creative Portfolio*, Upper Saddle River, Prentice Hall, 2003

Jain, S. C.: *Women and Technology*, Jaipur, Rawat Publications, 1985.

Jefferson, Michael: *Breaking into Graphic Design*, New York, Allworth Press, 2005.

Jensen, Clayne R.: *Opportunities in Recreation and Leisure Careers*, Lincolnwood, VGM Career Horizons, 2000.

Jones, Sue Jenklyn: *Fashion Design*, New York, Watson-Guptill, 2002.

Kieffer, John: *The Photographer's Assistant*, New York, Allworth, 2001.

Kirkham, P.: *The Gendered Object*, Manchester, Manchester University Press, 1996.

Kissane, Sharon F.: *Career Success for People with Physical Disabilities*, Lincolnwood, VGM Career Horizons, 1997.

Kring, Robin: *Party Creations: Book of Theme Event Design*, Denver, Clear Creek Pub., 1993.

Kurzweil, R.: *The Age of Spiritual Machines*, New York, Viking, 1999.

Lavery, P.: *Tourism Marketing and Management Handbook*, New York, Prentice Hall, 1989.

Lewis, Robert C.: *Cases in Hospitality Marketing and Management*, New York, John Wiley, 1997.

MacCloskey, Monro: *How to Qualify for the Service Academies*, New York, Richards Rosen Press, 1964.

Maclay, Edgar Stanton: *A History of the United States Navy 1771-1893*, New York, Appleton Co., 1894.

Mauro, Lucia: *Careers for Fashion Plates and Other Trendsetters*, Chicago, VGM Career Horizons, 2003.

McGuire-Lytle, Erin: *Careers in Graphic Arts and Computer Graphics*, New York, Rosen, 1999.

Miller, Samuel D.: *An Aerospace Bibliography*, Washington. Office of Air Force History, 1978.

Mitchell, Leslie Scott: *Freelancing for Television and Radio*. London; Routledge, 2005.

Mogel, Leonard: *Creating Your Career in Communications and Entertainment*, Sewickley, GATF Press, 1998.

Noronha, Shonan F. R.: *Opportunities in Television and Video Careers*, Chicago: VGM Career Books, 2003.

Orlik, Peter B.: *Career Perspectives in Electronic Media*, Ames, Blackwell Pub., 2004.

Packard, Sidney: *The Fashion Business: Dynamics and Careers*, New York, Holt, Rinehart, and Winston, 1983.

Parks, Peggy J.: *The News Media*, San Diego, Lucent Books, 2002.

Paullin, C.O.: *The Navy of the American Revolution*, Cleveland, The Burrows Brothers Co., 1906.

Perna, Rita: *Fashion Forecasting*, New York, Fairchild Publications, 1987.

Rachlis, Eugene: *The Story of the U.S. Coast Guard*, New York, Random House, 1961.

Reis, Ronald A.: *Careers in Art and Graphic Design*, Hauppage, Barrons, 2001.

Rocha, Tony L.: *Careers in Magazine Publishing*, New York, Rosen, 2001.

Rubinstein, Donna: *The Modeling Life*, New York, Berkeley Publishing Group, 1998.

Satterthwaite, Frank: *The Career Portfolio Workbook*, New York, McGraw-Hill, 2003.

Seguin, James: *Media Career Guide*, Boston, St. Martin's, 2006.

Sones, Melissa: *Getting into Fashion: A Career Guide*, New York, Ballantine, 1984.

Vogt, Peter: *Career Opportunities in the Fashion Industry*, New York, Facts on File, 2002.

Wilson, Wayne: *Careers in Publishing and Communications*, Bear, Mitchell Lane, 2002.

Yager, Fred, & Jan Yager: *Career Opportunities in the Film Industry*, New York, Ferguson, 2003.

Zahler, Karen Gantz.: *Superchefs: Signature Recipes From America's New Royalty*, New York, John Wiley & Sons, 1996.

Index

A

Administration, 67, 73, 102, 182, 213, 221, 223, 232.
Advertising Jobs, 193.
Agents, 71, 72, 76, 136, 182, 183, 198, 199, 200, 201, 202, 203, 204, 205, 211, 212, 216, 223, 239, 240, 242, 243, 245.
Animation, 6, 40, 128, 169.
Art, 6, 55, 89, 155, 190, 192, 193, 197, 198, 199, 209, 210, 212, 213, 217, 218.
Assistant, 22, 37, 56, 67, 69, 70, 80, 105, 116, 118, 121, 122, 128, 129, 134, 135, 137, 141, 144, 154, 155, 158, 159, 160, 165, 170, 171, 174, 175, 179, 180, 183, 213, 214, 234.

B

Broadcast Assistant, 105.
Broadcast Journalist, 99.
Broadcasting, 1, 17, 29, 31, 32, 33, 34, 35, 37, 40, 41, 63, 64, 65, 66, 67, 68, 70, 71, 72, 73, 74, 75, 76, 77, 78, 79, 81, 82, 83, 87, 88, 97, 101, 108, 109, 113, 115, 118, 124, 125, 126, 127, 128, 129, 137, 141, 144, 150, 151, 152, 154, 156, 158, 160, 161, 164, 166, 174, 176, 177, 178, 180, 203, 205.
Budget, 117, 123, 142, 143, 144, 159, 164, 189, 190, 196.

C

Camera, 1, 10, 32, 33, 58, 66, 67, 70, 71, 76, 77, 83, 84, 85, 86, 87, 88, 97, 98, 100, 104, 111, 115, 122, 136, 152, 153, 158, 159, 161, 170, 171, 172, 173, 174, 175, 242.
Career Development, 16, 22, 28, 104, 110, 116, 122, 128, 134, 141, 146, 152, 158, 164, 170, 175, 180, 185.
Career Options, 3, 56, 57, 95, 98, 188, 189, 192, 223.
Clerks, 72, 73, 76, 211, 212, 213, 216.
Commission, 15, 65, 81, 181.
Community, 7, 11, 12, 32, 40, 51, 73, 74, 77, 79, 80, 85, 91, 109, 126, 131, 132, 133, 139, 141, 145, 168, 193, 210, 220, 221, 230, 231.
Computer, 31, 32, 38, 40, 41, 43, 46, 48, 50, 58, 65, 68, 70, 71, 74, 77, 78, 79, 81, 82, 87, 88, 89, 91, 93, 100, 108, 142, 153, 156, 157, 165, 185,

197, 203, 210, 212, 223, 232, 233, 236, 237.
Conditions, 6, 12, 19, 24, 29, 30, 38, 49, 56, 57, 66, 69, 79, 85, 90, 100, 106, 112, 118, 119, 124, 130, 137, 143, 148, 154, 160, 166, 171, 172, 177, 178, 182, 201, 204, 208, 231, 240.

D

Demand, 13, 34, 35, 42, 52, 53, 54, 58, 59, 82, 92, 96, 98, 112, 115, 118, 158, 170, 175, 181, 187, 203, 215, 235, 244, 245.
Designer, 117, 165, 170, 194, 239.
Designing, 147, 165, 188, 191, 205.
Detective, 59.
Development, 1, 7, 16, 17, 20, 22, 23, 28, 104, 105, 109, 110, 115, 116, 122, 127, 128, 130, 134, 135, 141, 146, 152, 158, 159, 162, 164, 169, 170, 175, 180, 181, 185, 220, 223, 226, 227, 232, 243.

E

Editing, 1, 3, 10, 13, 16, 17, 18, 19, 21, 22, 24, 27, 28, 31, 32, 35, 40, 41, 42, 45, 65, 66, 67, 68, 75, 78, 83, 85, 100, 106, 110, 124, 129, 130, 134, 135, 144, 153, 154, 155, 156, 157, 174, 183, 184, 185, 186, 227.
Education, 7, 16, 30, 31, 32, 54, 73, 80, 85, 86, 108, 109, 133, 150, 162, 168, 202, 214, 218, 221, 224, 226, 228, 236, 241.
Entertainment, 11, 46, 64, 84, 85, 87, 115, 116, 118, 137, 154, 158, 160, 165, 166, 179, 180, 221.
Executive, 37, 72, 147, 189, 190, 192, 193, 195, 213, 214, 216, 217, 218, 227, 229, 231, 234.

F

Film, 6, 58, 69, 71, 77, 83, 84, 85, 86, 87, 88, 90, 98, 99, 100, 110, 113, 115, 117, 119, 120, 121, 122, 123, 124, 126, 127, 128, 134, 139, 140, 141, 142, 143, 144, 145, 146, 147, 151, 152, 153, 154, 155, 156, 157, 158, 159, 160, 161, 162, 163, 164, 166, 169, 170, 173, 174, 189, 191, 210, 223, 224, 227, 230, 238, 242.
Finance, 2, 5, 10, 23, 51, 178, 182, 232.
Financial Management, 141, 166.
Future trends, 6.

G

Government, 2, 4, 27, 41, 52, 53, 54, 56, 57, 59, 61, 64, 102, 124, 146, 220, 221, 222, 223, 224, 225, 226, 229, 231, 232, 234, 235.
Graphic design, 36, 91, 93, 197.

I

Installation, 72, 211.
Institutes, 2, 56, 85, 91, 223.
Institutions, 31, 52, 64, 73, 109,

133, 169, 188, 206, 207, 223, 225, 234.
Insurance, 182, 205.
Internet, 17, 26, 35, 36, 38, 39, 41, 42, 46, 48, 54, 68, 76, 81, 82, 87, 88, 94, 109, 117, 124, 153, 182, 187, 188, 193, 196, 199, 201, 205, 206, 209, 210, 211, 215.

J

Job Description, 11, 17, 23, 105, 111, 116, 123, 129, 135, 141, 147, 152, 159, 165, 170, 176, 181.
Job Prospects, 3, 56, 95, 98, 188, 223.
Journalism, 1, 2, 3, 5, 7, 8, 9, 10, 11, 13, 14, 15, 16, 17, 18, 20, 21, 22, 23, 24, 25, 26, 28, 29, 31, 32, 33, 34, 35, 39, 42, 61, 62, 73, 75, 99, 102, 103, 104, 105, 125, 126, 129, 132, 139, 178, 179, 180, 195, 214, 229, 230, 232, 235.
Journalist, 1, 2, 3, 6, 8, 11, 16, 23, 59, 99, 104, 105, 183.

L

Labour, 41, 43, 81, 204, 235.
Law, 2, 8, 16, 18, 21, 26, 27, 31, 39, 42, 54, 59, 135, 139.
Library, 9, 36, 39.
Location Manager, 117, 118, 122, 141.

M

Magazine, 4, 6, 19, 20, 23, 24, 25, 26, 27, 28, 29, 31, 109, 114, 135, 146, 181, 183, 184, 185, 210, 230, 238.
Marketing Communications, 195, 220.
Markets, 65, 73, 74, 82, 86, 93, 181.
Membership, 37, 94, 109, 163, 232.
Modelling, 99, 197, 236, 238, 239, 241, 242, 243, 244, 245.
Multimedia, 5, 6, 36, 110, 114, 134, 144, 147, 151, 155, 157, 197, 212, 237.

N

Networking, 24, 77, 78, 79, 116, 148, 158, 162.
News Analysts, 29.
Newspaper, 4, 7, 8, 9, 11, 14, 15, 16, 17, 19, 21, 22, 23, 27, 28, 31, 33, 34, 41, 43, 60, 61, 92, 94, 126, 178, 179, 181, 192, 203, 205, 210, 230.

O

Occupation, 34, 35, 42, 43, 52, 53, 61, 68, 71, 72, 76, 94, 202, 204, 212, 213, 216, 233, 235, 242, 244.
Operators, 66, 70, 71, 76, 77, 78, 79, 80, 81, 82, 83, 84, 85, 86, 87, 88, 172, 174, 175, 213, 216.
Organization, 36, 46, 202, 209, 219, 220, 230, 231.

P

Photography, 6, 32, 55, 56, 57, 58, 59, 60, 61, 62, 86, 113, 117, 119, 120, 144,

155, 159, 161, 163, 164, 171, 173, 175.
Preparation, 4, 30, 32, 38, 67, 77, 101, 111, 153, 177, 231.
Producer, 86, 103, 105, 106, 111, 116, 118, 123, 128, 129, 132, 134, 135, 136, 141, 143, 144, 147, 154, 160, 176, 177, 194.
Psychology, 32, 195, 213, 223, 232, 233.

R

Remuneration, 2, 55, 96, 99, 188, 224.
Reporters, 1, 2, 3, 5, 6, 10, 11, 12, 16, 17, 18, 29, 30, 31, 32, 33, 34, 35, 37, 57, 66, 69, 71, 76, 101, 104.
Reporting, 1, 2, 4, 5, 9, 12, 16, 17, 27, 31, 32, 66, 69, 84, 101, 104, 105.
Responsibilities, 32, 37, 69, 73, 124, 129, 130, 201, 204, 209.

S

Sales Agents, 71, 72, 76, 199, 200, 201, 202, 203, 204, 205, 211, 212, 216.
Scientists, 40, 69.
Selection, 3, 15, 16, 21, 27, 96, 98, 103, 109, 121, 127, 133, 140, 157, 163, 174, 179, 242.
Sports, 2, 5, 10, 18, 29, 30, 37, 57, 58, 59, 60, 68, 69, 75, 77, 87, 112, 129, 221.
Strategies, 170, 192, 194, 207, 219.
Supervisors, 71, 72, 73, 79, 212.

T

Technician, 70, 78, 79, 81, 88, 89, 91, 93, 150, 159, 160, 162, 164, 165, 170.
Theatre, 27, 30, 77, 99, 113, 115, 118, 132, 137, 154, 158, 160, 161, 162, 163, 164, 166, 168, 173, 180.
Traffic, 68, 94, 176, 212.
Translators, 43, 44, 45, 46, 47, 48, 49, 50, 51, 52, 53, 54, 55.

U

University, 8, 28, 48, 51, 120, 132, 139, 145, 162, 198.

V

Video, 10, 29, 30, 32, 40, 65, 67, 68, 69, 70, 71, 76, 77, 78, 80, 81, 82, 83, 84, 85, 86, 87, 88, 90, 97, 98, 120, 122, 123, 124, 141, 142, 145, 146, 147, 152, 153, 156, 157, 161, 163, 164, 173, 237.

W

Website, 14, 21, 106, 110, 114, 115, 121, 126, 129, 130, 133, 135, 144, 146, 151, 152, 154, 157, 162, 163, 166, 181, 185.
Working Conditions, 30, 38, 49, 66, 79, 85, 90, 201, 208, 231, 240.
Working conditions, 85, 177.

Y

Youth, 97.

□□□